OUTWITTING THE GESTAPO BY LUCIE AUBRAC

Lucie Aubrac

Outwitting the Gestapo

Translated by Konrad Bieber
with the assistance of Betsy Wing

With an introduction by
Margaret Collins Weitz

University of Nebraska Press
Lincoln and London

© 1993 by the University of
Nebraska Press. Originally
published as *Ils partiront dans
l'ivresse*, © Éditions du Seuil,
1984. All rights reserved.
Manufactured in the United
States of America. The paper
in this book meets the
minimum requirements of
American National Standard
for Information Sciences—
Permanence of Paper for
Printed Library Materials,
ANSI Z39.48—1984 Library
of Congress Cataloging-in-
Publication Data. Aubrac,
Lucie, 1912– [Ils partiront
dans l'ivresse. English]
Outwitting the Gestapo /
by Lucie Aubrac ; translated
by Konrad Bieber, with the
assistance of Betsy Wing ;
with an introduction
by Margaret Collins Weitz.
p.   cm. ISBN 0-8032-1029-9
(cloth)   1. Aubrac, Lucie,
1912– —Diaries.
2. World War, 1939–1945—
Underground movements—
France. 3. World War, 1939–
1945—Personal narratives,
French. 4. France—History—
German occupation, 1940–
1945. 5. Guerrillas—France—
Diaries.   I. Title.
D802.F8A7913   1992
940.53′44—dc20
92-26861 CIP

CONTENTS

All photographs except those of Lucie Aubrac courtesy of
the Secrétariat d'Etat Chargé des Anciens Combattants et
des Victimes de Guerre Mission Permanente aux
Commémorations et à l'Information Historique.
Photographs of Lucie Aubrac courtesy of Lucie Aubrac.

INTRODUCTION

by Margaret Collins Weitz

Lucie Aubrac's memoirs chronicle nine months of her activities in the French Resistance, from May 1943 to February 1944, the nine months of her second pregnancy. By any standard her account is one of exceptional heroism and commitment as well as of intense love and devotion. As she recounts in flashbacks, Aubrac and her husband helped found the Resistance group Libération Sud in the early days of the German occupation. For them this was simply a continuation of their prewar activism on behalf of human rights in the fight against fascism. They were part of a small group of French patriots who tried to hinder the Nazis and to inform the French population of the true nature of the Vichy government of Marshal Pétain, who had signed an armistice with Hitler. Few French were involved in Resistance activities at this stage, in part because the situation in France was far from clear.

When Hitler's deeds began to match the designs set forth in his writings, the majority of the French chose to believe that they were not in serious danger. Part of the problem was France's internal crises. The country was still recovering from the depression. From an attempted rightist coup in 1934 to the Popular Front coalition government of 1936–37, France was in a state of social turbulence. The Spanish civil war, British pressures, and then the Munich Pact added to internal dissension. When the Popular Front disintegrated, its members followed their separate ideological bents. Many Socialists were pacifists; the Communists focused on the concerns of the workers of the world, not those of "imperialist" nations. In 1938 Edouard Daladier of the Radical party put together a government whose solution to a steadily deteriorating situation was to pass decree-laws that circumvented the legislature. His government thought that Hitler could be appeased, as did France's ally, Britain, even after the invasion of Czechoslovakia in the fall of 1938. When German troops invaded Poland on September 1, 1939, however, France and Great Britain honored their alliance and declared war on Nazi Germany. The first six months of the war were marked only by a brief incursion into the German Saarland and an unsuccessful Anglo-French military expedition to support Norway against the Germans, ending a long period of waiting, what the French called the *drôle de guerre*, the phony war.

As events were to prove, the French High Command had not sufficiently studied or kept up with the new military techniques. They put most of their resources—and confidence—into the Maginot Line, a series of fortifications along the eastern border, little suspecting how vulnerable a fixed fortification was. Flexibility and maneuverability were now key factors in waging war, as at least one officer, named Charles de Gaulle, recognized. Although de Gaulle advocated the extensive use of tank units, his suggestions had been ignored by his countrymen—but not by their enemies. The senior French military also assumed if the Germans invaded, they would follow roughly the same route that they had in the First World War. Not wishing to antagonize their neighbors, the French did not extend the Maginot Line northward to the sea along the Franco-Belgian border. Instead, their neighbors the Belgians were charged with that defense. The long period of inactivity following Hitler's victories in eastern Europe in the early fall of 1939 lulled France into complacency. Rationing was not implemented; military preparation lagged.

Consequently, when the German blitzkrieg overran Holland and Belgium in May 1940, the French High Command was caught off guard by the German panzer attacks. There was some opposition from Allied forces, which included eighty thousand British troops and the belatedly called up French reserves. A massive evacuation from Dunkirk of those trapped by the German pincer-like movement followed. The rest of the army fought in retreat. The French nation was devastated and in shock. There were no contingency plans for the occupation of Paris. As the Germans marched toward the capital in the early days of June, one-tenth of the French nation was heading south, fleeing the approaching German army. The chaos and disruption of this flight added to the military's problems and to the general demoralization.

Paris was declared an open city and surrendered without resistance on June 14, 1940. Four days earlier the French government had joined the exodus southward. After a brief stop in Tours, it reassembled in the port city of Bordeaux. Changes in the cabinet and government ensued; Pierre Laval and others maneuvered to name Marshal Pétain, the First World War hero of Verdun, as head of the new French government. Although Pétain was in his eighties, his name inspired hope. On June 17 Pétain went on national radio to inform the French nation that he had asked the Germans for an armistice. The following day, Charles de Gaulle (who had been promoted to general a few weeks earlier), speaking from London on the BBC, told the French people that "the flame of French resistance must not die and will not die." Like de Gaulle, some French people had fled to England or one of France's colonies to carry on the fight. Ten days later the Churchill government recognized de Gaulle as head of the Free French.

De Gaulle was forced to devote much time to asserting his authority. Throughout the war he had to contend with power struggles among French military and political figures, who, while in agreement about continuing the fight against the Germans, often disagreed over tactics and leadership. Tensions existed between de Gaulle and his followers, the Free French, and the various Resistance groups formed by those who had remained in France. The Vichy government openly criticized the general for having "abandoned" France and indeed tried and condemned him to death for treason. His comparative isolation in London left de Gaulle largely unaware of the development of the Resistance on French soil, the Resistance of the interior. A career military man, he could not conceive of groups and movements composed mainly of civilians fighting the enemy in an improvised manner, their recruitment subject to circumstantial vagaries. Further, the very secrecy required for Resistance undertakings made it difficult to grasp their scope and nature. (This secrecy was also to hinder postwar efforts to write the history of the French Resistance.)

De Gaulle viewed resistance from a military perspective. He set about organizing networks, as did the British, to collect information that would be useful for military missions and for an eventual landing. The situation was complicated further when the United States entered the war in December 1941 and began establishing its own networks. Because of Roosevelt's hostility to the leader of the Free French, the Americans seemed willing to support any French commander but de Gaulle. Nevertheless, thanks in large measure to the dedicated efforts of Jean Moulin and other representatives of de Gaulle, most networks and groups on French soil had rallied to his authority by 1943, when the National Council of the Resistance was created. In addition to representatives of the principal Resistance movements, after considerable discussion, political parties, including the Communists, were also included in the council. This decision was to be debated (and criticized) throughout the postwar years. Then, as in the 1930s, the real enemy for many French was Soviet Russia.

The French Communist party, a partner in the Popular Front, had been outlawed following the signing of the German-Soviet pact on August 23, 1939. Shortly thereafter, those Communist leaders who had not gone underground were imprisoned. Until Hitler invaded the Soviet Union in June 1941, French Communists faced a genuine dilemma: to accept the Nazi-Soviet pact or to join a non-Communist-dominated movement to fight the Germans. After Hitler's attack on the USSR, the French Communist party could and did set up its own Resistance organizations. The Communists' considerable experience in clandestine operations was invaluable in fighting the Nazis. Many Communists had participated in the Spanish civil war. Even so, their presence in non-Communist movements and later, in the Resistance councils and organizations, was a source of tension. The

Communists' true allegiance was always in question, a concern that later surfaced over their participation in the postwar government. For their part, the Communists claimed not to have received their fair share of arms, since their combat groups—unlike most others—had undertaken a policy of attacking Germans. For most Resistance groups, the large number of French hostages killed in reprisals militated against these attacks. The historian Robert Paxton holds that the issue of preemptive violence masked a deeper division between those who wanted to concentrate on removing the Germans from French soil and those who wanted to change French society altogether. Moreover, under the guise of Resistance activities there was some settling of old accounts.[1] German propaganda was quick to play on popular fears of anarchy and labeled résistants "anarchists," "bandits," or "Bolsheviks."

Having a French leader in exile recognized by Great Britain complicated the situation for the French remaining in metropolitan France. No other occupied country had a government on home territory functioning with German approval. French citizens had been brought up to respect legal authority, and the marshal claimed to have been properly invested (a point still debated). Pétain and his entourage moved to the spa town of Vichy in a "temporary" move that lasted until the liberation of France. There he presided over the demise of the Third Republic. Influenced by Laval's machinations, the national assembly voted itself out of existence and granted Pétain full powers. According to the terms of the armistice, France was obligated to pay exorbitant occupation costs; nearly two million French prisoners of war were not released. In September 1940 France was divided into two zones (excluding Alsace-Lorraine, which was annexed, the Nice area adjacent to Italy, all the coasts, and a forbidden zone in the northeast). The occupied zone, encompassing the northern three-fifths, had a larger population and greater resources than the so-called free zone of the south, which included Vichy. The fateful word *collaborate* appears in the text

1. Robert O. Paxton, *Vichy France: Old Guard and New Order, 1940–1944* (New York: Columbia University Press, 1972), 293.

of the armistice agreement: French officials and public servants were to "conform to the decisions of the German authorities and collaborate faithfully with them."

French resistance started with the German invasion. Patriotic individuals who could not bear the sight of German soldiers on their soil reacted instinctively. A French woman was assassinated on June 17, 1940, for berating and harassing the German soldiers who attempted to requisition her home. A youth was apprehended and executed for cutting communication lines. Individuals committed small acts of protest, such as wearing the French national colors and displaying "butterflies," stickers with anti-German slogans. Insignificant acts and occasional participation often evolved into full-time commitment. Nevertheless, after six weeks of fighting the vast majority of the French population viewed the armistice with relief. France would be spared the extensive death and destruction that characterized the First World War. They looked forward to stability, a return to "normal" life. Yet the situation in France at the outset of the occupation was far from clear. An eighty-four-year-old hero of the First World War headed a new government. The general feeling was that Pétain would once again outfox the Germans. But there were some who refused to accept accommodation and surrender. As Combat leader Claude Bourdet notes in *L'Aventure incertaine* (1975; an insightful study not yet translated), the aim and nature of efforts to continue the struggle were in large measure determined by location. The French in the occupied zone had to confront the German presence; collaborationists were in charge. Consequently the early Resistance there was directed against the Nazis, who were held responsible for Vichy's increasingly disconcerting measures. Even late in the war the French in the occupied zone supported the myth of the "grand old man" playing a double game and doing his best to save France. In reality, as Paxton convincingly shows, "Vichy sought neutrality, an early peace, and a final settlement on gentle terms with Germany."[2] There was little substance to the postwar myth of Vichy's passivity.

2. Ibid., 46.

Pétain set about implementing what he termed a National Revolution. His regime blamed the Popular Front for France's ignominious defeat. More generally, the Third Republic (1871–1940) was blamed for France's decline and decadence. Under the guise of patriotism, those who had been out of favor during the Third Republic set about imposing their vision of France, what Stanley Hoffmann terms the "revenge of the minorities." A Vichy regime composed of traditionalists, industrialists, financiers, lawyers, technocrats, much of the Catholic hierarchy, many military figures seduced by Pétain's reputation, reactionaries, and opportunists of various stripes sought revenge against those they charged with France's defeat: leftists, Communists, trade unionists, civil libertarians, Freemasons, and Jews.

Without an assembly to hinder him, Pétain passed a series of laws and decrees aimed at strengthening the French state. His government made overtures to the Reich, suggesting a policy of "faithful collaboration," although initially the Germans showed little interest in following the marshal "down the path of collaboration."[3] It was in Germany's interest for France to contribute to the Reich's extensive needs. Vichy replaced the republican motto "Liberty, Equality, and Fraternity" with "Work, Family, and Country." The nation was to be purified and its moral tone strengthened; harmful individualism would be suppressed. Such broad changes were made possible by the acquiescence of a demoralized country coming to terms with defeat.

Efforts to purify the French state focused on the Jews. At Vichy's initiative, Jews were placed under special statutes, not just the foreigners who had fled to France from Eastern Europe in the 1920s and 1930s, but those with French citizenship. Jews were virtually excluded from the professions and from teaching, and their property was confiscated. Foreign Jews were interned in special French camps. All French Jews were required to register, which greatly facilitated the later Nazi decision to enforce the Final Solution. Only 2,500 of the more than 75,000 Jews deported from France survived. Under Nazi occupation, the French police continued their work, often in tandem with the German

3. Pétain used this language in a radio broadcast of October 31, 1940.

police. French police rounded up Jews for internment or deportation (even children, whom the Nazis had not requested) and helped pursue *résistants*. In January 1943 the Milice, the French equivalent of the SS, was formed from elements of the Veterans' Legion. Those who joined swore to combat democracy, Jewish "leprosy," and Gaullist dissent, that is, the Resistance.

In the southern zone, Resistance groups and movements formed as Vichy's true colors became more apparent. When the Germans entered the southern zone in November 1942 and the demarcation line was eliminated, some Resistance movements joined with those that had been formed in the northern zone. Although there were few *résistants* at the outset of the occupation, by the end of the hostilities a considerable number of French men and women belonged to Resistance organizations. (The exact number can never be known, but 220,000 were officially recognized.)[4] In addition to those who became active by joining groups or movements, a far larger number of French patriots helped in other ways, for example, the individuals who sheltered the Aubracs while they waited for a rescue plane and the villagers who helped free that plane from the mud. It should be remembered that a woman who sheltered or fed someone sought by the Gestapo—a political refugee, a Jew, an Allied aviator, or a *résistant*—risked death if caught (some were executed), whereas the aviator would have been sent to a prisoner-of-war camp. Yet such a woman did not necessarily belong to any Resistance organization.

Groups and movements were formed mainly through family, friends, and professional contacts. Open recruiting was out of the question. Any new, unknown colleague inevitably was regarded with suspicion (suspicions justified in some cases, for there were double agents and traitors). Because of the improvised, nontraditional nature of the Resistance, women could and did apply. They played an important role in this war within a war.

Life went on for those in the Resistance, often more intensely,

4. Margaret Collins Weitz, "As I Was Then: Women in the French Resistance," *Contemporary French Civilization* 10, no. 1 (1986).

for many of them were experiencing what was to be the high point of their lives. Romantic liaisons were discouraged since they could lead to capture, but some couples did meet through their Resistance involvement. Needless to say, the presence of children complicated one's decision to join the Resistance. Children were potential hostages. Some parents, like the Aubracs, were able to lead double lives—as a family and as active *résistants*—until forced to go underground. The Aubracs were married in December 1939, shortly after the outbreak of the war, and had their first child in the spring of 1941, when both were working for Libération Sud. For Lucie Aubrac her son, Jean-Pierre, was a joyous little fellow, the only child in their group. His presence promised a return to the happiness and security of former days; he reminded their clandestine visitors of what they were fighting for—a home and all that that implied.

Like most women involved in the underground existence of the Resistance, Aubrac had to assume the burden of household chores. She continued to teach at a lycée as well. Daily tasks became more difficult during the occupation: feeding and clothing a family when food and clothing were rationed; washing clothes (including those of her husband's fellow inmates when he was imprisoned) when soap was difficult to find; and heating a home during the cold winter months when heating materials were scarce. Women's traditional ability to improvise and adapt served them well during the German occupation. The conventional and stereotypical view of French women was to prove quite useful, as Aubrac's account reveals. The Germans did not suspect them of being "terrorists" (another term they used for *résistants*), at least not in the early days of the war.

Women, particularly young women, were used extensively as liaison agents, performing the "usual" errands and commissions. Baskets, shopping bags, even baby carriages could conceal documents and weapons. "Fiancées" accompanied male agents or visited prisoners, collecting information. Lucie Aubrac posed at times as her own husband's fiancée or girlfriend. The clandestine military units, the maquis, which sprang up in the last years of the war, particularly after the compulsory labor laws were passed in early 1943, could not have survived without the support of women who procured false papers, provisions, and arms. As large numbers of young French men chose to go into hiding rather than be sent to work in the Reich, the logistics entailed in helping them were overwhelming.

Those who undertook Resistance missions generally did so in spite of fears for themselves and their families. Some *résistants* cut themselves off completely from their families. Moreover, the independence and nonconformism of some *résistants*, particularly the strong personalities among the Resistance leaders, sometimes led to internecine power struggles and diverging opinions on policy and objectives. Secrecy contributed to these tensions. To be successful, Resistance groups had to observe *cloisonnement* (compartmentalization). One had to know as little as possible about others in the group in order to limit the information one could divulge under torture. The negative aspect of this policy was the difficulty in determining guilt in the event of betrayal. The best-known example is that of René Hardy, accused of being responsible for the capture and death of Jean Moulin. Despite Hardy's two acquittals, some Resistance colleagues continue to believe that he was guilty, as the film *Hotel Terminus* reveals. Although he was present, Hardy had not been scheduled to attend the June 21, 1943, meeting in a Lyon suburb where Moulin and other Resistance leaders, including Lucie Aubrac's husband, who was on the staff of General Delestreint, head of the Secret Army of the Resistance, were arrested by Klaus Barbie and the Gestapo.

The first efforts of those who felt compelled to "do something" generally focused on information: providing the French public with truthful, accurate information. This held for both zones. In 1940 there were no such things as television, transistor radios, and tape recorders. Newspapers were the principal source of information, but they were censored by the Germans; Vichy issued "guidelines." The radio was also censored, and getting sufficient power for reception created an additional problem. The Germans broadcast much false information, such as the claim that they had landed in England, so the underground press countered with news picked up from English or Swiss radio stations. They exposed secret agreements and detailed the extensive shipments of France's harvest and wealth to Germany, news that the occupiers tried to conceal. The printing, distribution, and consumption of underground papers were dangerous and difficult activities. German efforts to suppress these papers led to mutual assistance and efforts to protect those who had gone underground and needed food, shelter, and forged documents.

Responses to the German occupation brought many changes in French society. Traditional social barriers broke down as Resistance activities brought together French people from all levels of society, from the aristocrat to the factory worker. Women's participation in the Resistance helped bring about changes in their status. Some of these changes became permanent, while others did not outlive the war. Conventional morality was overturned during the occupation in the face of the suppression of traditional liberties. In the course of Resistance work respectable citizens became counterfeiters and thieves, even killers.

The family has always been central to French society. Vichy reinforced this traditional concern for family and youth. Vichy propaganda held French women partially responsible for the defeat. On June 20, 1940, Pétain declared that there had been "too few children, too few arms, too few Allies." The women of France had "neglected" their duty to the state by not producing enough children. (These natalist concerns, which had developed during the interwar years, were to be continued by de Gaulle and France's postwar governments.) An already stringent 1920 law prohibiting contraception and abortion was strengthened. At least one woman abortionist was guillotined (a case dramatized in the film Une Affaire de femmes [A Story of Women]). The Code of the Family, first decreed on the eve of the war under Daladier, was amplified. Families were to receive financial benefits: fathers of large families were given job preference and bachelors were penalized (although France's dire situation prevented many proposals, including those destined to favor families, from being realized). At the same time, divorce became more difficult to obtain.

The Catholic Church applauded the imposition of measures intended to bolster the family and the morals of the French nation. To please the church, Pétain (a notorious ladies' man) had his twenty-one-year civil marriage to a divorcée annulled, and the couple were reunited in a religious ceremony. This event says much about the opportunism of Pétain and his followers. Early in the war Vichy instituted laws prohibiting married women from outside work if their husbands' salaries were deemed adequate. They were placed on "special availability"; a woman's place was in the home. As the war advanced, however, Vichy had to do an about-face and urge women to work outside the home because of the increasing shortage of manpower.

Education was also a major concern to the Vichy government, which blamed France's secular education system for the country's ignominious defeat. Conservatives and clerics saw their opportunity to change the French education system, one of the major achievements of the Third Republic, which had instituted a clear separation between church and state. Now public schools could provide time for prayer and municipalities were free to fund parochial schools. Vichy set the example by awarding Catholic schools a large grant in 1941. When Vichy started to arrest Jews for deportation in 1942, however, most of the clergy protested.

A major component of the National Revolution was the cult of Pétain, the father figure. Schoolchildren saluted his picture and expressed their loyalty in song: "Maréchal, nous voilà" (Marshal, here we are [to follow you]). Clubs, organizations, and programs for young people were established, the best known being the Chantiers de Jeunesse. At these obligatory camps in the southern zone, young non-Jewish French males attended lectures and worked on outdoor projects, the emphasis being on moral and physical development. Young girls could voluntarily attend one of the 380 centers set up for them, where they were to receive professional training, mainly limited to sewing, embroidery, dressmaking and flower arranging. Indeed, the different elementary education offered girls suggests that Vichy preferred women barefoot and pregnant in the kitchen.[5] There was no question of French women being given the right to vote.

5. Paxton, Vichy France, 168.

Pétain changed the paternalistic Napoleonic Code in women's favor only when circumstances made it unavoidable. The legal code placed married women under the authority of their husbands, without which a married woman could not open a bank account or cash a check, enroll in a university or apply for a passport. With a million and a half French men prisoners of war, many French women found themselves heads of households and Vichy found it necessary to pass legislation to assist them. While continuing the practice of separating sexes in the classroom, Vichy had to appoint women to teach boys' classes because of the shortage of male teachers. The absence of men provided French women with opportunities for professional advancement that had not existed in prewar France. Lucie Aubrac was among the small number of women who received advanced degrees before the war, qualifying them to teach at the university level. During the war years, the number of women professors, as well as women doctors and lawyers, increased although women lawyers were still kept from the bar. Women also assumed managerial positions in firms and factories. And it was French women by and large who ran the country's many farms during the war. In short, women became directly responsible in a wide range of spheres. Aubrac credits the Resistance with bringing about a profound change in French women's thinking.[6] For some this was the logical outcome of their pre-1940 development; for many others it was a discovery that disposed them to act in ways they would have considered illegal, even unthinkable, before the war.

General de Gaulle awarded French women the right to vote and to stand for office in 1944 (first exercised in 1946). Aubrac became the first French woman parliamentarian when she was designated to represent the United Resistance Movements at the consultative assembly of the French Committee of National Liberation in Algiers in 1944. The end of the war nevertheless brought a return to prewar life, with women assigned for the most part to their traditional roles. After achieving considerable success in the first postwar elections, women became less of a

6. Lucie Aubrac, "Présence des femmes dans toutes les activités de la Résistance," in *Femmes dans la Résistance* (Monaco: Editions du Rocher, 1977).

presence in the political arena. Women's wartime activities did not carry over to extensive postwar political activism, which is not altogether surprising given that the war was fought at least in part to regain prewar conditions. Still, the major changes in women's status in postwar France were facilitated and to some extent accelerated by the many and varied activities of French women during the Second World War.

During the war, women who joined underground movements shared with men equal rights, responsibilities, and risks. Assignments were based on aptitude and ability. Yet French women's participation in the Resistance has not been adequately examined or documented. The relative invisibility of women in histories of the French Resistance can be attributed to a narrow definition of resistance, to the women themselves, and to the nature of much of their work. Despite the risks women accepted, the continuities between their Resistance assignments and their lives before and after the war tended to obscure the exceptional nature of their actions. Women's underground work was frequently an extension of traditional female activities: typing; doing errands (liaison); providing food and shelter (for those who needed to be hidden). In the context of the occupation, however, these everyday activities took on new meaning.

The phenomenon of domestication or normalization may help explain why women's Resistance participation did not always politicize them and why their wartime participation in unconventional roles did not serve as a platform for postwar feminist mobilization. Only the largely Communist-dominated Union of French Women provided a framework for women's activities. The war provided some French women with the chance to play different roles, but those roles were of limited length and often gender-bound. At the end of the war, Lucie Aubrac resumed full-time teaching along with raising a family. She never sought celebrity as a heroine or as the first woman parliamentarian, titles she had earned. But she continued to speak out on issues that concerned her. It is in that context that she decided to write her memoirs, which were first published in France in 1984.

The recent trial of Klaus Barbie brought the occupation period to the forefront. The French are still coming to terms with this difficult and complex period of their history. Vichy's role in aiding Nazi policy, including the Final Solution, is being discussed after decades of national amnesia. A few historians and political extremists continue to deny the existence of extermination camps. For the most part the French public was at best ambivalent about the return of Barbie to France for trial, fearing the prospect of disclosure of French complicity with the Germans or of betrayals within the Resistance. But for those who lived and fought during the war or whose loved ones were captured and tortured by the "Butcher of Lyon," it was indeed time for the events of that period to be brought to public attention, particularly that of the younger generation. After forty years of silence, Lucie Aubrac believed that the time had come for her to document the daily activities—both domestic and clandestine—of *résistants* and to attest to the presence of women in the French Resistance.

Selected Bibliography

Azéma, Jean-Pierre. *From Munich to the Liberation, 1938–1944*. Cambridge: Cambridge University Press, 1986. French edition, Paris: Seuil, 1979.

Hoffmann, Stanley, et al. *In Search of France*. Cambridge: Harvard University Press, 1963.

Kedward, H. Roderick, and Roger Austin, eds. *Vichy France and the Resistance: Culture and Ideology*. New York: Barnes and Noble, 1985.

Kline, Rayna. "Partisans, Godmothers, Bicyclists and Other Terrorists: Women in the French Resistance and Under Vichy." *Proceedings of the Western Society for French History* no. 5 (1977).

Paxton, Robert O. *Vichy France: Old Guard and New Order, 1940–1944*. New York: Columbia University Press, 1972.

Rossiter, Margaret L. *Women in the Resistance*. New York: Praeger, 1986.

Schoenbrun, David. *Soldiers of the Night*. New York: Meridian, 1980.

Schwartz, Paula. "Redefining Resistance: Women's Activism in Wartime France." In *Behind the Lines: Gender and the Two World Wars*, edited by Margaret Randolph Higonnet, Jane Jenson, Sonya Michel and Margaret Collins Weitz. New Haven: Yale University Press, 1987.

Weitz, Margaret Collins, "As I Was Then: Women in the French Resistance." *Contemporary French Civilization* 10, no. 1, (1985).

PREFACE

I was born into a family of winegrowers in the Mâcon area of Burgundy on June 29, 1912. Thanks to my father, who had been gravely wounded during the First World War, I became a passionate pacifist in my youth. During my university studies at the Sorbonne, from 1931 to 1938, I for the first time confronted the problems of fascism and racism, through a number of foreign youths as well as Communist students—young Poles, Hungarians, Rumanians, and Germans—all of whom described the racial and political persecution in their countries. My first assignment as a history teacher was at the Strasbourg lycée for girls.[1] On the other side of the Rhine was Hitler, backed by a fanaticized nation. We knew that leftists and German Jews were being rounded up and thrown into camps, guarded by the ss and the police. We already called them "concentration camps."

During the 1938–39 school year, I met a young engineer who was doing his military service as a second lieutenant in the Engineer Corps, building roads and bridges. He had just spent a year at the Massachusetts Institute of Technology—and I was to go to the United States on a fellowship the following year to begin my dissertation. He became my source of information on life in

1. Lucie Aubrac's title, *agrégée d'histoire*, indicates that she had earned one of the highest academic degrees offered in France. Those holding the *agrégation* received teaching assignments at lycées, or secondary schools, in choice locations.

America. He also became much more. We fell in love and agreed to marry when I returned from the United States. But war broke out on September 3, 1939, and I decided not to leave France. On December 14, 1939, we were married.

Raymond Samuel was of Jewish origin; his ancestors had come from Poland at the beginning of the eighteenth century. After the collapse of the French army in 1940, and following his own escape from a prisoner-of-war camp, his professors in Boston offered him a job as an assistant. I still had my fellowship, so in September 1940 we applied for American visas in order to go to the United States. But then we changed our minds; could we really leave our families and our friends behind, while our country was occupied by the Germans?

With the decision to stay, our destiny became clear: to participate in the creation and development of a resistance movement, an everyday life, professional and clandestine, with a child born in 1941. We had the incredible good fortune to live as ourselves— we did not have to adopt false identities or go into hiding—until the spring of 1943.

During this period we led two sharply distinct lives. Just as geometry defines parallel lines, we did everything possible to avoid the collision of our two lives. One of our major concerns was keeping up the appearance of normalcy. Our home was for us a refuge of relaxation, of equilibrium. In our clandestine world we were a rarity—a couple, a family capable of sheltering solitary, furtive passersby. We were just Raymond and Lucie Samuel, completely aboveboard.

Officially, beginning in the autumn of 1941, we lived in the city of Lyon, in a small house on the avenue Esquirol, with a maid, Maria, and our little boy. I taught at the lycée for girls on the place Edgar-Quinet. Raymond was working as an engineer for the Chemin Company, directing repair work on the landing strips at Bron Airport.

That was our everyday, respectable routine, but we were totally different persons in our parallel life. In 1943, to all his Resistance contacts Raymond was Balmont and later Aubrac, an officer of the secret army of the Libération movement. In case he were to be stopped by the police, or even worse, arrested, he had

4

been given a fabricated identity. He carried forged papers in the name of François Vallet and an identity card with the address of a small apartment in the silk workers' district on the Croix-Rousse hill. For many months we thought it wise to stockpile provisions there, even though we would rather have eaten them with our friends. We had to be able to hold out, alone, in hiding, in the event of a serious incident.

As for me, my Resistance comrades knew me as Catherine. For any missions that ran the risk of interception, I used the identity papers I had carried as a single woman, which had the address of my student lodgings in Paris: Miss Lucie Bernard, rue Rataud, Paris.

In February 1943 a new decree creating compulsory labor service suddenly altered the priorities within the Resistance. The German defeats in Russia obliged Hitler's General Staff to comb the factories of the Reich for every possible recruit, giving rise to the idea of replacing German manpower with young people from the occupied countries. The labor decree, promulgated simultaneously by the collaborationist Vichy government and the German occupation authorities, was not met with enthusiasm in the occupied areas. Large numbers of young people left their jobs and their homes to escape forced deportation to Germany.

In early March a meeting was held at our avenue Esquirol home. The Resistance was to attempt to organize the assembly, induction, and training of these *réfractaires*, who were resisting compulsory labor. Suddenly the secret army was presented with unexpected forces. Raymond and another Resistance leader, Morin-Forestier, had sent scouts into the Jura and Savoy regions to look into how all these people could be absorbed into the movement. Several meetings were set up for March 15 to review their findings. Raymond was to meet his deputies, Ravanel and Valrimont, in a borrowed fifth-floor apartment at 7, rue de l'Hôtel-de-Ville.

In the course of these hasty preparations, through a stupid error one of our couriers was arrested at the railroad station in Ambérieu. The Resistance had issued him a blank identity card, and he had written his date of birth in the space intended for the

5

date of issue. He broke down during interrogation and began to talk, and as a result many names and addresses fell into the hands of the French police. There were mass arrests between March 10 and 15, including twenty liaison people and two leaders of the secret army of the Resistance with their deputies.

Raymond thus walked into a trap when he went to the meeting on March 15. Valrimont had already been arrested. Serge Ravanel arrived shortly afterward and immediately attempted a spectacular escape. When he rang the doorbell, a policeman opened the door, threatening him with his revolver: "Empty your pockets!" Serge obeyed, grabbed a small folding blackjack from his coat, whacked the cop over the head, and raced downstairs, only to collide with another policeman who was on his way up the stairs. In their struggle they fell to the floor, but just as Serge was gaining the upper hand two more cops came to their partner's rescue. Needless to say, the party was over.

Ravanel had bungled his escape attempt; Raymond too was seized when the police came to search the apartment. And to make matters worse, Valrimont had the same bad luck when he tried to escape. He had fled at daybreak from the police station where he was being held, pursued by a policeman who turned out to be less sleepy than he had seemed. Valrimont had raced ahead, turning into a small street at the corner. It was a dead end.

Then we went through the usual routine: police station, police headquarters, prison, after a cursory interrogation by the police court judge . . .

In June, after several betrayals, the Gestapo managed a string of arrests, catastrophic for the Resistance. In Paris, they caught General Delestraint, chief of staff of the secret army. In Lyon, on June 21, 1943, Jean Moulin, representative of General de Gaulle in occupied France and president of the National Council of the Resistance, was arrested by Klaus Barbie and tortured to death. Fortunately, it was too late to jeopardize his mission. He died under torture, but the chain of command remained intact.

As these tragic events took place, life continued, with its material difficulties and daily responsibilities; the underground fight had to go on. Repression grew more and more brutal, as Vichy police forces and Gestapo agents grew in numbers.

6

I had my place in the Resistance. A young woman passionately attached to my husband, I had succeeded in freeing him, in May, from the French prison where he had been held since March 15. I now mustered all my spirit, and my comrades in the *groupe-franc*[2] all their courage, to save him from the firing squad that the Gestapo had promised would be his fate after his arrest in Caluire with Jean Moulin. At the same time, I was pregnant with my second child. Because of my deep involvement in the underground war, keeping a diary was out of the question. That, however, is the form I want my narrative to take. It covers nine months—from May 1943 to February 1944—of my life as a member of the Resistance, a wife, and a mother. I have tried to tell things as accurately as possible. I was helped in this effort by my own memory, that of my husband, and the testimony of our comrades.

In November 1943, and again in January and February 1944, among the numerous messages—all in code—that the BBC broadcast from London to the Resistance in France, there was one for the Aubrac family. Because of bad weather, the British plane could not land in November 1943 or in January 1944 on the secret landing strip where our reception team was waiting for it.

On February 8, 1944, under a full moon, the plane got through to the rendezvous. That day the BBC had repeated three times the following message: "Ils partiront dans l'ivresse"—"They will leave with joy."

2. *Groupes-francs* were small armed resistance units, often more effective and secure than combined forces, in view of the Nazi military power.

February 12, 1944

As I wake up, everything is hazy. Hospital odors, whispers . . .
I raise my head, then, lifting myself on my elbows, I see an iron
bassinet hanging from a rack. Inside is a sleeping baby, its head
down at the end. Our daughter . . .

"Stay in bed. Your daughter weighs ten pounds; she's the big-
gest baby in maternity."

Mechanically I register the nurse's words, spoken in school-
girl French. I obey; my haziness slowly dissolves. Nearby in the
room I hear other women chattering in a language I don't understand. I am in London. It's February 12, 1944. I am thirty-one
years old. My name is Lucie Aubrac.

The nurse places the baby on my bed for a moment. She un-
wraps the baby from a large white woolen shawl. My naked
daughter thrusts her long, awkward limbs in every direction and
screws her face up tight. Her scalp is covered with pale down.

"We mustn't traumatize her," the nurse says, putting her back
in her cradle. "You can nurse her tomorrow."

I am exhausted. With the sheet pulled up to my chin, I cry
silently. My pillow is drenched. I've got to get rid of this haziness and reassemble my memories one by one. London, February 1944—Catherine weighs ten English pounds: nearly five
kilograms, after all.

9

Now I start to remember: last night, London was bombed at dinner time. The Germans choose full moon nights for bombing, as the British do for their parachute drops. I was with Jérôme, the head of the maquis, who like me arrived on a secret airplane flight.[3] We followed everybody else into the shelters. Down there, on a couch, I felt sick. I had a sharp pain in my back. The bombing was interrupted, then resumed almost at the same pace as my pains. Jérôme was leaning over me—would I be scared this time?

"Jérôme, I have to get to a hospital. I'm going to have the baby. I feel it." I thought of my suitcase back in my room at the Savoy Hotel. There was a whole layette inside it. And what a layette! Diapers cut from old sheets, swaddling clothes sewn from pieces of blanket, baby vests made out of cotton shirts . . . This time, no one said "pink for a girl, blue for a boy." In my child's layette there is one yellow jacket, which I knit; the rest is in every shade—from gray and brown to green and red.

Yes, ten English pounds is about four and a half kilograms in France . . . I'm more awake now. My English roommates keep up their chatter. I'm no longer crying. Memories fall into place: against the advice of the young woman in charge of security, I had left the shelter to get my suitcase, clenching my teeth and tightening my fists to keep from screaming when the contractions came. The hotel manager, alerted by Jérôme, came upstairs carrying a hot-water bottle, thinking I had indigestion. He then called for an ambulance. "You're lucky the air raid alert is still on, otherwise they would all be out on emergency service."

It was eleven o'clock at night, a night lit by bombs and searchlight beams. The stretcher in the ambulance was hard, the London streets full of holes, and the rattle of the bursts of antiaircraft shells reverberated on the roof of the vehicle. I remember the woman driver sounding the siren. We finally reached the hospital.

3. *Maquis* originally referred to the Corsican underbrush where bandits were able to hide indefinitely from the police, but it later became a general term for all underground activities between 1940–1944 and in particular, armed resistance.

"Shut up, it's a war." The midwife didn't like my screaming with each contraction. She wanted to make me lie on my side to give birth, but I protested in French.

"For four years now we've been working with bombs exploding everywhere. Be brave, madame, we've never seen a woman like you."

The nurses had just put an asbestos bracelet around my wrist, with my name. They undressed me, rather roughly, shaved my pubic hair and my armpits, painted me with Mercurochrome, and gave me an enema. Stupefied and in pain, I couldn't understand any of their questions. These English are peculiar. Then, as I knelt on the delivery table, one of them came up behind me and pushed me down on my right side. I screamed. Another one held up my left leg. They're crazy! And a third one tried to put a mask over my face. I ripped it from her hands and bit down on it with all my strength. At that instant I felt a horrendous tearing pain between my thighs. I would not see the birth of my baby!

Now, in the ward, on my soaked pillow, I cry again. But this time without grief or anger. I'm crying peacefully—it's an overflow just oozing out of me. And now I know: Raymond is alive and Catherine was born on February 12, 1944, at three-thirty in the morning. In London. I have won my battle.

The first one to visit me is the French consul, Mr. Gauthier, who comes to my bedside to register the birth. He explains in English to the other women who I am and where I come from. One thing puzzles them: how could someone produce such a big baby in a country where people are starving? I listen as the consul answers at length. He talks about how we kept on the move in the Jura; how in our successive hideouts the French peasants had been solicitous of the fugitive heroine. In London now, they speak of me as "the heroine."

"A funny kind of heroine," mutters the matron later as she picks me up when I faint on the landing. The matron is the head of the maternity ward; she was escorting me to the elevator to take me to a private room.

My little girl is voracious. She sucks with fervor and grunts like a little animal; then she lets go and falls asleep. My nipples are leaking and are becoming painfully chapped. In my new room, a large table covered with a white cloth has been set up; bottles, glasses, and a dish with biscuits are brought in. About noon the matron comes back, along with a small group of men. Raymond is there. I recognize two others—François Morin-Forestier, whom I had freed in Lyon in May 1943, and François d'Astier, an Air Force general whose two children had started their Resistance apprenticeship with us in Lyon. D'Astier takes a document from his pocket and begins reading a citation from the army. It's about me. I'm amazed. In France, we were not accustomed to this sort of honor.

We fought, sometimes we won, sometimes we lost. We met in prisons or surreptitiously in the homes of sympathizers, and without ceremony. In this maternity bed, I suddenly understand what it is that separates a regular army from our secret organizations, whose leaders were accepted by all without need for rank or insignia and into which men and women of all ages were recruited. How I wish that the comrades of my *groupe-franc* were here so this citation could give them some measure of glory. The military men here fight the same enemy we fight, and they demonstrate their fraternal esteem by treating me like a soldier, by giving me what is for them recognition of military accomplishment—a medal. The general is deeply moved. He is going to pin the ribbon with that heavy medal on my chest. Disconcerted, being used to the thick fabric of military uniforms, he fumbles nervously with the light fabric of my hospital gown. Seeing the big black prongs of the medal, I fear for my vulnerable breasts, filled with milk. Raymond hugs me. He too is moved. He whispers a thank you in my ear; the most beautiful of gifts.

During the night the sirens wake me. I take my daughter in my arms. Using the elevator is not permitted during air raid alerts, so I walk down the stairs—seven flights—to the shelter, which is lined with armchairs and beds. I choose a bed near a corner, put the baby next to me, and fall asleep. I am awakened by some commotion overhead; I was sleeping so soundly that I didn't hear the all-clear signal. Perhaps that night I regained my status as a heroine.

Some phosphorus bombs fell on the hospital. One wing was destroyed. We have to find a new shelter! My war is not over yet!

In a few days, on February 20, 1944, as prearranged with my comrades in France, the BBC daily broadcast will include a message that only they will understand: "Boubou has a little sister, Catherine, born on the twelfth."

Like all mothers, I carried her for nine months (minus two days). She was conceived on May 14, 1943.

Lyon, Friday, May 14, 1943

About nine-thirty in the morning, I catch sight of Raymond from the window of my room. The prosecutor had signed his release, contingent on bail. For a long time I have been watching the street, lined with small bungalows and tiny yards, deserted up to now. There he is—holding a strange bundle at arm's length. I recognize it at once: tied by the coattails and sleeves, it is the overcoat he was wearing the day he was arrested. I wait for him at the garden gate. Once the door is closed, our initial effusiveness is cut short.

"I really need to wash up."

Some dry wood goes into the stove, a shovelful of coal is added, a large pan of water goes on top; it heats quickly. He undresses in the bathroom on the second floor and throws his clothes out the window into the yard.

"Those lice! I didn't have them anymore at the hospital, but they took me back to the prison office to be discharged. Also, my overcoat had been left in the office of the court clerk. It must be completely infested . . ."

Holding the coat by my finger tips, I spread it on the fence at the end of the garden. We bought it in the fall of 1940, thanks to Maurice, Raymond's cousin, who is in the retail business. It's a fine, warm weave in a raised blue and gray check. You can't find one like that today. Now it is filthy and wrinkled, with streaks of white plaster along the back and a reddish stain on the left shoulder. Looking at it up close, I see a round hole right through the shoulder pad.

Later, inside our house, stretched out on the bed, our longing for each other satisfied, I say nothing, but I already know: we will have that second child that I have been wishing for for months. I count: nine months—that would be mid-February.

Raymond is talking. He knows I saw the hole in his overcoat.

"The cop missed me. But not by much. When they took me to search the apartment in the Croix-Rousse district, the address on my identity papers, I had an idea. I asked the two police inspectors escorting me to stop the car a little before the house. I told them: 'For the sake of my reputation, you understand—I don't want my landlady to refuse to rent to me after seeing me get out of a police van. But if the three of us arrive on foot, it won't look so bad.' See, I wanted to give them the idea that I didn't have anything to hide except a little black marketeering and that I'd been caught in the police dragnet on the rue de l'Hôtel-de-Ville. They laughed at my attempt to appear respectable, but they agreed. I had my keys. I opened the door and left the key in the outside lock. I said: 'Come in, gentlemen, and do your job.' Then I opened the cupboard for them. There were about a dozen tins of sardines, another dozen packages of noodles and bags of sugar, several packages of tobacco, some rice, some salt, a little chocolate—my activities as a small-time dealer seemed established.

"I asked them for permission to wash and change clothes while they were ransacking the place. For a whole week I had been dragged from police station to prison and back again . . . . They said it would be all right, adding that I wasn't done with jail and that I was going to spend that very night at the Saint-Paul prison. I pretended to be upset at this news and stammered out a request to pack a toilet kit and a change of underwear. They looked at each other, laughing: 'Go ahead.' They must have thought: 'Poor idiot, he still doesn't understand what's happening.' I picked up my things—razor, shaving brush and soap, handkerchiefs, socks, and briefs—and set them on the table. Then, as if it were the most natural thing in the world, I took a chair into the hallway: 'I've got to get my suitcase from up there on the shelf.' They weren't even paying attention to me anymore.

"Then I opened the door, went out, and locked the door before bounding down the stairs. Alas, they wasted no time. Before I got to the street they were hanging out the window, waving their guns. They were shouting: 'Get back up here or we'll shoot!' At first I thought at that distance they couldn't miss. But then I took a gamble: if I went outside, they would surely shout another warning before they fired. So I dashed into the street, zigzagging. 'Stop!' they yelled. 'Stop him! Stop the murderer!' Then they both started shooting, and a bullet went through my overcoat, just above the shoulder. I think what made them miss was the driver of the police van chasing me.

"I dived into the *traboules*, those cavernous tunnels that you and I had explored, leading from house to house to the quay. I pushed in a door at random. Rotten luck! An old lady was on her way out with her shopping basket. I bumped into her so hard that she fell. As I helped her to her feet (simultaneously apologizing and trying to keep her from yelling for help), the barrel of the police driver's gun suddenly appeared under my nose.

"He took me back to the apartment. That was a bad moment, but I had one consolation: they hadn't found anything. An attempted escape isn't enough to build a criminal case. Of course now washing, changing, or taking a suitcase was out of the question.

"The whole neighborhood could see me being taken away in handcuffs in the van. I knew that you hadn't been there yet, but that it wouldn't be long before you heard of my attempted escape."

I had rushed over there the next day. I needed to recover the papers that we had hidden there. Our security rules stated strictly that the apartment of any *résistant*[4] who was arrested was to be emptied as soon as we were sure the place hadn't become a police trap.

Raymond had rented this apartment from a woman whose husband was a prisoner of war. She lived with her parents, while drawing a small income from renting the two furnished rooms with a kitchen. She had asked Raymond to take particular care of the furniture, which was still like new after ten years. Raymond

---

4. *Résistants* were all French people who rejected the policy of collaboration with Germany and participated in the underground struggle against the occupation and its police forces.

had introduced me to her as his fiancée, saying that if he were away on business too long she could trust me completely, and give me the keys. The neighbors knew him by sight. In Lyon, people are neither curious nor talkative, and it takes a long time to get acquainted, but this very reticence is a guarantee of discretion. They appreciated the polite, courteous young man who was not noisy and who often was away. Maybe he had to travel on business. Besides, they would say, it was no concern of theirs.

When I called on the landlady, after Raymond's arrest, to get the keys and recover the papers—the police obviously had not found anything—she told me everything. The place was still a shambles. "It's strange, just the same," she said, "for a man to risk his life for a black market operation, and for such a small amount of merchandise. They could have killed him, you know; they emptied their clips firing at him. Now, you understand, I'm not asking you any questions," she added with a smile.

"Naturally; besides, the less one knows these days, the less one risks telling."

I think she guessed the truth. "It was that old lady Raymond knocked down that put a flea in our ear. A black marketeer or a murderer, as they called him, would never have stopped to help her up and apologize so politely. She said she'd never forgive herself for screaming. She told us that after Dunkirk, her grandson got to England and she was sure that he had joined de Gaulle."[5]

While Raymond and I trade thoughts of whatever comes to mind about these two months of separation, the morning passes quietly. Relaxed, scrubbed clean, satisfied, Raymond lights his pipe after drinking the roasted barley "coffee," which we are all used to now. He still can't believe that he is here this morning. His lawyer had requested bail, which is standard procedure for an indictment for black market activities. Raymond knew that the police court judge favored a release on bail, but that the

5. The extraordinary evacuation of British and French troops at Dunkirk, surrounded by overwhelming German forces, was accomplished by a myriad of small boats and, of course, some large warships, while under German air bombardment.

prosecutor opposed it. That clever bloodhound of a prosecutor had five young men in custody; he had proof that two of them were not mere small-time racketeers. His hatred of Gaullism and of Communism as well as his racism made him a fearsome adversary for *résistants*. To him, they were all enemies to be destroyed.

While Raymond, still amazed to be free, paces the floor, leafs through a book, straightens a picture on the wall where I have hung snapshots of our little boy, I keep asking him questions. It will take days to satisfy my curiosity. How did it go with the police and with the judge? The lawyer had mentioned interrogation by the Gestapo; what was that like?

Raymond takes plenty of time in answering me; he circles and hovers, giving me long kisses as he goes by. He follows me downstairs and fiddles with his pipe while I fix lunch.

"Our first judge was relatively good-natured," he says. "He entered a vague charge of black marketeering against the three of us. For Morin-Forestier, who was arrested with his secretary, his office clerk, and all his records, it was trickier. Well, the judge filled out our arrest warrant as a group, so as to minimize Morin's case. How did the Gestapo come into this? Some zealous French cop probably was in touch with the Germans. One day, a German police officer and two French inspectors arrived at the prison. They said: "The German police wish to interrogate three of the detainees." They used the names under which we were held: Asher (that's Serge Ravanel); Kriegel (that's Valrimont); and Vallet—that's me. First they took Ravanel out and questioned him for a very long time. When he was arrested he was carrying some Michelin maps with notes on reception centers for those refusing to accept compulsory labor service. When he returned after three hours of questioning, we were relieved and happy to see him again. Then it was our turn—Valrimont's and mine. The French police signed a regulation prison administration discharge, just as they had for Serge, and off we went.

"There were three people in the office of the German police chief. We steadfastly maintained our cover as petty black marketeers. Valrimont, who understands German, heard them discussing us. 'We're wasting our time with these guys—they're not

17

worth the trouble. Send them back to the French.' Once back in our cell at Saint-Paul prison, we breathed a big sigh of relief."

I shiver. Knowing about the collusion between the Vichy government and Hitler is one thing; to be confronted with the reality is another matter. I swear to remember this after the war: these were French policemen, real government employees, not just fascist rabble like the Milice, obeying German orders as a matter of routine![6] They had agreed to hand over to the Gestapo some Frenchmen whom they themselves had arrested and whose cases were being investigated by French judicial authorities. It is inconceivable!

There were exceptions. When Raymond was being held at the police station inside the Palais de Justice, where he remained almost a week with his comrades, French police and officials seemed to take the mandatory close watch over their prisoners quite lightly. One pleasant policeman who was on duty at the police station had even suggested to Julien and me as we were waiting around that we could visit the prisoners. At first we were suspicious, thinking it was a trap. But he convinced us of his sincerity. This is how we were able to find out, roughly, the circumstances of their arrest on March 15 in the rue de l'Hôtel-de-Ville. The policeman led us to the basement of the Palais de Justice, the dark corridors and musty cellars, but we didn't have time to help our friends escape before they were transferred to the prison.

"When the Germans were around," Raymond tells me, "French inspectors behaved like real doormats. They escorted us to the office of the Gestapo, saluted, and left. After interrogation, we met the French officials again—they had been waiting downstairs, by their car, like obedient children. Since the Germans considered us small fry, they hadn't sent along any of their own personnel to take us back to the French prison. As the inspectors

6. The innocuous designation Milice referred to the infamous military hordes that Vichy authorized to parallel and eventually supplant regular police forces. It had started honorably, as a veterans' organization, the Légion des Combattants, but early on was permitted to serve as the arm of the fascist Vichy government.

delivered us back to the warden I told them: 'You can really be proud! A fine job you're doing and you call yourselves French!' One of them replied: 'Your buddy said the same thing this morning. But we're just following orders.' "

The kitchen table is set for a meal. On the plates is everyday fare: potatoes in their skins (we waste less by peeling them after they are boiled) and a salad of dandelion greens. Today is a feast! A tin of paté, a whole salami, and a bottle of Moulin à Vent, set aside for such an occasion.

Under Raymond's napkin is a small package; he is really touched to find a brand-new pipe. We are celebrating not only his freedom, which is still almost impossible for him to comprehend, but also an anniversary very dear to us. Four years ago, on May 14, 1939, in Strasbourg, we realized we were truly in love. Not just love at first sight, but a harmony so definitive that we swore always to be together on the fourteenth of May as long as we lived.

Sitting at the table across from each other, in silence, deeply moved, we could stay like this forever. Raymond still can't get over being free, and just in time for our fourteenth of May. He suspects me of being involved in that miracle. How on earth did I manage this?

"Since you hadn't succeeded in escaping on your own, we decided, with the help of the groupe-franc, to get you out. There wasn't much spare 'human material' with which to replace you, and the Resistance needed you, your skills and your contacts. It's not that easy to get out of jail, so I thought we would repeat the trick that enabled you to escape from the POW camp on August 25, 1940."

At that time, Raymond's brother, a physician, had given me some pills that would make Raymond feverish. I was able to slip them to him in the Uhlans barracks at Sarrebourg, where his whole regiment was confined. The pills worked, and the German military command transferred him to the hospital run by the Red Cross. In 1940 the Germans still observed the

Geneva Convention on prisoners of war. That night Raymond scaled the wall of the hospital and escaped, wearing the blue overalls that I had brought to replace his uniform.

"This time, my problem was to get all of you transferred out of the prison and into the disciplinary section of the Antiquaille hospital. An obliging prison guard gave you some medication, which he thought was candy. You were in civilian clothes, so no change of clothes was needed. On the other hand, we had to neutralize the French police who were guarding you. With the groupe-franc, we tried to organize a way for you to get out, the most plausible being that the German police had come to take you to be interrogated. But the earliest date this plan would work was the twentieth of May, because we didn't have the necessary transportation. We knew you could manage to stay at the hospital by raising your temperatures when they came to take them. Though poor Serge didn't have to pretend, with his bronchitis and bad cough . . ."

Raymond listens without interrupting.

"The plan had to be put off for so long that I wondered how we would be together on May 14. I said to myself: This man who hates de Gaulle and the Resistance, this ferocious prosecutor, perhaps he makes such a fuss because at heart he is a coward. I found his address, and the day before yesterday I rang his doorbell. I told the woman who opened the door that I had a personal message for the prosecuter. She gave me a funny look. Maybe she thought it was a lovers' tryst. The prosecutor agreed to see me. I told him straight out: 'You have in your prison a man named François Vallet. Twice you have refused to sign his release on bail. The police court judge understood immediately that it was better to sign it, and you'll soon see why. Of course, his lawyer has not been told what this case is all about. As for me, I am here representing General de Gaulle, who is Vallet's supreme commander. If you don't sign this release tomorrow at the Palais de Justice, if Vallet is not free on the morning of May 14, you will not see the sun go down that evening. I can substantiate what I'm saying. Listen just this once to tonight's BBC broadcast. Among the personal messages you will hear the following: 'Continue to scale the mountain.' That message is for you personally. You have heard correctly: 'Continue to scale the mountain.' The prosecutor was speechless, and I didn't want to waste time. Before he could come to his senses, I opened the door, calling out for good measure: 'See you tomorrow! And don't forget our rendezvous on the fourteenth.'

"Until I got to the bridge over the Saône, I was terrified of being caught by the police. You know, all he had to do was call the Saint-Jean police station nearby. On that stretch of road, along the high bank of the river, there's no place to hide, and with so few trolleys running."

"And so here you are!"

Raymond is stunned: "And if the message hadn't been broadcast?"

"Yes, it was taking a chance, but at one o'clock the message was broadcast. Besides, I'm always lucky; isn't this the best proof?"

"Now listen, Lucie, if you keep tempting fate, you'll run into trouble."

"But now you are here and at six-thirty I have an appointment with your lawyer, Fauconnet, who must already know about your release. We'll go together."

"If you think he's going to be overjoyed by your blackmail, get ready for a good lecture!"

"We'll see. For the moment, we have a whole afternoon to make love, to make plans."

As a precautionary measure, we decide to go separately and meet at the lawyer's door. When we get to Fauconnet's office, all the other clients have gone. The big dark waiting room with its somber paneling and drapes, its empty chairs, retains the odors of the people who came to see him that afternoon. I rather like this man, whom I have known for only two months. He is from Lyon, unmarried, Catholic and liberal, full of good sense. He is a learned jurist and absolutely opposed to Vichy collaboration.[7]

Our cousin Maurice, who knows everybody in Lyon, had recommended him to me after Raymond's arrest on March 15. The

7. Vichy advocated full collaboration with the Germans. The term *collaborator* eventually became a synonym for *traitor*.

first time I entered his office I naively expected a sort of spontaneous complicity between us. However, he was not exactly a backslapping type. He was about ten years older than I, not very tall, a bit stout, with blue eyes and graying hair.

Fauconnet dressed conservatively, and a slightly misshapen upper lip gave him a rather sarcastic expression. He received me quite formally: "Madam, the only client I know is François Vallet, a seedy black marketeer. You are willing to take an interest in his legal defense and therefore will pay my honorarium; I will in turn keep you informed of the steps I take and eventually of my conversations with him."

This is how we began, and our weekly meetings remained rather formal. Once I remarked on the magnificent bindings of his library and on his valuable collection of snuffboxes. Still later, with Raymond, in the visiting room at the prison, there were some confidential exchanges of information, matters were hinted at or alluded to obliquely, and a sense of trust created. One day, Fauconnet took a wedding ring from his vest pocket and gave it to me, smiling: "Mr. Vallet asks you to keep this for him. Of course, you and I have already forgotten this transaction."

"Of course, sir."

Either because he is shy or because he has the typical Lyon reserve, he does not show emotion easily. Today, as he welcomes us warmly, I begin to understand that.

"Sit down. How happy I am to see you together! It's a miracle. But I must confess I don't understand it at all. Just the day before yesterday, the prosecutor seemed deaf to everything I said."

"Well, sir, when you gave me the wedding ring that Raymond had succeeded in passing to you, I said to you: 'I will give it back to him on May 14.' And I did."

Once again I describe my intervention and the bluff I used with the prosecutor. Raymond watches me out of the corner of his eye. I am much less relaxed than I was with him this morning, all the more so as the lawyer seems shocked, becoming more and more distant and reproachful. I feel uneasy, even guilty, as if in this proper office I had committed some unseemly act or had burst out swearing.

Suddenly, he explodes: "But you can't do this, it's simply not done! You have threatened an officer of the court, and that's a very serious matter. What would become of the independence and dignity of the law if everyone acted like you?"

I rise to my defense: "Well, in this case it was effective, and you know very well that your justice is not what it was before 1939. In any event we're fighting it. Besides, if your prosecutor had a clear conscience or even was able to act independently, he would never have signed the release!"

From a low sideboard, the lawyer takes three glasses and a bottle of Izarra liqueur, its color a wonderful gold. "Let's say no more about it; let's drink to your reunion, to your freedom that you are going to have so much trouble keeping, for I suppose you will go on with what you do."

Clinking our glasses in a toast, this good man looks at me severely: "My dear child, those are not legal procedures; after the war, you'll have to be sure not to use them again, not even think of them." My eyes fill with tears, like a naughty child who has been scolded, then forgiven.

We go home without lingering. It is seven-thirty at night. The sun is red in the west. The sky with all its constellations reflects our joy. We decide to wait until Monday before asking Maria, our maid, who is staying with my in-laws, to come back. Tomorrow morning, Saturday, I have to teach two hours of classes. We will still have the whole afternoon to ourselves!

Sunday, May 16, 1943

Our family is once again complete. My sister-in-law brought back our Jean-Pierre from the Auvergne, where she had left him with very dear friends after Raymond's arrest on March 15.

His life as our cherished little boy picks up where it left off. Outside the underground life of the Resistance, with its more or less dangerous activity, daily life must be confronted—for a woman more than a man: a household to take care of, a husband and child to feed, clothes to be washed. Raymond is watching me soak the weekend's dirty clothes in a tub filled with water warmed in the sun.

"At least now you won't have to do the wash for five prisoners."

"And what wash!" I told him of my difficulties with the disgusting rags brought back periodically from Saint-Paul prison. "First I had to delouse your undershorts and shirts, your underwear. That was awful. How could you live with those lice? There were so many of them, big black ones. You know, a louse is extraordinarily tough and nearly indestructible. Even after boiling the wash, I found some in the seams; by then they were transparent, completely bloodless, but still moving! I finally got them with a hot iron."

"It was worth it, though," Raymond says. "You can't imagine what a pleasure it is to put on clean underwear. We were all right until nighttime, but then the whole business started again with the lice-infested straw mattresses. They don't allow even the smallest can of Fly-Tox in that jail. It had never occurred to me that lice could become the number one problem. I told my buddies, 'Sparks will fly over these socks; Lucie with her suffragette mentality has made them the symbol of feminine independence. She's liable to throw them out!' When they came back clean, the others all made fun of me."

"You don't understand. The socks belonged to prisoners. I was a free person. So there was no dependence. It was only natural that I washed the socks and the rest of the clothes. But one thing was totally disgusting: the handkerchiefs. Oh—that slimy stuff that came out when I scrubbed them under running water! I often told myself that after the war a woman would surely invent paper handkerchiefs to be thrown away after they're used."

On my desk is a batch of papers to be corrected; it's the map of France's subterranean resources. I also have a class tomorrow with my third-year students: agriculture in France. My preparation consists of just two short paragraphs devoted to soil conditions and climate, and sneakily develops at length what fits with present reality—the shortage of manpower resulting from more than a million being held as prisoners of war, three-quarters of whom are farmers. Agricultural equipment is wearing out. Spare parts are extremely rare, obtainable only with a coupon. Then there is fuel, distributed in dribbles because it is the most valuable commodity of all for the occupying power. I examine agricultural resources and outlets at even greater length: prewar statistics showing the surpluses of wine, wheat, and meat. A wheat office had even been created to help farmers sell the harvest. I found a terrific passage reprinted in a 1938 economics journal, encouraging the French to consume more bread and pastry: "Advice to mothers: French pastry, the finest in the world, so attractive and diverse, is a complete food. Made from fine flour, butter, eggs, and milk, it is a pleasant way to feed your children and aid their growth."

This course will be taught on the very same day the authorities are releasing the coupons: KC, which entitles "hard laborers" to five ounces of cold cuts and K8, which provides an extra half-pound of sugar to the three youth categories (J1, J2, J3)—these children certainly will have something to talk about at home!

These ration cards and coupons that you have to get every month at the municipal offices are a real headache. When are you entitled to what? Unless you consult the announcements posted at the town hall and in store windows, you have to read the newspaper announcements to find out. The whole population is divided into categories. And what conversations you hear at the stores!

"Do you have a J3, madam?" (J3s are the adolescents.)

"No, but I have two 'hard laborers.'" (These are also given to pregnant women.)

What labor isn't hard these days, when rutabagas replace potatoes, when you have to be on intimate terms with the fishmonger to buy even a carp's head without a ration coupon?

Each adult is entitled to one liter of wine every ten days. So there are three liters per month, for adults only, and even this works only if the store has been supplied. As you have to return empty bottles, I am always carrying six empties in my bicycle rack that I try to get filled during my various trips.

It's also a ten-day cycle for tobacco. One pouch of tobacco or two packs of Gauloises—for adult men only, of course. This is where there is the most bartering: one loaf of bread, two liters of wine for one pack of cigarettes. It is all so degrading. Adults show the same kind of raw energy, the same serious intensity, as children do trading marbles or candy.

I have to decide before I leave to run my errands whether

it's safe to use the coupons that are still valid on François Vallet's ration card—the identity that Raymond has just abandoned. That could mean three rations for two. When Raymond arrived at Saint-Paul prison, he surrendered all his ration cards to the jail dietician, who gave them back to him when he left. I still had his genuine card under his own name, which I used to make up the food packages that I sent with the clean clothes for the prisoners. Since Jean-Pierre was being fed decently in the Auvergne, I also had the baby's flour, milk, sugar, and cocoa coupons. When they got out, every one of Raymond's companions told me he had never eaten so well as during those two months in prison.

Besides the prison food that the prisoners got, the money their lawyers gave them made it possible to buy certain items from the prison canteen. Pathetic purchases of whatever was available without ration cards, things like bran biscuits and fruit jelly made with grape sugar. Also the social services of the Resistance gave me some canned food, which enriched the weekly package.

Raymond told me, "Your chocolate crepes! Only in jail could one hope to get them." And in the same vein of black humor: "You know, when it comes to that, it wasn't all that bad a life there."

Silly jokes.

Monday, May 17, 1943

At the lycée, when I open my mailbox in the teachers' lounge there isn't much mail, but I recognize two items from their distinctive folds and shape: underground newspapers. An issue of *Combat* and one of *Libération*. I will read them later in the toilet and find out what's in them. But for the time being I calmly pick them up with the other mail. If it is a trick, people will plainly see that I'm not reading them. But if someone is really distributing them, that means there are other *résistants* here besides myself.

I get along very well with my students; the final-year students and I had a good laugh together on May 8. That day, following a government directive, all history professors were required to pay homage to Joan of Arc, whose birthday, May 9, the state was officially celebrating. They were to show that Marshal Pétain[8] was her "worthy heir" and that the personal qualities of these heroes were identical. I called two students to the blackboard, which I had divided into two sections with a vertical line; on one side, Marshal Pétain; on the other, Joan of Arc. Then the game began: age, sex, profession, personal situation (married or single), enemy or ally. As I wrote down the responses, the class kept inventing new categories, and they all laughed until tears came to their eyes. There was no reaction from parents during the next few days. However, not all the parents opposed the Vichy regime, but I believe that for the young, school is a private domain that does not concern their parents.

Today I have chosen to discuss the presidency of Marshal MacMahon after the 1870 defeat in the Franco-Prussian War. To be sure, it's not every week that I find such marvelous opportunities to dramatize today's situation while keeping up my role as teacher. This afternoon no one was missing, none of the girls with biblical or foreign names, emigrants from Paris or even farther away who hoped that Lyon would be their last stop. When the school secretary comes around toward the end of the class with the register of absentee students, I am unconcerned and sign the book promptly. In this Lyon lycée, its population increased by the arrival of refugees from the north, enrollment has changed considerably. There are several Jewish or foreign students in every class. At the beginning of the month, among my third-year students, the little Lehmann girl stopped coming. Why? Nobody knows. One of her classmates went to her home, but nobody answered the doorbell. The shutters were closed; the mailbox was overflowing; the concierge had received no instruc-

8. Pétain was credited (though some of the best military historians and analysts dispute his merit) with winning the crucial battle of Verdun (1916) during the First World War. He took over the government after the fall of France in June 1940. His authoritarian regime tried to safeguard France's interests. Too weak to resist German demands, however, it soon became a mere puppet government, although it did a great deal of harm to the population in general and to minorities in particular.

tions. All my students fell silent at this news. My history class did not go well that day.

Tonight I come home after slipping the newspapers I found in my mailbox into two neighboring mailboxes. It was out of the question for me to take them home; we must be prepared at any time for the house to be searched.

All week long my time is divided between the lycée, my home, and the *groupe-franc*. Our three comrades arrested with Raymond on March 15 are still at the Antiquaille hospital, and we have to get them out of there as soon as possible. Two men are sent out to reconnoiter the place during the visiting hours for regular patients; they are to make a precise map of the reception and administration offices, as well as of the section reserved for prisoners. The drivers run through a plan in advance with our two cars; arrival, parking, and especially departure must be swift and without mishaps. We are also making an escape route study of Lyon in order to evacuate our liberated comrades.

Raymond finds inactivity hard to bear. He plays with his son—but only for a time. He wrote the editorial on foreign policy for the newspaper *Libération*. Pascal Copeau came to see him when he returned from Paris, where the National Council of the Resistance is being formed.

Our various resistance movements were created in the fall of 1940; within two years, they grew in parallel and along similar lines. There were regional organizations and the different services were established: for manufacture of false identity papers, social services, the underground press, propaganda, information and intelligence, the secret army, and labor action. During the winter of 1942–43, Max, General de Gaulle's representative within France, contacted every leader of every resistance group with the intention of fusing them all into a single organization: the MUR (Mouvements Unis de Résistance). All had foreseen such a union and most were successful in implementing it. The various newspapers maintained their autonomy and kept their names—*Combat, Libération, Franc-Tireur*. They were printed whenever they had the good fortune to find a cooperative print shop and a supply of newsprint, which was so severely rationed that we had to either steal it or buy it on the black market.

Max (Jean Moulin) arrived in France from London on December 31, 1941. At that time, he used the name Rex. In early January, Raymond welcomed him to Lyon on behalf of our group. They met under the theater arcades. Rex took Raymond to a small room near the town hall, produced a box of matches from his pocket, and emptied it on the table. He then handed Raymond the box, together with a magnifying glass. At the bottom of the match box was a microphoto of the official military order signed "de Gaulle" identifying Max as the representative to the resistance movements.

"You must destroy that," Raymond said to him. "It's no proof in my eyes—the proof for me is that d'Astier vouches for you. But if the police find this, it means your arrest and perhaps your death."

Once the unification of the Resistance movements was a reality, Rex, who then changed his name to Max, undertook to convince the different parts of the newly unified movement to create a national organization that would combine the Resistance movements from all France, as well as all the political parties opposed to Vichy and Hitler—which was no easy task. He also proposed that the National Council of the Resistance take over the political direction of the Resistance. He succeeded in having the paramilitary groups form a single secret army led by an officer designated by de Gaulle whose staff would be made up of secret army representatives from the various movements.

Raymond is fascinated by the methodical way the Resistance is being organized, which he takes to be a sign both of growth and of vigor. He accepts Pascal Copeau's suggestion to postpone decisions on the resumption of his own activities until after the escape from Antiquaille hospital has been carried out.

That escape has been set for Monday, May 24, in the morning. I have no classes on Monday mornings so I can be part of it. This afternoon we'll reconnoiter at the hospital as a last-minute precaution. No one will notice us among the many Sunday visitors.

What the hell are they doing? We are getting nervous. Christophe, one of the members of the group, is at the wheel of the car, sitting next to me, ready to take off as soon as Raymond and André Lassagne get here. The other car, driven by Daniel, is closer to the hospital gate; it will be the one to carry to safety the freed comrades and the fellow from Luxembourg in German uniform, who lends an air of authenticity to the whole expedition.

I don't doubt for an instant that we will succeed, but I am anxious about letting Raymond participate in the operation. Out of solidarity with his three comrades who were still locked up, he was determined to be in on the venture.

"Good," said Ambre (he is a member of the *groupe-franc*). "Here, Raymond, this is the last pistol we have. It has no hammer, so it's useless; you stay in the hallway, near the office, and keep the secretaries away from the phone. The pistol should be enough to scare them. André, no one here knows you, so you come up with us."

André is a professor of Italian at the Ampère lycée; he is a childhood friend of one of our cousins. He is in his thirties, handsome, dark-haired; his sense of humor is irrepressible, he always has a funny story to tell. He doesn't even hesitate. "Listen, I'll be the cop, with a raincoat and a felt hat and a loud voice. You'll see, it's going to be perfect."

The *groupe-franc* of the Libération movement found a man from Luxembourg who had been forced into German military service and had then deserted. They subjected him to all sorts of clever tests and finally became convinced that he wasn't a spy. His German uniform and flawless German make him an invaluable accomplice.

"Here they come now . . ."

They all bolt from the hospital. Engines start. The cars are heading in the right direction. Serge Ravanel gets in between Raymond and André, and we're off.

There is a lot of joyful shoulder slapping to ease the nervous tension that we all had so carefully concealed. Serge Ravanel describes what happened: "They charged into the room, followed by the hospital director and a male nurse, shouting, 'German police! Get dressed quickly! Come with us for interrogation!' For a moment, I thought they were the real thing—I was panic-stricken. I didn't know these three men and the one in uniform was much too natural to be fake. So I said to them, 'Show me your identification.' That really made them laugh. The director protested, 'Gentlemen, these men are ill, they were entrusted to my care by the health services of Saint-Paul prison. They are in my charge; I can't let them go even if I wanted to. Besides, these two policemen on guard duty will confirm it.' But when he turned around, they were gone! After seeing how these guys broke in, they wisely took off, not caring either to interfere or even to witness the action."

"So then," Serge continues, "to make the whole thing look even better, on the staircase André kicked me in the pants, and I went down faster than I meant to."

We leave our Ravanel on the Rhône embankment. He is the youngest of the trio: at age twenty, having just graduated from the Ecole Polytechnique, he has the serious, systematic bent of the young mathematician working hard to succeed in the rigorous competition of his school. But with all that serious side, he moves easily from his role as the amazed innocent to clobbering a policeman who threatens him with a gun.

Raymond has stuffed his hat into a pocket of the gabardine raincoat, which he carries over his arm. Hand in hand we take the trolley home.

At the house, Jean-Pierre is quietly playing with his building blocks. Viewed from the outside, the Art Deco stained-glass windows of the dining room, with their black lead frames, seem dull. But indoors, on this sunny morning, bright spots and all the colors of the rainbow vibrate on the wooden floor. Our little two-year-old patiently tries to line up his blocks with these patterns. It all has to be redone in a few minutes. As the sun moves, the colors go with it, and he tirelessly starts again. Our good little guy, our joy, wanted and made after Raymond's escape from the POW camp. We of course think he's the most beautiful child in the world, and hope with all our might for a second baby. I already know we started it on May 14 . . .

Pascal Copeau, who has been watching for our return, arrives with a bottle of wine, his deep, beautiful voice booming: "I was sure it would work—let's drink to it! But now you'll have to go away for a while. The French police won't take this slap in the face very well—the Krauts even worse. There will be a big fuss. Get away until all this blows over. Off you go! Take a ten-day vacation."

"I have obligations as a teacher—I can't just stay away from the lycée without giving notice."

"Come now; it won't be the first time Dr. Riva will discover that you are in bad need of a rest so you can undertake a special mission. The mountains are no longer safe, what with all the men who have gone there to escape the forced labor edicts and the organization of new maquis units. Anyway, there's no place for you to stay there. Why not the seaside? The Mediterranean, maybe, near Saint-Aygulf—so far there are only garrisons of Italians there."

As soon as the meal is over, while the child takes a nap, I only feel like doing one thing: being in those welcoming arms. But I have to see the doctor right away.

As usual, I'm lucky. It's not his consulting day, but he's just coming home between house calls. He knows me well, as he was the one who examined my baby in 1942. At that time, he quickly understood what we were doing, and he brought me—I was still nursing—a famished baby. The parents had to flee and weren't able to take the baby. They were German Jews who had been warned, just in time, that the Vichy police were on the way to their apartment.[9] While efforts were made to find the parents, the baby had to be fed, and so he shared my milk with Jean-Pierre for a week. It was also this doctor who procured the medication

9. The Vichy government agreed to hand over to the Nazis thousands of foreign Jewish refugees. Many others—like the translator of the present book—were warned in time by French police officials loyal to the Republic and were able to survive underground, with the help of both Catholic and Protestant French people. Those interned by Vichy were transported by cattle car to the German concentration camps, which turned out to be extermination centers, like Auschwitz.

that made it possible to get Raymond and the others in prison transferred to the hospital.

The doctor has established a solid medical file on me, because from time to time I've had to carry out a mission while school was in session. According to that file, I am a former tuberculosis patient, with convincing X-rays, medical records with proper dates, and a clinical analysis of my recovery. There were four examinations that showed no disease, since one cannot teach if contagious. Still, according to the file, I'm anemic and have a tendency to tire easily. That's easy to verify; at five feet eight I weigh only 118 pounds. I nursed my son for fourteen months and really did have a decalcification, which my clever doctor had a colleague diagnose. However, I am actually in good health, vigorous, and without the least scruple about deceiving the school administration.

So I'm off now to the lycée office, where they agree I look really sick. I hand in the medical certificate recommending two weeks of complete rest, which means a leave of absence. When I say good-bye to the principal, she tells me, "You have been nursing far too long, my dear, and now you must suffer the consequences; try to rest up someplace where you can find some milk, that's the best recalcifier."

Tuesday, May 25, 1943

We can't even think of boarding the train at Perrache, the main Lyon station, since it is probably even more closely watched than usual. With our backpacks, and our little boy trotting along, we barely manage to catch a trolley for the suburbs, to La Mulatière. There we have a hard time finding seats on the bus that is leaving for Vienne, in the Isère department. While the T-shirted driver busily stirs the fire of the wood-gas engine,[10] we look at each other in loving complicity. People don't kiss in public, in

10. Because the Germans confiscated almost all oil and gasoline resources, French engineers adapted automobile engines to wood gas; buses, trucks, and cars were equipped with these burners, difficult to control.

1943, under the Vichy regime. But our lips are sending kisses—once more we've made it!

At Vienne, the train for the Côte d'Azur is ready to leave. What a horror! It's jam-packed. People in the compartments, the corridors, even in the toilets and between the cars! The train has accumulated all the heat of this early summer day. Black smoke and cinders coming through the open windows make all the travelers look alike—dark skinned. We sit on our backpacks in the corridor, where, luckily, nobody can pass. The child is stretched out over our laps, asleep. Nobody moves; besides, where could they go? There's no dining car on this train, a semi-local, and the toilets can't be used. We all warily watch our luggage—it isn't easy to replace a wardrobe or a picnic basket when everything is rationed.

"Would you like me to take your kid for a moment?" A traveler seated in the neighboring compartment takes Jean-Pierre in his arms without waking him.

At Avignon, the police examine everyone's documents. No one makes it easy for the cops to go up and down the corridor. We are okay; our genuine identity papers, my baptismal certificate, my medical report, and Raymond's demobilization card are all seen and approved.

"The kid's asleep," the traveler says. "If I wake him up suddenly he's going to scream and bother everybody. Finish checking this coach while I wake him gently, and then I can get out my papers to show you."

"All right." The cops move on, climbing over suitcases, duffel bags, and people sitting on the floor. When they reach the end of the coach they turn around. The traveler, who still hasn't awakened the boy, is waving his wallet at arm's length. The policemen hesitate at the coupling between the cars. The first one mumbles something, the other shrugs his shoulders. They are not coming back. In the crowded compartment and in the corridor, nobody says a word, then there is a sigh of relief. Of course, the traveler is someone illegal: a Jew or an escaped prisoner, perhaps one of those dodging the compulsory labor service, or a *résistant* on a mission? There are some strange people on the train these days . . .

In July 1941, Raymond was given the task of taking a suitcase full of newspapers to Grenoble. To be on the safe side, he put the suitcase in the baggage rack of the compartment next to his. When he went to retrieve it at Grenoble, it was gone; yet two days later all the papers had been distributed! Later we learned that a railroad worker had found the abandoned suitcase in the Grenoble station waiting room. The thief obviously didn't wish to be caught with such a load.

For the moment, our marvelous little one still sleeps. He's sucking his thumb, while with the other hand he strokes the smooth button on the traveler's coat. When the man gets off at Marseille, I take his seat. He hands the child over to me carefully. "He's been a great help to me."

Nothing more. I will never know anything more about him, nor will he ever know that on that very morning we had been waiting at the gate of a Lyon hospital for three *résistants* arrested two months earlier. The police—so many different kinds! Everyone is afraid of them, from the male nurse at the Antiquaille hospital to the travelers on the train. Everybody is subjected to their presence and fears their huge power. Whether they're in uniform or not, nobody challenges the order "Police. Your papers!" Ah, to be safely in order—but who can ever boast that they are completely? Fortunately, people develop a sense of community, and they are shrewd. This train trip marks one more victory, although we don't know for what, or for how long.

Night falls; impossible to catch a wink. I am numb from the weight of the child, who clings to my chest. His head jounces with the train, so hard it bruises my breasts. I can't stop kissing his soft young skin.

Raymond dozes impassively. The jail cell provided some training in putting up with discomfort and lack of privacy. The train rolls along in the dark through the short night of the longer days of summer. A tiny blue night light gives everyone a cadaverous look. Once in a while, between the cracks of the poorly drawn curtains, the rapid flash of a shooting star appears. Should we make a wish? It's not really a shooting star, just a glowing cinder hitting the window pane. Is it because of this ghastly light? There has never been such a noisy train. Its whistle is unbearable, the coach rattles and creaks and at every joint in the tracks the double clack of the wheels makes an unsynchronized bang. I'm obsessed with it, I count the clacks, trying to guess their frequency. I'm fed up and so sleepy.

At dawn it turns chilly. Everyone looks ugly, dirty, completely exhausted. Seeing Raymond in this condition, I now understand why people look like criminals in identification photos. Unshaven, disheveled, and to top it off, swollen lips and a black eye from being roughed up—a portrait of the typical terrorist. It would make a great "wanted" poster: Marxist Jew, a foreigner, and a Gaullist!

In February I went on behalf of the movement to Paris and from there north to Valenciennes. I can still see myself, at daybreak in winter, on that train with its wooden benches, the only woman, freezing, surrounded by workers on their way to work in the coal mines. They were all undernourished, and despite their different ages, they all looked alike: exhausted and miserable. I even wondered whether they still had the strength to think. The coach was open at either end; rough boards served as seat backs for the long wooden benches running the length of the car. These were the only trains that the German requisition services had left behind, and now they carried their cargos of coal miners to the north.

At Saint-Raphaël, we get off and go to the station cafeteria. Our ration coupons provide us with three slices of bread and butter and some roasted barley coffee, sweetened with saccharine. A can of condensed milk bought on the black market makes a decent breakfast for Jean-Pierre. We clean up as best we can. Raymond even shaves after a fashion. Our little boy, whom all our friends call Boubou, is delighted to be in new surroundings. He is all bright eyed; he at least has slept well.

We pay a surprise visit to my sister, who is convalescing at a nearby heliotherapy center.[11] She knows the area and gives us the address of a little pension at Carqueiranne.

11. Heliotherapy, intense exposure to the sun, was for some time believed to be a cure for certain ailments.

"You'll see, they will have room for you; it's been three-quarters requisitioned for Italian officers. Nobody wants to go there."

"That's stupid," Raymond grumbles, "to go there means throwing ourselves to the wolves . . ."

But I'm delighted. "On the contrary—it's excellent camouflage. A young couple so obviously in love—who would suspect us? And such a beautiful little boy. You know, on the Mediterranean coast, a child is king." I've won.

The owner, a blonde, blue-eyed Provençal woman, is so pleased with the unexpected guests—French people, just think! The prices are reasonable. She shows me the room right away; it has a large bed with a white hand-crocheted cover. She adds a child's bed. There is a washstand; certainly no shower or bath. "I'll bring you some warm water so your husband can shave. The toilet is at the end of the corridor. And I'll get a potty for the child."

There is a large garden, and in it a pond with papyrus plants; there are rabbits in a hutch and a fenced-in space with a hen and her chicks. (On the first day, we had a near-tragedy. One of the chicks managed to squeeze through the mesh of the fence, and Jean-Pierre caught it. He brought it to me triumphantly, while the hen clucked angrily. I put the chick back, a little groggy from its adventures, on the other side of the fence.) The sea draws us right away. The water is warm, the little bay deserted. There are more stones and pebbles than sand, but so what? We stretch out in the sun. Raymond is whiter than I am, after two months behind bars, and that night he is covered with freckles. "You'll see—tomorrow they'll blend and I'll have a good tan."

In short, it is a honeymoon. We got married during the war, in December 1939, and here we are together at the seashore for the first time. We've never been so happy. The organization of the Resistance, the meetings, the dangers—how far all that seems now! No need to make an effort to act like a carefree couple with nothing to do but get a suntan while our little one marvels at everything: the rolling waves, the seashells, the smooth and shiny pebbles revealed by the receding water. We prattle to him in his language, making him repeat new words—"hello sea, hello waves." But "seashell" trips him up, and we laugh happily.

It's out of the question for us to caress each other on the beach —it's not done! And what would the innkeeper say? Behind the curtains some lovelorn Italian soldier probably is watching us. I'm lying on the rather hard ground, with my stomach as Raymond's pillow. How I love him and how he stirs my senses! I feel our two bodies as strongly united as when we make love. I couldn't stand losing him. During this quiet vacation we have plenty of time to talk. Little by little, Raymond tells me the details of his arrest, of life in a cell with four companions.

"You know, it's strange when you arrive in prison. First, you have to repeat all the personal information that you've already given the police and the police court judge. Name, first name, place and date of birth, father's first name, mother's maiden name, place of residence, profession—everything has to be recorded. I felt completely at ease being François Vallet, an orphan, an only son, and a bachelor. But now that man has ceased to exist, even though there's no death certificate. I wonder what name I'll have now. Where am I going to be born this time?

"After the entry in the prison register we were led into a room with one guard per prisoner for a ceremony that you simply can't imagine. All of us stark naked, and then came this silly order: 'Turn around, bend over, cough!' "

I laugh until the tears come to my eyes. I can just see all five guards inspecting my friends' bottoms, making sure that nothing falls out at the word "cough." I've read enough detective stories to know that it's the classic hiding place for the criminal. But here were two graduates of the polytechnic, one road and bridge engineer, one law graduate, and an adolescent, all five bending over for this humiliation, which is merely routine for their guards.

"And yet," Raymond goes on, "they must have noticed we were a different breed from their usual catch. They didn't call us by our first names. But wait, that's not all. Another order: 'Spread your legs, raise your arms!' They felt our pubic hair and our armpits. Then they stuck their fingers between our jaws and cheeks. After that, we could dress; they let us keep our shoelaces and belts, but no neckties. Then we were taken to the bedding distribution center, where we were given three straw mattresses and three blankets; then on to the cell block. Our cell contained only two beds. We took turns sleeping on them. Besides, they were no better than the mattress on the ground. We were lucky to remain together. We all knew each other slightly, except for Hégo, whom I had never seen before. He was a liaison agent from the north. He had been too young, of course, to be a soldier and came to Lyon to avoid compulsory labor service.

"You know, Lucie, it's not easy to use a toilet bucket when there are five to a cell, five men inside four walls. We decided that two of us would hold a blanket stretched in front of the bucket while one man used it. That still left the problem of the noise and the odor! We four who were older were used to a certain degree of communal living because of scouting or dormitories in graduate school. But even in the barracks we enjoyed certain privileges as officers in training.

"Here it was entirely different, a pretty strange initiation, and we were all good-humored about it. We agreed at once that we should find things to do with our time and get maximum benefit from the right to walk around at certain times and the chances to wash. Of course there were endless discussions about the organization of the Resistance, how we had been arrested, what we planned for the future. Each of us dreamed endlessly of escape.

"Morin-Forestier, one of the students from the Ecole Polytechnique, came from a musical family and was able to whistle and hum whole symphonies without mistakes. From our memories we dug up poems learned during our not-so-distant adolescence. It was easy enough to recite La Fontaine's *Fables*, or Corneille's *Le Cid*. Rimbaud's *Le Bateau ivre* gave us more trouble. I don't know why, perhaps the irregular rhythms, but also its eroticism; it was damned seductive for five young men without women.

"Valrimont had already started studying law and I, too, had had a taste of it. Together we could recite any number of statutes and articles while the two young students from the polytechnical institute made up tricky math problems. We even made a chess set out of paper. Hégo was a particularly devoted and alert student of our game—above all to please our egos, I think. But despite all this activity, a day in jail is long!"

In the dining room of the pension we are the only "civilians." At mealtime, the Italian officers all have white-gloved orderlies standing behind them, to prepare their fish and peel their fruit. We can't help staring. They notice our fascination and keep looking our way.

"They're getting on my nerves," Raymond says. "Why do they keep looking at us like that?"

"It's not me they're interested in. You know how children in Italy are always protected and noticed. Our "bambino" is so beautiful, so chubby in his green rompers. They're probably thinking about their own kids."

"Well, let them go home, then!"

Sometimes an orderly is sent over to our table with a nice filet of sole, a helping of lasagna, or a slice of cheese. The baby claps his hands, and I thank the officers with a discreet nod and a vague smile.

"What!" says Raymond, furious. "You're accepting, and on top of that you thank them?"

I always justify myself: "It isn't for us. It's good for the baby, and don't forget, Italy is not Nazi."

"No, except Mussolini started it all, ten years before Hitler," Raymond replies.

"But think, those guys aren't so bad. They've been mobilized. They're an occupying force and it seems to me they'd rather be ignored since they can't be loved."

"We'd like them a lot better at a distance," Raymond persists. I can't help thinking about the centuries of civilization behind them. After all, it's the same civilization that we inherited. But only one argument carries any weight with Raymond: "For our own security we have to be a little friendly."

While I talk I am conscious that my little boy is getting his stomach filled with good food. Still, I know I wouldn't have accepted anything at all from German officers. Would they even have thought of offering anything?

We all take long naps in the heat of the day. Jean-Pierre sleeps, and we make love until we fall asleep. These ten days mean total relaxation. We're rested, tanned, and confident about the future.

Every morning Raymond studies his moustache. He grew it to change his looks after being freed on bail. But alas, we have to accept the fact: his hair is dark and all his body hair is dark, but he has a red moustache! A big help for going unnoticed! A barber who is sympathetic to the Resistance gave him some advice as well as two tiny flasks, one containing bleach, the other black dye. As soon as a millimeter of red hair appears, he shouts: "My roots!" He sets to work like any coquette with dyed hair. Then he has to trim the ends so they won't hang down over his lips. It cracks us up every time.

We spend as much time as possible outdoors. Raymond is slowly recovering from the two months of confinement in a cell. He needs silence and solitude. In prison he registered as a Catholic, so he was allowed to attend mass on Sundays. Enclosed in a stall completely separated from his neighbors, he appreciated that one short hour alone, when he could escape the presence of his four fellow prisoners, even though they were his friends.

He had no contact with the world outside the prison, except with his lawyer. According to his fake identity card, he was a bachelor, an orphan, an only child, and he didn't have the right to receive visitors. So I never saw Raymond at Saint-Paul, though I delivered packages to be shared by the five occupants of the cell. I insisted on being the one to take them because of the secret correspondence that I hid in the packages.

It's no fun to find yourself at the gates of a prison. You have to wait in line for the doors to open. The warden says: "Two lines, visitors in one, packages in the other." I really felt embarrassed standing on that sidewalk with a package under my arm. It was poorly wrapped and tied with string that was likely to snap at any moment. How hard it is to change your social status. As a professor at the lycée, I am always greeted with respect by the students' parents. There, under an assumed name, I was surrounded by women who seemed perfectly at home. I was always afraid of being recognized while I waited my turn, and then waited again for the bundle of dirty clothes that the guard

41

would bring back when he got around to it, calling me loudly by name.

Only women waited in those lines, giving the impression that prison inmates have no male pals or relatives, at least not when they are under arrest. These women apparently had no misgivings, felt no shame about coming on visiting days to see "their prisoner." Those prisoners were common criminals. I heard the women talking among themselves: they knew everything about the judges, the lawyers, prison life, the way to handle some of the guards, and above all the tricks used to communicate with prisoners without being caught. They had quickly perceived that I wasn't quite like them, and their discretion surprised me. Often destitute, vulgar and loudmouthed, they found out I was taking care of a whole cell. As for the guards, they called me "the D 57." They would shout: "Mrs. Bernard, dirty clothes from D 57," and when I came forward, the man on duty would throw me the bundle. All the women wondered why I wasn't allowed to visit.

"You should go to court to insist on your rights," they advised.

"I'm not married to any of the five prisoners," I told them. Then they were really incensed. They never asked, whether because of intuition or indifference, why these five were in prison, but they said: "Someday it's going to change; the same people won't always be in control . . ." Was that a hint? I became aware that I might recruit some allies in this marginal world. I already knew that middle-class people had no monopoly on courage, common sense, and loyalty. Raymond had told me that when he served as second lieutenant in Alsace, in the winter of 1939–40 during the phony war, it was invariably the tough guys, the black sheep, who volunteered for dangerous missions.

In February this year, during the midterm vacation, while we were in Paris with d'Astier, the head of our movement, we stayed in a brothel, between the elegant rue de la Paix and the avenue de l'Opéra! I slept in a room that was plastered with mirrors, even on the ceiling. It made me seasick! D'Astier knew a pimp who vouched for the safety of the place. If the world of pimps and madams was riddled with police informers, it also was one of solidarity. The proof of this was that there were never any raids on this house, which the Resistance often used as a shelter. However, I really didn't want to spend another night under the mirrors, and the next day we slept at the Norgeus' apartment on the rue des Pyrénées.

Mrs. Norgeu was my sister's mother-in-law. She and her daughter operated the small print shop in Belleville that her husband had founded. They agreed to print *Libération Nord* when I asked them to—quite a change from their specialty of religious pictures and texts. They also had to let the foreman in on the secret, because, of course, it was imperative that the printing be done outside of normal working hours. D'Astier thus lived with them for several days. He had never set foot in this neighborhood before the war and therefore hardly risked meeting any of his acquaintances.

D'Astier is six feet four and very skinny. His Don Quixote silhouette is impossible to disguise. In the Resistance, he was first known as Bernard, then later as Merlin. And like the wizard, he was seductive, courageous, and poetic as well as totally unmindful of danger; material things were not his strong point.

One day while we were still living on the rue Pierre Corneille he arrived with his overcoat on his arm.

"Lucie—I need your opinion: I feel like everybody's looking at me when I wear this coat."

He put it on. It was made of a beautiful dark brown material and fitted down to the waist like a morning coat, then got wider and wider like a bell at the bottom. I burst out laughing: "Where on earth did you get that?"

"I bought it on the black market. Apparently it's a Russian officer's coat. But it came down to my ankles; I asked my niece Bertrande to shorten it by putting in a hem. But I'm afraid she didn't quite succeed."

"That's an understatement!"

Bertrande had folded the cloth under, inside out, so it stuck out like a tutu, a dancer's skirt! We had to take it apart and redo it completely by cutting off a lot of material. With the leftover cloth I made myself a bolero jacket, and there was still enough material to make a fine pair of pants for Jean-Pierre.

43

Jean-Pierre is cuter and cuter—a delectable nectarine! The Italians simply worship him. We're making plans; maybe next summer we'll come back here with the new baby. This war can't last forever. We'll have plenty of happy years and plenty of children!

D'Astier's secretary, Maurice Cuvillon, came from Marseille to see us. We have to get ready to go home. The movement needs us, the Vichy police and the Gestapo are more and more of a threat, more and more efficient. It has been decided that Raymond won't return to work at the Chemin factory where he has been employed since early 1942. Instead, he will work full-time for the Resistance. We'll have my salary, to be complemented whenever possible through subsidies from the movement. My leave is coming to an end, I have to go back to teaching.

Jean-Pierre takes along a few shells and some sand from the beach. "Bye-bye, sea," he says, and "Hello, train." The return trip is long. The innkeeper reserved two seats for us. We travel at night in the same heat, in the same packed compartments, with the same noises and the same pervasive dust as on the trip down to the coast. We arrive at Perrache in Lyon dirty and tired, but we don't seem to attract any interest from the police or the economic inspectors. We're not carrying any black-market merchandise. Besides, where on the starving Côte d'Azur would we have found anything? Everything there is prohibitively expensive. Our travel documents are in order. The kid is on his father's shoulders, hanging on tight with both hands clasped around Raymond's forehead. What expert eye could recognize, just by looking at the bottom half of this tanned face with its dark moustache, the prisoner who jumped bail?

Monday, June 7, 1943

Our house is waiting for us. Grass is growing everywhere. The petunias and marigolds I planted have started blooming. And in the back yard the apple tree is covered with small green apples, promising a fine harvest.

At the lycée all my colleagues and students think I look great. There is some nervous tension in the air because in a month

44

the third-year students will take their exams and the graduating students must take the *baccalauréat*. The compositions to be assigned this last term and a practice exam are being planned. When I get home in the evening I sense that Raymond is eager to talk. Pascal Copeau has just paid a visit.

"I was glad to see him again. He's still as lively and full of spunk as ever. He played with the kid; he also brought a bottle of Juliénas and three or four goat cheeses. We've left you some. He brought me up to date. Morin-Forestier is on his way to London; Henri Frenay (the leader of the Combat movememt, whose code name is Charvet) arranged his departure. It was too risky for him to stay in France after the confiscation of his records and the escape of his secretary, Christine. 'But you're different,' Pascal told me, 'you're not in any jeopardy. The MUR command is going to use you to inspect the secret army. So here you are inspector general for the whole southern French zone. You'll begin with a visit to Toulouse. Tomorrow Lucie will go to see Pierre-the-forger to get everything concerning your new identity." "It's a good thing," Raymond adds, "that in Carqueiranne I had passport pictures made with my new moustache.

"They also decided, Salard (that's Pascal Copeau's assumed name) told me, that the various commands for all sections of the MUR were to be transferred to Paris because in Lyon we are too well known now. Of course the maquis section and the print shops will stay here. And, he said, they might want me to work in the north. As for you, Lucie, Pascal plans for you to spend school vacations covering the south."

Even though this morning we were back to the old routine with chores and worries like everybody else, now at the same time, we're back in the secret network with its encounters and its missions. We stay up late talking about it after the child is asleep. We have to be ready to move, so we should see if an Austrian woman who has stayed here before is willing to stay with us again, at least until the end of the summer. A friend of ours working in the social services managed to get her out of the concentration camp in Gurs, where the Vichy regime confined those who had fled German National Socialism before 1939. This woman adored Jean-Pierre and he was very fond of her. If she stays with us we won't have to drag our child around to strange places. He'll stay in Lyon and we'll see him during our stopovers.

This morning my first class is at ten. So I have just enough time to ride my bicycle over to pick up the new identification papers for Raymond and ride back. I know Pierre's address, or rather that of his outfit. This past year he and I have become good friends even though, theoretically, that's not the best policy in the underground. We introduced our friend Jean Jeanssen to Pierre; Jean was "first forger" in the Libération movement. Jean, who has both the gift and the minute accuracy of an engraver, copied—as his first work of art—the German documents that enabled my brother-in-law to leave the stalag where he was being held. Subsequently Jean was able to overcome his moral principles and agreed to produce false identification cards for some of the early *résistants* who were on the run and for fugitive foreigners and Jews. He soothed his conscience by telling himself "Of course I'm a forger, but for one thing I don't get paid for my work, and for another, my way of helping these people who are hiding from the police and the Gestapo is related to what I have to offer. I don't have any money, but I have a specialty and I'm using it to help others."

As the Resistance consolidated, Jean was no longer able to fill all the requests. So Pierre became the actual inventor of the "false paper service." This young man had been in charge of a metals business in Paris before the war, and he was never able to get rid of his middle-class Parisian accent, not even after a prolonged stay in Lyon. He was methodical in his organization. He knew all the towns in which the records office had been destroyed during the war, and he had built up a genuine file of people who had gone abroad or were prisoners of war. He had an impressive collection of various models of official identity cards, passes and permits, certificates, town hall and rubber stamps from local police. On the basis of these originals, he made fake documents that sometimes looked almost too good to be true. He also had found some accomplices inside the administrative bureaucracy and was able to tell us places we could raid for blank identity cards and even German passes.

46

Pierre-the-forger was just scrutinizing the batch of papers meant for Raymond when I rang the doorbell.

"Look—Claude Ermelin, a bachelor, an only son born in Sedan, repatriated last April from Tunisia, where he was a soldier until the arrival of the English and American forces. Here's his demobilization paper. It's a gem. You've got to check Raymond's automatic response to any interrogation; his memory must really function flawlessly concerning his new identity. Check his clothes carefully for laundry marks and monograms, even tailors' and cleaners' labels. As for his previous papers, burn them right away. No kidding! Even ration cards—for tobacco or cloth!"

He has thought of everything, briefly and clearly listing, with the authority of a commander, all the rules. And then, with a sudden sweet smile: "How is our Boubou?"

At that, Catherine, his liaison agent, who is still as superbly elegant as ever, and Isidore, his collaborator, come over to listen. After all, our little man is the only child in our group of *résistants*. None of us are used to the rigors and cautious discipline of the Communist groups, and hence everybody knows everybody. Raymond and I live our everyday lives with our actual identities, and for many people our home, first the one on the rue Pierre Corneille and now on the avenue Esquirol, is a place to stop for a quick meal or to spend a night. Our friends who live solitary lives far from their families like to come and share our life as a couple and as parents, just for a moment. Jacques Copeau, Pascal's father, named our little boy Boubou when he was passing through Lyon. Jean-Pierre was just a year and a half old then and hardly talked; sitting on Jacques Copeau's lap, he rapturously sucked his thumb while stroking his new friend's silk shirt. Grunting with pleasure, he made a kind of onomatopoeia, bou . . . bou . . . bou. That nickname stuck with him. Now I must think of some anecdote to tell about him. This little moment of innocence makes the three of them happy.

I pedal back up to the avenue Esquirol. Really, we are odd people: engineers, draftsmen, teachers, middle-class or workers, every one of us entered the world of cheating and lies with the utmost serenity. Only Jeanssen had a hard time at first and had to look for reasons before yielding to necessity. But a lot of us think that what we are doing quite naturally entails reversing our moral order. How many of us are going to be able to respect legality once the war is over?

I attack the last hill between the Grange-Blanche hospital and the morgue. A police van is just entering the gate; this is where people shot in the streets end up when the Gestapo permits the bodies to be removed. Morgue employees secretly photograph the anonymous faces so they can perhaps be identified later. Women come furtively when they hear the news, trying to recognize some loved one who has disappeared.

Tonight, despite the heat of a continental summer, we have to close the windows. It's time to listen to the radio. Let's hope the power is on! At nine-thirty we receive a breath of fresh air. We listen with ears glued to the set. An exasperating hum from the worn-out radio tubes adds to the usual noise made by jamming on the part of Vichy and the German forces. Managing to hear a French voice coming from London presents a daily problem. Sometimes one of our friends speaks, using his own name or the pseudonym he disclosed to us when he spent a night or even a brief moment in our home.

Tonight, June 8, is the "one thousand and eightieth day of the French people's struggle for their liberation." Pierre Brossolette is speaking. I knew him at the Sorbonne, where he was a brilliant graduate student in the history department. He was older than I, and a militant in the Young Socialists movement, and I'm deeply moved recognizing his precise, rather dry voice. Tonight, that voice has a tone I have not heard in it before, like the explosion of victorious pride.

He is both reading and commenting on a text—the "orders" as they say in Gaullist circles—establishing the French Liberation Committee. We take notes as fast as we can. If only there were some machine that could record what is being said! What a marvelous propaganda tool we would have! The speaker concludes by saying that there is one central government in France and that resides in the French Liberation Committee! He adds: "For all of us and henceforth for all of you, that's the basis for legality, that's where the flag flies, that's where your duty lies—outside of it, there is only usurpation and violence."

I have no classes on Friday morning or, of course, on Thursday, which is a weekly day off for all schools. For several days now I have wanted to go on a "food expedition" to my family, who live in the department of Saône-et-Loire. We have invited Raymond's parents and his sister to visit us on Sunday, June 13. They have scarcely seen him since he got out of Saint-Paul prison, and I want to have something good to feed them.

Miracles do happen! Raymond was able to get a car from the place he used to work. He has just been to visit the Chemin factory, where he was employed as an engineer until he was arrested in March. Naturally, I had tried to conceal the truth, providing medical certificates to justify his absence. Raymond decided to take a chance and confide in his direct superior, his fellow student at the engineering school, and in old man Chemin, his boss, a longtime member of the Radical party and a friend of Herriot.[12] Raymond came back beaming.

"They were absolutely dumbfounded by my story. 'What, you, a Jew, you have the courage to get mixed up in that outfit?' 'Jew or not, for me it's a matter of honor and survival. You'll see, Vichy won't always be in control of keeping an eye on your man Herriot; one day the Germans will get him, and that means they'll get his friends too . . .'

"At this, Chemin said: 'Okay, we'll keep you on the job with your real name on our personnel roster, and your function listed as site inspector. From time to time, you can use one of the company cars. Just be careful about gasoline, because our rations are more and more restricted. We'll continue to pay your salary.

12. The Radical party was the main centrist or slightly left-of-center political party of the Third Republic (1870–1940). Edouard Herriot (1873–1957) was the perennial mayor of Lyon and deputy from that city, sometime prime minister and cabinet member in numerous governments of the Third Republic and a highly regarded literary author and historian.

So at the end of each month, you'll get your envelope with the pay slip. Of course, if ever there's a hitch, we know absolutely nothing. Now if you were able to bring us a baptismal certificate, we'd be completely covered in case of inspection.' I thanked him warmly of course. So Wednesday night, after your last class, we'll set out in the car, all three of us, for Salornay."

My parents are surprised to see us and delighted to see their grandson. I'm a teacher, but Raymond is an engineer: he has brought my father half a bag of cement to repair the roof of his rabbit hutches. Tomorrow morning, my father is going to take a walk among his vines to cut the few late asparagus poking up between the rows.

"You'll eat them on Sunday and think of us. These asparagus won't have wilted on a truck or in a store window."

Dear papa! He can't imagine that asparagus—a luxury item—hasn't been available in the shops for at least three years; you can find it only in black market restaurants or on the dinner table of the occupation army. He also digs some of the first new potatoes for us, another luxury! I had forgotten their honey color and the silky texture of their delicate skin.

Thursday, June 10, 1943

In Besanceuil, on the border of the Charolais region, my Aunt Jennie has a cattle and poultry farm. Although she is not known for her generosity, she sells me, at a reasonable price, a dozen eggs, a quart of cream, a big rabbit, and a fine piece of bacon from the salt box. As a bonus, she even adds a small bag of wheat. "But don't you say a word about this to your parents; I can't begin to supply the whole family. It gets around so quickly—such news snowballs. I need my produce for barter to get fertilizer and clothes for my menfolk . . . But you, Lucie, you don't come here often and you look so much like my poor mother, your grandmother whom you hardly knew."

From there we return to my parents' house to pick up the potatoes and asparagus. My father adds a couple of pounds of strawberries from his yard, kept cool under plane tree leaves.

Then it's over to Vinzelles near Mâcon to see Uncle Carrage. We knew we would receive a hearty welcome here. Earlier this year he came to see us in Lyon—he was beside himself: *his* Marshal Pétain, "victorious at Verdun," had betrayed him ignominiously. Vichy economic units had come to inspect his stock of wine in order to requisition it for fuel alcohol. When they finished, they poured a glass of heating oil into every barrel so as to adulterate the wine and thus make it unfit for consumption. That way, they ensured its delivery.

"The wine, that's really nothing; we had taken some precautions and hidden what we need, the best wine, of course. But the casks! They've been here since my father's day. The older the cask, the better the wine. They're lost. That stinking oil leaves an odor that never goes away. They're good only for burning!" Uncle Carrage wept over this act of vandalism. "And to think—all this just to send wine to be distilled for fuel for the Boches.[13] They may have enough to go all the way into Russia but they won't have any left to come back—they'll all die. Ah—that Marshal's a fine man! He deserves to be shot twelve times!"

It wasn't easy to calm down Uncle Carrage and make him talk less loudly. More than any rational argument, more than any patriotic explanation, these glasses of heating oil adulterating a fine Pouilly-fuissé swung the winegrowers of the Mâcon hills to the Resistance.

These rocky hills are the exclusive domain of the wine. I know every path here from the days I spent as a little girl accompanying my Grandmother Vincent from Chaintré to Solutré. There's no room for meadows, but then milk never was the favorite drink in this area! The only animals raised here are a goat to trim the hedges, a pig, some chickens and rabbits. A few vegetables grow in these small plots, among the vines tended as carefully as a garden by these winegrowers, who are used to frugality, to a hard life. Right now, the peaches are ripe, small velvety bush peaches with their red pulp, so easy to halve. I stuff myself with them and fill my basket. When I was little, I spent hours after school

---

13. A derogatory name for Germans, originated during the First World War.

stoning them for the pig's mash. What's lacking here above all is bread. No cereals grow in the area and rationing is hard on the people.

"How can somebody work all day in the vineyard on just one slice of bread—the ration for consumptive people," my aunt laments. I give her one of my bread ration cards; thanks to the new identity, once again I have three of them for two people.

"That calls for a drink," my uncle says, taking Raymond with him to his vineyard. They are gone a long time. When they finally return, their eyes are shining, they're grinning from ear to ear, and they quickly finish off the pot of red beans that my aunt had simmering on the stove.

It's time to leave if we are to be back in Lyon before the curfew. Jean-Pierre falls asleep in the back of the car. He has been fed an enormous pancake known in these parts as a "hunger-damper." We used to eat them with bread when we were kids. The company car is a great passport for the police checkpoints, and the sleeping child spares us any prying searches. Raymond is in high spirits.

"No one could guess," he says, "how much can be stored behind the tools and bundles of kindling in that tiny hut at the vineyard. I assure you it's larger inside than outside! With his pipette, your uncle siphoned from the seven casks—yes! that's what I said! seven casks—marvelous white wines, dry and cool. They were a pale yellow and tinged with green. He made me taste every single one of them. And each time, we toasted: 'Here's another one that Pétain won't give to the Boches!' Then he suddenly became serious, and he said, 'You see, Raymond, if you run into trouble you could come and hide here. Nobody would ever bother you here. Lucie and the baby would stay with us. And if I was ever late bringing you supper, you'd always have enough to quench your thirst!'

"I answered him: 'Thanks, this could be a temporary hideout before I join the maquis, where there's plenty of space and plenty of action.' And, Lucie, see what a deep impression Vichy propaganda has made. He said, 'Yeah, but you Jews have to be twice as cautious.' And when I answered, 'Therefore, twice as active,' he retorted: 'Well, I was sure you were in the Resistance and certainly Lucie will never stand in your way! You two are going to go far. You'll see, someday she'll be a deputy in the National Assembly. She sure has guts.' "

Sitting next to my talkative husband, I sigh audibly with pride. Raymond drives slowly, but could he do otherwise in this ancient Renault with its recapped tires? There is a moment of silence, then Raymond blows up: "What are we going to do with that live rabbit?' If it's going to be like that goose, I'm turning it loose!"

"Don't worry; while you were happily drinking away in the vineyard, I asked my aunt to kill and skin it; she even cleaned it. It's in a clean cloth, ready to cook."

On All Saints' Day of 1942, I visited Luçay in the Indre department, and I brought a live goose back to Lyon, which we planned to fatten as a Christmas treat for our scattered and lonely friends. That goose was more trouble than it was worth! It was never satisfied, always noisy and belligerent. I went around to all the neighbors, collecting all sorts of peelings and scraps that I made into mash. It gobbled them all up at top speed. As soon as the goose had finished eating, it started to honk again as loudly as it could. All the neighbors knew it was there and people kept asking: "Well, when are you going to eat your goose?"

At night I locked it up in the basement so that it wouldn't be stolen. In the morning it came out, black with coal dust, having rolled our winter's allotment of coal all over the basement, now ready to insult us. It had taken a dislike to the kid, who was scared stiff of it ever since it nastily pinched his arm with its beak.

At Christmas, d'Astier was still not back from London, and neither Copeau nor the Hervés were in Lyon. We decided to wait for their return, and the goose spent the holidays devouring our scant reserve of rutabagas and even our ration of noodles. In early January it was decided: the feast would take place on Twelfth Night.

"We're going to chop it's head off," Raymond had said. We set up a large rock in the yard. I caught the beast and held it with both hands on the improvised block. Whoop—with a blow of the ax, Raymond decapitated it. It jerked and jumped and I turned it loose. What a horrible sight! We watched our goose take off down the alley, spurting high from its neck a jet of blood that only gradually subsided. It felt like an eternity to us. When the blood finally stopped flowing, the beast collapsed in the alley.

Anyone who has never plucked a goose cannot conceive of what slave labor it is. There are three layers of feathers: the thickest ones, which you pull with all your might, come out with bloody goo on the tips. The medium ones are relatively easy to pull out, but then there is still an unbelievable mass of down and hair. The more you pull out, the more there is, floating everywhere. You breathe it in, it sticks to your clothes and nests in your hair.

And when we cleaned the goose, what a disappointment! Its liver was even smaller than a chicken's. We were dreaming of goose liver, not enormous, perhaps, but surely nice and fat. "Livers are only fat when geese are fat," Pascal pronounced with authority. With its feathers off our goose was really skinny, and it took a long, long time to cook. But we were all young and had young teeth. D'Astier's teeth were the oldest and they were only forty. So the feast was a success. Copeau and Farge[14] had unearthed some wine and were telling thousands of risqué stories. We were all having a great time when an unexpected guest arrived: Jean Cavaillès! Our friend Jean, whose nickname was Sully, had been my philosophy colleague in Amiens. We met again in Strasbourg when he became a university professor, and again in Clermont-Ferrand in the fall of 1940. He served as my link between d'Astier and Rochon when the Resistance movement was just starting. The French police had arrested Jean together with Christian Pineau on the Mediterranean coast when their planned depar-

14. Yves Farge was one of the leaders of the Resistance. After the liberation in 1944, he was appointed governor (Commissaire de la République) of the Lyon area. Farge died in an automobile accident in the Soviet Union, during a visit in the 1950s.

ture for London was botched. They were sent to the military prison in Montpellier; General de Lattre de Tassigny was then commander of that garrison.[15]

Jean's sister, whom I had known since before the war, got in touch with me. Vincent Badie, who shared our political views, met me in Montpellier and obtained a visiting permit for me as Cavaillès's supposed fiancée. I had elaborated an escape plan with the help of our local Resistance group. When I visited Jean for the first time, I brought some metal files with me to saw the bars of the cell, which was on the second floor of the prison overlooking the yard. We drew very close to each other for the chastest possible kiss, Cavaillès and I, so the files went from my chest to his. He understood that we would be waiting for him under the prison walls, at night, with two bicycles for the escapees. But the escape never materialized. The police had placed an informer in the cell with them, and though I brought them a sleeping powder to put him out of commission they were unable to use it.

A week later, Cavaillès and Pineau were transferred by train to the internment camp at Saint-Paul-d'Eyjeaux, near Limoges. During that trip, Pineau managed to escape. So there we were, with Jean's Parisian comrades, trying to find a new way to finally get him out for good.

Surprise! He arrived unannounced at our home in Lyon. He had escaped by himself, taking advantage of the more relaxed surveillance at the camp during the holiday celebrations. He looked quite extraordinary! He was the color of an orange, and unshaven, with bluish spots on his face.

"After the war, I'm going to patent a method for rapid, indelible tanning! They fed us nothing but carrots for three months,

15. Jean Cavaillès, whose numerous escapes were legendary, was eventually caught and executed. Christian Pineau, a Socialist, was later deported by the Nazis to a concentration camp. He survived and after the war became a government official. General Jean de Lattre de Tassigny, commander of the Nîmes garrison, refused to surrender after the occupation of all of France in November 1942. He later became the commander of the French army that liberated Alsace and invaded Germany.

so everybody in camp turned this color. Then, on top of that, I came down with impetigo. In the infirmary, they daubed me with methylene blue. You can see the result! Not a chance of going unnoticed! I might as well forget it. But something smells good here—what are you eating?"

We told him about the goose's last moments, and all of us had a good laugh.

Today, however, as we head back to Lyon, we know we won't have the same problem we had with the goose; the rabbit has been killed, completely killed, it's ready to cook. We enter Lyon by driving along the left bank of the Saône. There is much less traffic here than on the main road, where German convoys roll along and gangs of French militia operate for their own profit: certain of impunity, they stop cars, arrest and rob people, often killing them. We cross the Saône at Romanèche and drive peacefully through the beautiful Bresse countryside, where the meadows are still green despite the summer heat.

At Bron, Raymond stops for a moment at the construction yard where he was in charge before his arrest. He wants to find out if anything new has happened and talks to a worker who shares our commitment. Nothing has happened these past two days. At home, we unload our treasures, and I carry Jean-Pierre to his bed without waking him up.

Raymond drives the car back to the factory garage and stops at his parents' house to let them know we're back. They have left Dijon and settled in Villeurbanne in a vast warehouse, which his mother's taste has transformed into a pleasant apartment. They have enormous cupboards partitioning the rooms, and the grand piano seems perfectly at home on the Persian rug covering the cement floor. They live here under their real names. We had intended to provide them with a new identity, corroborated by baptismal certificates, as soon as they arrived in Lyon, but they refused: "My family goes back for five generations in Lorraine," my father-in-law said. "I fought in the war of 1914, my two sons are officers, one of them an army doctor, at present a prisoner of war. We have nothing to fear."

56

We throw caution to the winds. No holding back today, for this family celebration—which is a little late for Boubou's birthday (he was born on May 3, 1941), and for Raymond's being set free on May 14, and a little early for my birthday, on June 29.

Aunt Jenny had carefully wrapped eleven eggs instead of twelve! That's how she is. But still, it's plenty to make a huge soufflé with asparagus tips—a dish fit for kings! After that comes the rabbit fried with bacon and served with little new potatoes. And I made Chantilly cream to go with the strawberries from my father's yard. My pretty mother-in-law had unraveled a woolen cardigan and knit a suit from the wool for her cherished grandson to wear next winter. Of course, he wanted to put on his new pants right away but then he ate so much whipped cream that he had an accident. The pants are dishonored! My son and I, both ashamed, disappear to clean up the mess while my indulgent father-in-law smiles tenderly at his wife and children, who laughingly comment on this minor catastrophe.

Like happy people without a care in the world, the six of us fully enjoy the calm, exceptional climate of mutual affection. We take pictures with my Tenax, the first small camera, which I received as a wedding gift in December 1939; it has thirty-six exposures. Here we are, my family and Raymond's. Tomorrow after school I'll take the film to the photographer who specializes in snapshots, next to Lardanchet's bookstore.

Late at night, in bed, Raymond has second thoughts: "Don't you think we should destroy that film? Right now. If anything happens to us, if we are caught, those pictures would implicate our parents."

I'm tired after this great day, and from all these delicious foods that I'm no longer used to; I feel extraordinarily sleepy, like a vegetable.

"What do you think is going to happen to us? You know our good luck, our baraka! I don't know why, but tonight my nipples are itching, maybe I'm pregnant."

"Let's see," says Raymond, taking me in his arms.

Monday, June 14, 1943

It's Whitsuntide Monday, a legal holiday, so I don't teach today. Our house is quiet; Jean-Pierre keeps himself busy, which is rare for an only child. He has set up all the wooden animals of his zoo under the Henri II table in the dining room. At Christmas time I found him some animals meant for a crèche, oxen and donkeys, rather roughly made out of clay, which he added to his collection of wild animals. He has now organized his own sort of battle on the wooden bars connecting the ornate feet of the table. On one side, the oxen, the donkeys, the crocodile (which he insists on calling a lizard), and the lion (which he calls a dog). On the other, the ones that will be defeated because he doesn't like them: the goats, monkeys, giraffes, and hippopotamuses, his villains. He commands each army in turn. Completely absorbed in his game, he sometimes bumps his head into the edge of the table. "It's nothing, it's nothing," he mumbles, rubbing his head.

I don't interfere. I have my work table in a corner of the room. I'm looking through my papers for something to illustrate my course on the Pharaohs, for my class of first-year students tomorrow. It's an hour for dreaming. We'll take off for the banks of the Nile, for the Pyramids, the Sphinx, and all those gods with animal faces, heirs of the primitive totems. The little girls of eleven and twelve are enchanted by this world narrated through pictures on the walls of tombs. Maybe that way of telling history will be a modern method of teaching when my little boy is their age. In 1938, I saw a comic book from the United States, what they called a "cartoon." *The War of Fire* was told in a sequence of drawings; bubbles enclosing short easy-to-read sentences came out of the mouths of the characters. Will we have to accept this way of reading? Where style is so unimportant?

Tuesday, June 15, 1943

This morning Raymond met with André Lassagne. There have been important changes in the organization of the secret army. The unified movements had acknowledged General Delestraint as leader of the unified secret army and he had been confirmed by General de Gaulle. Then came a whole series of arrests in

Marseille: one of the heads of Combat was worked over by the Gestapo and talked; another *résistant* carelessly failed to "neutralize" a mailbox—an uncoded message in that mailbox led to the arrest of General Delestraint in Paris along with his chief of staff, Gastaldo, and his liaison officer, Théobald, who is said to be the son of a senior officer. Raymond and André give a lot of thought, as Max had requested, to the best way of establishing a new leadership for the secret army—one likely to be accepted by all the movements, a far from easy task.

Raymond comes home for lunch; he is accompanied by Vergaville, whose real name is Robert Ducasse. We still call him "Kari" the way we did in the Latin Quarter before the war. He was one of a group of gifted young math students, some of whom went to the Ecole Polytechnique, others to the Ecole Normale Supérieure, still others to Raymond's school, the Ecole des Ponts et Chaussées, or to the Ecole Centrale.[16] At the outset of the war, these young men served as officers, most of whom we met again in the Resistance. Barel, the son of a Communist deputy from Nice, belongs to a Communist party organization made up of physicists and chemists. He is a secretive, cautious theoretician. We know very little about his activities, but we think that in addition to propaganda work among his engineering colleagues who hold various factory jobs, he is using laboratories at the university and is skilled in crafting explosives.

It is true, the Communists receive fewer parachute drops than we do. Since General de Gaulle made his headquarters in Algiers, the Communist deputies imprisoned at Maison Carrée in 1940 have been freed. When Fernand Grenier, the Communist deputy from Saint-Denis, arrived in London this past January after escaping from Châteaubriant with the help of Colonel Rémy, he explained to the Allies the role of the Communist party within the Resistance. Now the Communist Resistance is better supplied.

16. The Ecole Normale Supérieure is intended, theoretically, to train future teachers. In fact, many of its graduates enter diplomatic service or other high government service. The Ecole des Ponts et Chaussées trains civil engineers; many of its graduates also enter government service. The Ecole Centrale is the oldest engineering school in France.

Our comrades from the Latin Quarter were among those initially in charge of organizing the secret army in southern France. Thus our friend Kari, an engineering graduate, a naval officer, and the son of a Protestant minister from Dieuze in the Moselle, ended up with his family somewhere in the Gard department after the collapse of the French army in 1940. I knew his whole family, three sisters and two brothers; he is the oldest. He is a tall, quiet fellow, athletic, somewhat mysterious even to his close friends, and he was part of all our student adventures. We went down the Tarn in a kayak, with him and his friend Maurice Rousselier, a graduate of the Ecole Polytechnique who is now the head of the secret army in Limoges. He was also along when about ten of us set out with sealskins under our skis to climb the snowy peaks of the Queyras and then descend them in a snowy apotheosis. One night Kari took us to the Paris observatory and under its cupola initiated us to knowledge of the sky. He also took excellent photographs. He was the best of all possible friends, a fine sailor and a great hiker. But there always seemed to be secret gardens that were his alone and that we could not explore.

He was demobilized in Toulon when the French fleet was scuttled; he became Raymond's assistant in the Libération movement. Together they organized the transfer of weapons from the armistice army to the Resistance when the Germans invaded the southern zone in November of 1942. Both of them were persuasive with the officers to whom they were sent as envoys by the former military governor of Strasbourg, General Frère. This was not always the case, of course. Once Raymond came back from Grenoble disappointed and furious. He had met with the colonel in charge of the barracks and the arms depot; he had started out by stating all the reasons that should have led the officer to turn over his stock of arms. The colonel let him finish and then said: "Sir, I should have you arrested for your insulting remarks about Marshal Pétain, but this is not done among officers. So I choose to forget that I ever saw you or heard any of the opinions of General Frère, and I ask you to leave immediately."

Another time, Kari turned up at our house in the middle of the night with a truckload of ammunition cases and light machine guns. He woke us up, furious: the address for the storage facilities where his load was to be hidden was wrong. What a mess! Raymond and he had to look for a long time before they finally found, in a small street in Villeurbanne, the owner of the plant, who agreed to store this dangerous cargo.

Raymond and Kari had enormous respect for General Frère. Together, they had gone to tell him about visits to various barracks, providing him with valuable information for the Resistance organization he was trying to create within the army.

General Frère is a man of admirable integrity and rectitude; he is one of the few generals totally devoted to the cause of the Resistance and not afraid to show it. I went to see him, in March, at Chamalières, near Clermont-Ferrand, where he was living. He had great regard for Raymond and was very upset to hear of his arrest. He promised to explore his connections with military judges to see if one of them could intervene with the Lyon police court judge to suggest that Raymond be released on bail. He was already getting on in years, rather short and bony with a stiff leg, a "souvenir" from the 1914–18 war. He showed me, on his wall, a huge map of the world. On it, he was following the evolution of the worldwide conflict, and he pointed to the different seats of military operations. He commmented on the enormous dispersion of Japanese forces in the Pacific, the many islands being so scattered and so distant from one another. He was encouraged by what was happening in eastern Europe, with the German armies immobilized, having been partly annihilated at Stalingrad and outside Moscow. I was an attentive audience, and I later conveyed this lesson to my comrades in Lyon.

Kari, Raymond, and I make a meal of yesterday's leftovers, and naturally we discuss our clandestine action. We realize how much elbowroom we've lost since the beginning of the year. The Germans are now solidly entrenched in Lyon. They have imposed a curfew, making our nocturnal action difficult if not impossible. They control everything, traffic, food supplies, municipal life; they censor the newspapers and the movies; they rule the police and the French government officials. They have total power and are paying informers very well. Our apprenticeship in clandestine life happens on the spot, and not all of our members are aware that silence is the first safeguard. We discuss the transfer to Paris of the national organization of the Resistance. There, the city and its suburbs lend themselves better to the requirements of clandestine strategy. Raymond says Max suggested it. All that would remain outside of Paris, in the various regions, would be the social services, the underground press, and of course the information services.

It will be mid-June before we mend the damage done by the arrests in Marseille. Our buddies from the Combat movement know that one of their members, Multon, has talked. He became a Gestapo informer and is responsible for the arrest of more than fifty of their comrades; the mailbox in Lyon that he knew about can't be used now.

Saturday, June 19, 1943

When you step on an anthill, the surviving ants rush in to put everything back in order and reestablish all connections in their society. Every time we experience a new blow, we do the same thing. In our shadowy world, everything frequently has to be started all over again, reorganized from scratch.

Raymond has had long talks with Pascal Copeau. We have to change appointments, check to see whether offices, lodgings, and mailboxes are still safe. Liaison agents will probably have to be switched and possibly regional leaders as well. Raymond takes a quick trip to Montpellier and Toulouse. Today, he met Aubry and Lassagne on the quai de Serbie, at the home of a friend of Lassagne's.

At home tonight Raymond tells me: "Lassagne saw Max this morning; he told me Max is planning a summit meeting, soon, to install the new general staff of the secret army. Lassagne took over the organization of the meeting. He also said Max wanted to see me tomorrow afternoon and that he wishes to meet you, to make your acquaintance, Lucie. We are to meet at three, at the Tête-d'Or park, on the path leading to the puppet theater. We'll take Boubou along, that will look more normal."

Sunday, June 20, 1943

After lunch, while Jean-Pierre naps, I spruce up, brushing my reddish-brown hair. It's a splendid summer day. I'm wearing a pretty skirt, made from upholstery material, with a flowery design. Digging around in what my mother calls her "oldies," I turned up a *cache-corset*, a kind of low-cut sleeveless tunic of embroidered cotton, tight-fitting over the chest. Now that its been washed, starched, and ironed, it is superb. At thirty, one can take liberties with one's fancies.

"I could eat you up, my Lucette," Raymond flatters me. "You bet Jean-Pierre and I will have to keep an eye on you this afternoon."

I'm immensely impressed by the idea that I'm to meet the envoy of General de Gaulle. Thanks to d'Astier, we know something about the rather difficult conversations Max has had with the various leaders of the movements in France. They accepted the concept of unification, but putting it into practice is a different matter. The secret army remained the thorniest question. On the whole, the Resistance inside France insisted on keeping control over it, whereas Max thought that an officer from outside the movements, one under direct authority from London, should direct it. There were also some differences of opinion concerning the representation of the political parties within the National Council of the Resistance. The movements ended up by agreeing to the commonsensical and political reasons put forward by Max, but nevertheless created, parallel to his structure, a central committee of the movements as well.

Max's task was far from easy. Raymond respects and admires this man, who is at least ten years older than he. "He must have had some experience as a high government official to show such an extraordinary flair for organization and efficiency," Raymond said.

Today, around three o'clock, we stroll down the agreed upon path in the Tête-d'Or park, with Jean-Pierre happily gamboling around us. Twenty yards ahead, we see a man coming toward us, feigning friendly surprise. He greets me and then shakes hands with my husband. "This is Max," Raymond says. Max is a man of medium build, dark haired, with beautiful black eyes and an animated face. He tells me what a pleasure it is to meet me, and his courtesy seems very genuine.

"I come from a family of teachers," he tells me, "my parents are both retired, but my sister still teaches. We'll talk more at length, however, tomorrow night. I'd like to invite you both to dinner and introduce you to the man who works with me. He's nick-named Sophie. And I hope you'll bring me some positive results from the conversation you'll have tonight with your husband. He and I will figure out where we can meet. Will you be free?"

It's out of the question for me to miss such an opportunity; besides, what else could I have to do at dinner time? I have registered his remarks about a conversation, an agreement. What is this all about? I run after my little boy, who trots ahead down the path, and leave them to their talk.

A mother with her child, what could be more transparently innocent in a public park on a Sunday afternoon? I'm happy to provide some slight cover for this meeting between these two ré-sistants. And I'm all the happier because Max, the accomplished diplomat, has indicated that I have a place alongside them. He knows that our commitment to the cause is inseparable from our agreement as a couple. They walk along behind us, at the kid's haphazard pace—stopping to show him a white pebble, taking him by the hand, one on each side. But he quickly tires of this and drags them off to the little puppet theater which has a twenty-minute show every hour. It is very funny and daring and skillfully done in the local dialect of Lyon. In it a mean drunkard is forever clobbering an ugly, ignorant, stupid gendarme. These skits strike home nowadays, and the grown-ups laugh just as hard as the children. When the show is over, my two conspirators laugh and applaud with all their might. For a brief instant, they have recaptured the joyous, carefree feeling of their childhood.

There is still some leftover laughter in our voices when we part. "See you tomorrow night," we all say.

When we get home, before we listen to the radio, Raymond starts to fill his pipe and says:

"Sit down and listen: Max asked me to brief you. This is a decision we both have to agree on. As you surely know, the general staff of the secret army must be modified. He suggests entrusting the general overseeing of the southern zone to André Lassagne, and he wants me to accept responsibility for the northern zone.[17] Here are his reasons: I am not known in the northern zone, and my experience of the region (and, he says to flatter me, my connections) ought to make possible the restructuring of a secret army along the same lines as in the south—on the one hand, large formations of maquis wherever geography lends itself to this, and, on the other hand, smaller units to be grouped in hierarchical order for more efficiency in the towns, that is, what we call groupes-francs and workers' action groups. Of course, that means we're to leave Lyon. You heard me say 'we.' You are still living legally, and a normal home obviously is the best cover; we have to try to keep it. But this is the end of the school year; it shouldn't be difficult for you to get a different appointment. It's not too hard now to get an assignment in Paris. Given your academic credentials and your seniority, plus the fact that many male teachers are absent because they're still prisoners of war, you could easily find a job in Paris. Now, what do you think?"

I don't say anything for a moment. My home is here, familiar things, my friends and relatives nearby. All the surroundings to my nest. I know the shopkeepers—something invaluable in these times of scarcity. My family in the country is close by in the Saône-et-Loire if we need more food. Since 1940, however, I have been wrapped up in the Resistance. It's part of what I do. I do have friends in Paris, and our safety here in Lyon may be jeopardized any day. I realize that my imagination, my sense of risk, my liking to take chances in spite of, even because of the danger all push me in the direction of new commitments. But above all, it is inconceivable for Raymond to turn down this great responsibility. When you commit yourself you have to go all the way.

So I conclude my thoughts out loud: "Of course you'll accept, but it's out of the question for us to separate. We're the three of us, maybe four next year—so let's go!"

Not at all surprised, Raymond kisses me. "I was right," he

17. The northern zone referred to occupied France, from the Pyrenees to the Belgian border.

65

says, "when I told Max your agreement was a sure thing. Tomorrow, we'll celebrate this with a good dinner. He's taking us to Mère Brasier's, and we're to meet him at six-thirty at the place Tolozan."

It still isn't time for the radio. I reread a small book. About sixty pages long, on thick gray paper, it's called *The Silence of the Sea*. The author is Vercors; the publisher is Editions de Minuit—Midnight Press. Silence, Midnight—two words of our daily lives, two words that are the accomplices of our meetings and our operations, connected by this beautiful name, Vercors, a place of broad limestone plateaus above the Rhône, at the foot of the Alps where valleys have dug deep gorges. I have some splendid photographs of the Vercors to illustrate my geography course at the lycée.

In this book, a father and his daughter, landed gentry in Brittany, keep their dignity in the face of the occupying force. A German officer has been billeted with them. He, however, is no ruffian. He resembles the young students I used to know in the youth hostels of the Black Forest in Germany, before the war: a musician and a poet, rather romantic, full of goodwill. In those days, we young French students were trying to persuade them to accept the victory of 1918 and the Versailles peace treaty!

Tonight, on the BBC broadcast, Grenier speaks. He is the Communist deputy who escaped from the Châteaubriant camp. That's where a Vichy official handed over hostages to the Germans for execution, in reprisal for attacks on German soldiers and military installations. We have read a wrenching story about the twenty-seven hostages from this camp, among them a seventeen-year-old boy, who were shot by the Germans; it is rumored to be by Aragon.[18]

Grenier says: "Paris has been occupied now for 1,095 days." As the Communist deputy of Paris, he speaks of the starving

18. Louis Aragon, one of the greatest French poets, at first outwitted the censors by choosing medieval themes and names for his poems on contemporary events. Later he became one of the leaders of the literary Resistance. See *Aragon, Poet of the French Resistance*, ed. Hannah Josephson and Malcolm Cowley (New York: Duell, Sloan, and Pearce, 1945).

city, bound-and-gagged, with its prisons full of patriots. He describes the bicycle arena near the Eiffel Tower where they are putting Jews arrested during the day. He says: "You can hear the heartrending cries of mothers whose children are being torn from them, even newborn babies—to be sent without any mark of identification to the cursed Reich's reeducation centers."

A huge shudder runs from the back of my head to my heels, a wave swells and twists in my stomach. Suddenly, I see my marvelous child, my twenty-eight-month-old baby, forgetting his name, his parents, being raised in an ice-cold universe, learning to respect only force and to value, as their national anthem proclaims, "Deutschland über alles"!

"Yes, Raymond, tomorrow we're going to tell Max that we've agreed on Paris and that we're both committed to go all the way, to win."

Monday, June 21, 1943

At the lycée, my schedule allows me to take care of whatever my little boy needs in the morning, and again at lunch time and in the late afternoon. The twelve hours I teach during the week are well spread out. Today, I'm at the lycée from ten to twelve and from three to five. For my first-year students I've put together a nice lesson on Egypt. Shuffling the official program around, I've combined my geography and history classes, and together we'll see the world's deserts. The girls in this grade love discovering a country they know about from history. Egypt and its climate, the vast oasis created by the Nile, the sedimentary rocks with all that sand, the dunes, the winds. So I'm all set. This afternoon, at the end of our two hours together, they'll be enraptured.

These days it's not easy to teach the youngsters. Around noon and again at five, their interest lags. Sometimes students almost fall asleep. The school physician calls it "hunger sleepiness." The small cup of skimmed milk with a scantily buttered slice of bread and the lunch consisting of a tiny bit of meat and green vegetables are long gone by the end of the morning and the late afternoon. At ten, two little cookies per child are distributed in the classes. The cookies supposedly contain vitamins.

The students think they smell like fish. One of the girls asserts that they are, in fact, made with fish meal imported from Latin America. Her father told her so. We teachers insist that they eat them because, after all, it's a bit of extra food for these young organisms.

When I come in this morning, the final-year students taking experimental science, who have two hours of written work ahead of them, are all excited: "Look at this morning's paper, Mrs. Samuel. There's a big celebration tonight, in Germany. For the summer solstice, young people everywhere are going to light huge fires and dance. It seems they're going to do this in the youth camps in France, too. The philosophy teacher just told us that this is a return to the ancestral traditions of Western Europe, which is how a nation rediscovers its origins."

This makes me sick! What happened to the happy Saint-Jean's fires of my childhood? Where certain paths crossed in the vineyards, bundles of dried vine clippings would be heaped to make a bright crackling fire that rapidly rose up against the starry sky. The fire went down as fast as it flared up. We used to say that the girls who could cross the blaze in one leap without scorching their skirts would find a lover within the year. My innocent Saint-Jean's fires! Enlisted now in the service of Nazi racism! I promise my students a long discussion about the myth of fire throughout history. I think a lot of it will be about Moses and the burning bush!

At noon, I pick up their essays and take off on my bike to exchange my bread coupons for the daily ration. Just on the off chance, I glance at the door of the butcher's shop, with its daily sign: two and a half ounces of meat for the J1 category. Jean-Pierre will have his little steak today. There are still a few potatoes left from last week's foray to my parents'. The baby will be content and will take a good nap. On the cours La Fayette, I get two pounds of cherries, and I stop at the herbalist's shop. Maria, who detests the roasted barley coffee, adores tea. It's impossible to find now, but she has discovered mint and chamomile tea. She will be pleased that I thought of her.

Raymond is home. This morning he finished revising an article for *Libération* and passed it on to Ségolène, his secretary who has a small shop selling notions. For the time being it serves as a very safe office for us. She will pass the article on to a liaison who will take it to the clandestine print shop.

"Let's eat quickly," Raymond says. "I'm to meet Max at 1:45 at the place Carnot. Lassagne must have told him this morning where we are to meet this afternoon."

The very idea of this meeting makes Raymond blissfully happy. He is so methodical, so orderly, and is expecting a lot from a reorganization of the Resistance. He's also happy that he can tell Max that as a couple we agree concerning our future in Paris. He is soon ready to go.

"Good-bye, my darling, see you tonight at six-thirty, place Tolozan. Don't be late, but not too early either. There are too many people meeting near the river. Go more toward the rue Puits-Gaillot."

He puts Boubou on his shoulders—a daily ritual now—and takes him upstairs to our room, where he dumps him on the bed for his usual nap. The kid wants more kisses, but Raymond quickly extricates himself.

"We'll meet right at the place Tolozan," he repeats, putting on his jacket. "If we're finished earlier, I'll go to the room at the Groses' house at the place des Jacobins. Until tonight, then."

After he was freed on May 14, Raymond turned over a new leaf. It was, of course, out of the question for him to return to the apartment in Croix-Rousse. A friend from our Latin Quarter days whose husband was a doctor in the Bresse region had given me her brother's address. Jean Gros was an architect who lived with his wife and their little boy in an apartment on the top floor, the sixth, on the place des Jacobins. They agreed to rent us a room that had a separate entrance on the landing. Obviously, it was critical not to be caught in that room, it was a real trap—no way to get out unseen. But Raymond's visits never bothered the other tenants. Architects have visitors, that's all. They also had a telephone, which was most convenient.

I have a free hour now. It takes me scarcely fifteen minutes by bike to get to the lycée. What am I going to wear this evening?

The night may be cool. I'll wear a light dress that I bought last summer—after all, Max has never seen it. I'll also take along the bolero jacket that I had cut from Bernard's coat. As for shoes, I have no choice—only the sandals with wooden soles; Raymond nailed two pieces of an old bicycle inner tube underneath. That tap-dance clatter on the sidewalk is so irritating. "Perfect for a silent getaway!" says Raymond.

I pace up and down. Raymond gave Maria two good sprinkles of tobacco, and she has rolled herself a cigarette so thin that I think she is really smoking nothing but paper. At any rate, she has to keep relighting it. She has also embarked on an amazing experiment: in a bucket she soaked old shredded newspapers, which she stirred into a thick mash. By sweeping the basement floor, she managed to come up with two big shovelfuls of coal dust, and she now mixes that in with the mash. Then with her hands she kneads and shapes black balls the size of eggs, which she then sets out in the sun on the steps leading to the garden.

"Don't laugh," she says. "This winter, you'll be glad to have these to keep warm."

The afternoon goes by wonderfully well. The students are pleased, and I am too. As I unlock my bike from the lycée's iron fence, one of my colleagues, Miss Vialtel, a professor of German whom I had said good-bye to already, seems in no hurry to leave.

"I'm waiting for a young relative who is passing through Lyon," she tells me, looking around in every direction.

Well, now! What could she be in on? "Young relatives passing through"—this smacks of clandestine activity. Somebody in hiding, or perhaps somebody working for us. But then, it's none of my business. I'm looking forward to a wonderful evening. Tonight will change our destinies and we'll be damned busy with this transfer to Paris.

On my way home, I find a pastry shop with fruit jellies in the window. What a luxury! I buy half a pound of the sweets, to the delight of Jean-Pierre and Maria.

"Where are you going, Mummy?"

"To see some friends, my pretty baby. You'll be very good for Maria, you'll have a nice tapioca soup, and there's a surprise for you in this little paper bag. Don't forget to have him brush his teeth, Maria. He knows now not to swallow the water when he rinses. And before he goes to bed, he has to pee. Don't cuddle him too long! Oh well—after all, tonight he's all yours."

I dress quickly and gleefully run to catch the trolley at the corner of Grange-Blanche. I get off near the theater. As I pass my Aunt Marcelle and my cousin Maurice's store, on the rue Puits-Gaillot, I run in to say hello and kiss them. That way, I'll approach the rendezvous from downtown and will be able to see whether or not the Rhône embankment looks dangerous. Raymond's worrying has finally made an impression on me.

I'm on time. It's six-thirty, and nobody's there. Ten minutes later, still nobody. Seven o'clock, nobody. I don't want to panic. I reason as calmly as possible—on principle I always refuse to believe bad news. I'll go to Maurice's store before he closes. From there I'll call the Groses to find out whether Raymond has been there. Maurice is sitting alone in his store, flushed and sweating—his eyes popping out of his head.

"Thank God, you are here! It's been awful! The Gestapo was at Dugoujon's! And other people were there besides the patients who came to see the doctor. I got a phone call just now from a road worker who knows me. It seems they arrested six or seven men but one of them got away."

I understand already.

"Raymond had a meeting with Max, de Gaulle's representative—Lassagne organized it. They've surely all been caught."

We call the Groses—we have agreed on a sort of code language with them. I say, "This is Suzanne, how's the kid today?" If there's no risk, she answers: "Hello, darling," and goes on from there. Otherwise she says: "Hello, Suzanne." Her "Hello, darling," and her normal tone of voice reassure me, but Raymond has not been there. I say I'll be over right away.

Maurice and I go to the cours La Fayette to prowl around Lassagne's house. The bicycle repair man across the street has not put out his danger signal: a child's tricycle on the sidewalk.

"Maurice, we'll have to warn everyone immediately. Go around to all the restaurants where our comrades might be and let them know what's up. I'll do the same. But first I'm going to empty the room at the place des Jacobins."

When I get there, Mrs. Gros has already taken all of Raymond's suits from the closet and mixed them in with her husband's. She has put his pipes in the living room and his toiletries in their bathroom. In Raymond's room she has set up her ironing board and a big basket full of clean clothes; she has put a sewing kit and some woolens to mend on the small desk. The sheets are off the bed, and one of her dresses is spread out on the neatly folded blanket.

"That's perfect," I say. "Now all that's left is that little volume of selected letters by Madame de Sévigné. Could you put it with your books?"

I don't tell her that this is the book Raymond uses to encode his messages and reports. Without the key, the code can't be broken.

"You never sublet to anyone, right? You don't know anyone by the name of Ermelin. Your husband's and your own profession (she teaches) make additional income unnecessary."

"Right."

Next I make the rounds of several cafés and chance upon Pascal. We make a rendezvous for tomorrow morning at ten in front of Grange-Blanche hospital, because during consultation hours, people are always coming and going there.

I find Maurice. It's nine o'clock, but it's still daylight. "Come and get some dinner," he says to me.

We sit down in a little restaurant on the place Morand. Downing dishes of cabbage cooked with a bit of bacon (amazing that I should be hungry!), we try to get a clear picture of what happened.

"I'm going to Caluire right away," Maurice says.

"You're going to get yourself arrested."

"Oh, no. If they arrested everybody, it would show what a meticulous setup it was. And there was so much fuss, the road worker said, that they can't possibly set up a trap there."

"Well, then, come tell us what you find out, tomorrow morning, in front of Grange-Blanche."

"Where are you going to spend the night?"

"At home, of course, it's still the safest place. I'm absolutely certain Raymond will never give away our home."

It's too late for Maurice to accompany me and still get back to his apartment before the curfew. I catch the last trolley home. The house is silent. On the second floor, the window of Jean-Pierre's little room is open to the summer night. Maria, who sleeps downstairs, scarcely responds to my whisper: "It's me, Maria, good night."

I undress quickly and now I am all alone in the big bed. Raymond's pajamas are under his pillow. I hug them to me. Breathing in the smell of the man who wears them, I finally break down. I cry and cry without stopping. Exhausted, I fall asleep with my grief.

Tuesday, June 22, 1943

Deep in the comfort of my bed, I hear Maria laughing with my little boy. The sun peeks through the open window. It's eight o'clock. How could I have slept so long, so heavily? Am I heartless? I feel guilty. I go downstairs, aching all over, worn out as if I had walked for miles. The kitchen stinks of the chamomile and mint that Maria so relishes. Jean-Pierre has finished his breakfast. He climbs on my lap and his milky breath nauseates me. To conceal my reaction, I kiss the nape of his neck, his shoulders, all along his arms. His cool skin makes me feel better. He is ticklish and wriggles with pleasure as I caress him. But Maria's not fooled. She scrutinizes me.

"Your face looks swollen, are you all right? Did you sleep well? Is there a little sister on the way? Your nausea is a good sign!"

"Oh, Maria, I'm still drowsy. I'll wash up and then I'll feel better."

I can't finish my cup of black coffee, my stomach is all upset. Boubou follows me upstairs. He is perplexed by the empty bed, because he was looking forward to snuggling with his father. "Papa isn't here, my little one; he's taking a trip."

Back downstairs, I have to think up something to tell Maria. A week's trip is fine, but if it's anything longer, it won't be credible. For the time being, there is more important business to attend to. I need free time, I have to be available these next few days. I don't have classes this morning, but this afternoon I have to teach three hours, then two hours Wednesday afternoon and three Saturday morning. Next week, I have to teach only four hours—just my little first-year students, because the third-year students will be in the middle of the Brevet Elementaire exams and the older students have time off to review for the *baccalauréat*.[19]

Maurice and Pascal are already there when I reach Grange-Blanche hospital. Maurice has been to Caluire. He saw Dr. Dugoujon's neighbors and also some people who witnessed what happened yesterday afternoon. He describes how fast it all happened, how brutal it was, and how the people who saw it all are baffled by the flight of one of those arrested.

"The road worker told me it was impossible for him not to have been in cahoots with the Gestapo. He shoved past one of the German police and ran zigzagging across the square to get to the path down to the Saône. The police fired a few shots, aiming everywhere except at him. One policeman went after him. How could he have failed to see him in the ditch? The grass there is mostly dried up at this time of year. The other Germans, who were in parked cars, called to him to come back. The cars, by the way, made two trips, there were so many people to take away . . ."

But who is it who got away? Max's secretary, whose name is Maurice, like my cousin, is a very young man, blond and full of vitality. Today, however, his face is serious, preoccupied. You can tell he is stunned. It doesn't surprise me that he is deeply attached to his boss. Max is not someone to provoke indifference! At first Maurice thinks, judging from the road worker's description, that the escaped man must be Bruno Larat, because Max had told him where the meeting was so that he could inform Colonel Lacaze. Last night, when Max's secretary first heard, he warned Sophie, who had just arrived from London to help out and whom we were supposed to have dinner with last night. All of us are aware that something very serious has happened. We know exactly who was there: Aubry, Lassagne, Bruno, Lacaze, on the one hand, and on the other, Max, Aubrac, and Colonel Schwartzfeld. None of these seven men showed up at home last

19. The Brevet Elémentaire exams were taken by students who chose to leave school at fourteen years of age.

74

night, and every possible hideout has been explored. So who escaped? It can't be Bruno, since he hasn't been found at any of his refuges.

Is it Dr. Dugoujon, as Pascal suggests? That's impossible, for he would have landed quickly with one of his many Lyon colleagues and friends. My cousin Maurice adds that the doctor has a cool head; he was not implicated in the meeting, and by running away he would have acted like a member of the group. Besides, the Caluire road worker saw him being pushed into one of the German police cars. So? Could there have been an eighth man? One more mystery! We were already wondering how the Gestapo knew about this meeting. The secret was well kept. Dr. Dugoujon's place had never been used before. The doctor himself was in poor health and had more than enough to do as a general practitioner; while sharing our ideas, he was not involved in the Resistance.

These arrests hit us hard, following so soon after those in the first two weeks of June. After the arrest of Vidal (Delestraint) in Paris, I was sent to warn General Frère. I met him in the same place as I had in April, near the seminary in Chamalières. Father Elchinger, who had been the chaplain of our social teams in Strasbourg, was head of this seminary. During a convivial dinner with some friends of mine from 1938–39, we all compared our various commitments within the Resistance, happy to find we were all in it together: the Teitgens were in Combat, we were in Libération-Sud, and some others were in Témoignage chrétien.

When I contacted the general about the safety rules he would have to observe, he was emphatic: "I'm a soldier, an officer. I won't give up the fight and I can face any situation." All I could do was report his determination to my comrades in Lyon, describing to them this already aged man standing erect and trim, even with his stiff leg, who walked me to the door of his office and said: "Good-bye, young lady, we'll meet again in Strasbourg to celebrate victory."

He was arrested on June 12 by the Gestapo, along with a number of military officers belonging to the Organization of

Army Resistance. This avalanche of arrests at the top was crippling.

Max's secretary has met with Sophie, who is to inform London of Max's arrest. Since Bruno Larat, chief of radio operations, is out of circulation, they have to use another channel to communicate with London. Now, where are Max and his companions who were caught at Caluire? Were they taken immediately to Paris? Are they at Gestapo headquarters? At Montluc? "I'm going to find out," I tell them.

"How are you going to do that?"

"I'll take a bundle of clothes to the prison guard house, for Ermelin. If the guards accept it, it means they are there. There's no reason why they should have been separated. We'll meet at five in front of the lycée."

At home, I gather up some underwear and socks, a towel, and a shaving kit. I also rip out a page from the newspaper Le Nouvelliste—the one with the crossword puzzle, where I scribble a few words—to wrap up the whole bundle. Before going to my classes, I ride my bike to the Montluc prison. It's half past one. The guard is relaxed at this time of day; the soldiers are digesting and smoking. I hold out my bundle.

"This is for Mr. Claude Ermelin," I say, and I write the name on a piece of paper, in block letters. A soldier takes it, consults a list, and says: "You, wait!" He goes off dragging his feet.

Suddenly I'm not so confident. "If I get arrested, I'll have asked for it! It's stupid to have come here myself!" But I've already prepared what to say just in case: "I'm a lycée teacher; we have a humanitarian organization that takes care of prisoners. I was given this name today to bring a package." I would even muster the cheek to add: "You know me, I come here every week."

After a very long quarter of an hour, the soldier returns. Wrapped in the newspaper are a shirt, some dirty socks, and the shaving kit. "This is forbidden," he says, showing it to me. I put everything into my saddlebag and dash off to the lycée.

During recess I look in my saddlebag; there's no message among the dirty clothes. Nothing. But my eye is drawn to the crossword puzzle of *Le Nouvelliste*, where the word *Maxwell* is very distinct. Definition: "physicist." Suddenly, revelation: Raymond is with Max, who is all right. At five I meet the others in front of the school and pass my discoveries on to them.

"Fine," says Max's secretary, "we'll figure out some way to help them escape. We're almost certain there was a betrayal. Max has a chance of remaining anonymous with his false identity card and his tight cover. If there is a traitor, he doesn't know Max."

"Do you know who tipped them off?"

Then Pascal tells us that just before he came to meet us, a *résistant* visited him, a police inspector, who told him a very strange story. Last night, at the Saône Quay police station, the phone rang. The caller indicated that he had helped a man whose arm was bleeding to walk to a certain address. The police rushed to the spot, where they found a young man who said he had escaped during an arrest made by the Gestapo in Caluire. The policemen took him to the Antiquaille hospital for treatment. After taking his deposition, they left him in the section for prisoners. According to the inspector, the man's name was René Hardy. Pascal has figured out that the eighth man, the one no one expected at Caluire, is a *résistant* in charge of the railroad sabotage service. He uses the name Didot, and belongs to the Combat movement. Pascal told Claude Bourdet all about this. Bourdet is taking over interim direction of Combat since Frenay is now in London. "Didot is a buddy," Bourdet said. "Why was he at the meeting?" "He probably ran into Aubry, our representative for the secret army, and Aubry, not quite feeling up to such a summit meeting, probably asked him to go along."

Just the same, such an easy escape seems suspicious. But then, in the Resistance so many unbelievable things happen! Is it courage, or just luck? For the time being, our most urgent task is to try to save Max.

Wednesday, June 23, 1943

On Wednesday morning, a man about forty years old, rather portly and well dressed, arrives from Paris, I believe. He is called Mr. Henry. He is said to have been the police commissioner under Max when the latter was a prefect. He is here as the strategist who is going to organize Max's liberation. We gather around a bench at the trolley terminus, facing Grange-Blanche. As I have a record of organizing successful escapes, and above all, since Raymond is involved, I'm brought into the discussions. Mr. Henry takes things in hand and runs through all the possibilities with us.

An attack on the prison? We can't carry it off: we don't have sufficient strength in numbers, and even if we did, before we ever found Max's cell, we would all be caught inside Montluc by German soldiers, who could easily race in from the adjoining fortress and from the Part-Dieu barracks. Should we attempt to transfer Max to the hospital in a repeat of the Antiquaille operation? But how can we get him the medication that would make the transfer necessary? We could send a parcel through the Red Cross to Montluc addressed to Martel, which is Max's name on his identity card. A *résistant* male nurse would then keep an eye on the prisoners arriving at Antiquaille, the French hospital. If they sent him to the German military hospital, we would try to find a contact there.

Or we could attack the German cars and trucks that leave Montluc every morning for the school of health, where interrogations take place. Every night, they reverse the itinerary. How would we know which car Max was in? We decide to set up surveillance around the prison complex to familiarize ourselves with the regular traffic and any contingency plans. Henry has an idea that seems, at first, a stroke of genius. On the far side of Montluc, on the boulevard running along the railroad tracks, he spotted a big wooden container used to store sand for icy road conditions. We'll make a hole in the side of the container facing Montluc and install a lookout with binoculars inside the box. Yes, but the lookout has to be able to recognize Max!

Well, as I have no classes on Thursday and as I met Max last Sunday, I get the job tomorrow morning! It's also been decided —counting on the complicity of railroad workers—to set up a watch at the railroad station overseeing departures in case there is a hurried transfer of prisoners to Paris. My cousin Maurice has lunch with me. In his native Lyon, he is like a fish in water, and he has found a mother who was in the doctor's office with her little girl at the very moment the Gestapo arrived. She was asked to leave the office, but she saw everyone who was in the waiting room.

"There were three gentlemen," she said, "who were not from Caluire." At any rate, she had never seen them before. A miracle! There is still a chance that Max, Raymond, and Colonel Schwartzfeld, who we know arrived there together, have not been identified. I don't hesitate for a minute. What General de Lattre de Tassigny and I did to contact Cavaillès may help Raymond. I'm back in my role as the fiancée. This afternoon I have two hours of classes. Too bad! I telephone the lycée, saying that Jean-Pierre is sick and that I have to wait for the doctor. I put on a very pretty checkered rayon suit, big white porcelain daisy earrings, and a tiny pillbox hat with a little veil. If Raymond saw me, he'd say: "You're looking mighty olé, olé, honey!" I hope I look like a society girl.

"Maurice, wait for me in your store. If I get out of there, I'll call you. But I will get out! Take my clothes, I'll change in your fitting room."

I trade my wedding band for a huge Mexican ring; in my purse, besides my comb and lipstick, I have a whole array of clandestine identity cards. My name is Miss de Barbentane. My food and textile ration cards indicate that the normal number of coupons have been used for the twenty-third of the month. Here I go!

There's a sentry at the gate.

"What do you want, miss?" he says.

"I'd like to see the people who made the arrest on Monday afternoon in Caluire, at a doctor's office."

The sentry calls an orderly, who goes to find out. A German in civilian clothes immediately appears. "Come with me." My heart beating wildly, I follow him up a beautiful stone staircase. On the second floor, he stops in a long, wide corridor in front of a door and knocks.

"*Herein.*"

I go into a large room flooded with daylight—into the wolf's jaws, too! Behind the desk, a man is putting on a light beige jacket over a pale green shirt. This man, about my age, with blue eyes, light hair and complexion, gets up and greets me coldly.

"I'd like to speak to the head of German police services." Silence. At a small table, a young German woman in a blue-gray uniform (we call them "gray mice") thumbs through a file. There's a moment's pause, then the answer rings out: "That's me." I'm flabbergasted. I would never have imagined that this rather run-of-the-mill, slightly vulgar young man was the om-nipotent master of the city of Lyon. It's Barbie. There's a lot of talk about him. They say he was living in France, running a silk business; that's why he speaks French and knows Lyon so well. Is it really possible that this little man has everyone scared? At his age, in the French police system, people haven't even reached the rank of first-class inspector!

Barbie gets up. He is shorter than I am. "I'm Obersturmführer Barbie; you know how to read, it's on the door. Now, what do you want?" Timidly and politely, I answer in an even tone of voice as if sure of my rights: "I haven't seen my fiancé since Monday, and I found out what happened. He had left me to go and see a physician. Some time ago, he had a bad bout with tuberculosis and he has to have a checkup. I was very worried when he didn't come back. I was afraid there'd been an accident, so I went to the police station, where I was told that you had arrested a lot of people at that doctor's in Caluire. I was also told he was in jail. So I came to ask you to let him out quickly, his health is so frail."

"What's his name?"

"Claude Ermelin."

With a queer smile, he immediately opens the drawer in front of him. He takes out a portfolio and throws it on the large leather-topped desk, which probably belonged to the commandant of the military school of health before the war. The portfolio opens, scattering various papers and cards, as well as a small snapshot of me in a bathing suit, on a beach, with a baby by my side.

I'm petrified.

"How long have you known him?"

"For about six weeks, sir. We met on the Mediterranean coast, just after his return from Tunisia. I was won over right away by his deep tan and his military past in Africa."

"He doesn't come from Tunisia, he comes from Saint-Paul," he sniggers.

"No, sir, he wasn't in Saint-Paul-de-Vence, but in Saint-Raphaël."

That retort was a miracle, out of the blue really, and the first piece of luck for me. I appear not to know that there is a prison in Lyon called Saint-Paul.

"His name is not Ermelin but Vallet, and you can believe me, he has just gotten out of prison. He has already been arrested as a Gaullist. It's out of the question that we release him, he's a terrorist."

Something snaps inside me. I can't help crying. Suddenly I realize I'm pregnant, and have been since May 14. We're going to have another child. I'm crying, and he just says: "It's not my fault; he deceived you, that's all."

"This is terrible, sir, we are to marry soon."

"Miss, I already told you, he won't be set free. He's a terrorist; he will have to pay."

"Sir, that's impossible, I must marry quickly before my parents notice I'm expecting a child. It's terrible. He promised to marry me. I don't want to be an unwed mother."

I'm crying, and this time it's no pretense. The tall German girl comes closer; he looks at her and so do I. Is she moved at all? I turn to her: "Miss, tell him that I have to get married quickly."

She shrugs her shoulders with a degree of pity, probably saving me. It's my second piece of luck!

"Go away, miss, we can't do anything for you," and she pushes me toward the door.

I still wonder how I got down the stairs and into the street. I bite my left forefinger until it bleeds to keep myself from howling. I cross the street and sit down on a bench, muttering and moaning behind clenched teeth so that no noise comes out of my mouth. I sit there without moving, tears running down my cheeks and wetting my jacket. I can't stand my earrings, I tear them off and throw them down on the road as hard as I can.

81

No more daisies—just a dozen tiny white splinters. A woman wearing an apron comes up to me, carrying a glass of water: "I'm the superintendent of the house behind you. Drink some water and stop crying." Then she whispers: "I've got a message for you. Your cousin is waiting for you in his store."

I drink the water. "Thank you, madam, I feel better now." The cousin, of course, is Maurice. He came here to find out what happened and to protect me. I get up and walk to the river, where I cross over the bridge and walk alongside the Rhône. I don't have to force myself to stop frequently. I vomit all the water I drank. I just hope I don't run into anyone I know. The quays at road crossings are our usual rendezvous. I walk slowly, but eventually I come to the town hall. I have to make sure I'm not being followed, so I go through the gates, cross the two courtyards of the town hall, and end up in the square surrounded by flocks of pigeons. I sit down for a moment on the edge of the fountain, then walk to the rue de la Martinière and come back by a traboule. It's okay. I'm not being shadowed.

At Maurice's store, Au Roi du Pantalon, I collapse on a chair in the fitting room. I take off my hat and pull my hair back with a wide band. Maurice tells me he followed me to the prison and never let the entrance to Gestapo headquarters out of his sight. When he saw me leaving, he asked the super to pass a message on to me. Then he followed me back to the town hall and when he was sure that nobody was tailing me, he came to wait for me in his shop.

"Rest a bit," he says. "Relax. Later, I'll take you out for a bite to eat, and then I'll take you home."

In the restaurant, I tell him about my meeting with the head of the Gestapo and my sudden sense of despair afterward.

"Just the same, you have to be sure you're pregnant. Go to see Dr. Eparvier tomorrow afternoon. I'll make an appointment for you."

I'm scarcely listening. The people in the restaurant make a lot of noise. The clatter of knives and forks on the plates gets on my nerves; the waitress's perfume makes me nauseated. I'm mesmerized by the massive metal shutters lowered to within seven feet of the ground. It is certainly menacing. I feel like the curtain will suddenly drop and I'll be caught in a trap.

"Let's go, Maurice, before they close. I'm afraid of getting stuck." He pays, grumbling that we've got plenty of time and that I'm being so capricious, he's sure I must be pregnant.

As we reach my doorstep, he asks: "Do you want me to stay?"

"No, Maria would think it was strange, and where would I put you? Also, I have to get used to this."

Thursday, June 24, 1943

Thursday morning, Boubou is not awake yet. I must be at our Part-Dieu lookout by seven so I can hide in the sand container. I'll have to choose a moment when nobody is passing by, and pray that no one in the neighborhood is watching the sidewalk from a window. Mr. Henry is there with binoculars. Maurice is furious. I still think the idea is great. Someone was there at the crack of dawn to pierce a hole and empty out some of the sand.

"We'll be back around ten o'clock. That's when the transfers from Montluc to the school of health will stop."

Sitting inside that big box, with the cover closed, I have the prison gate lined up with the hole. The railroad is between the gate and where I am and then there is the square in front of Montluc. Both the big gate and the little one are closed. I adjust the binoculars to my eyes and wait. At first the sand is comfortable but little by little I get stiff. I can't possibly budge and I can't see anything toward the sidewalk. I mustn't make any noise that could alert passersby . . .

Two black Citroëns drive up. The big gate opens and swallows them. It's seven-forty. I wait. At nine-thirty, the gate opens again. First comes a pickup truck with a tarpaulin and a streamlined cab; two soldiers are in the cab, one driving, the other with a rifle or submachine gun between his legs. When the truck turns, I can see in the back. It's full, and two armed soldiers are sitting on the sides. A little later the two black Citroëns, two people in front, three in the back—probably some more important quarry for the Germans. But it's impossible to see their faces. The sun bounces off the car windows, blinding me. This hiding place is idiotic; how am I going to get out of here? You could see much better just hanging around the prison in the open, replacing the observers every hour.

When they pick me up, the two guys from the groupe-franc, Robert and Julien, check out the area. Like Maurice, they are furious. Me too. The very idea of this hideout is preposterous. I deliver my "report," as he calls it, to Mr. Henry, and I season it with scathing remarks. I'll never see him again!

The afternoon is long. I don't have to meet my buddies again. Around five, my father-in-law comes to give his grandson a hug and to take him for a walk in the neighborhood. When they return, he says: "I'll wait for Raymond; he won't be late, I hope."

This is it! I have to explain. For the moment, only my cousin Maurice knows. How am I going to get around it? My brother-in-law is in a prisoner-of-war camp for officers; my in-laws, so proud of their children, had to give up their business in Dijon. They are now refugees in Lyon without any work, living on their savings. They don't even want to think about the ever-possible racial roundups. How can I break this to them? Their oldest son in the hands of the Gestapo! Here goes: "Listen, father, I'm going to let you in on a secret. I'd planned to come tomorrow to tell you both, because at one this afternoon I heard a message over the BBC: Raymond did get to London, and he has rejoined General de Gaulle."

My lie is rewarded. My father-in-law gets up, and just the way he always does when he is moved or surprised, he raises his left eyebrow, and says: "I was thinking that's what would happen. Raymond will be very useful over there. I thank you, Lucie, for letting him go. It's very brave of you. I'll tell Hélène. We'll look after you and Boubou."

Tears come to my eyes. In this climate of racist persecutions that a man in his situation can take on his role as head of the family this way and think of protecting me. With all my heart I embrace him. But still I have to warn him not to see me too often, and I have to explain that I plan to be separated once more from Boubou.

"He'll be fine up there in the mountains; with the climate and food, it's much better than Lyon during the summer."

"Why don't you go with him? You'll soon be on vacation."

"I'll think about it."

After he leaves, Maria, who has overheard everything, is excited.

"Oh, Mrs. Samuel, are we going to hear him on the radio?"

"Maria, he won't use his own name because his family is still here in France. By the way, if you don't feel safe staying in the house of Gaullists, I can find you another family."

"Don't even think of it. It's my house too, and Jean-Pierre is also my little boy. It's natural for him to go to the mountains during vacation. But when school starts again he'll need me."

Monday, June 28, 1943

Although I don't have any classes this morning, I go to the lycée office to ask if I can be relieved of proctoring the exams as well as of serving on the exam jury. Having a small child, I can exploit the fact that last week I had to cancel my classes at the last minute because he was sick.

I still have four hours of courses to finish up the school year with my first-year students. I will take them on an all-day excursion while the other teachers are busy with the *baccalauréat* exams. The administration agrees.

On my way home I meet Alphonse. "I was looking for you, Lucie. Vercingétorix wants to see you in an hour at Sept-Chemins."

I'm a little surprised. Georges Marrane, one of the leaders of the National Front serves as intermediary between his movement and the United Resistance, the MUR. All MUR leaders have frequent and easy relations with him. He understands quickly and cooperates honestly. We like him very much and even know his real name. How could he hide who he is—with his bowlegged cyclist's silhouette and the head of an Andalusian Moor? He grew a superb red moustache, which gained him his nickname. He is a Communist, organized and cautious and not exactly talkative. He rarely confides anything about himself, and when he does, it's very vague. He leads a clandestine life that is far from easy; he has very little money. One day, I gave him two cans of condensed milk and two pounds of sugar for his little boy, born the previous spring. But we have a close connection that is even older. I met him in 1932–34 when I was a member of the Young Communists. We were attending a congress in his town hall in Ivry in 1934 when we heard that fascist demonstrations were taking place in the place de la Concorde. All the young people attending the meeting wanted to go straight there. "Nobody is leaving!" Maurice Thorez declared; he was presiding. So we were left spoiling for a fight.

It takes just under an hour to reach Sept-Chemins, which is a little beyond Saint-Genis-Laval. My bike is fast, and I catch sight of Marrane, also on a bicycle. Before I can stop, he pulls up alongside me and whispers: "In ten minutes, second path on the left." Then he takes off, standing up to pedal.

We sit down in the shade of a hedge, in a meadow. Both our bikes lie in the grass. He starts: "You know the safety rules of the party."

I cut in: "I'm not a member of the party."

"I know, but there are a number of Communists inside your movement. The orders are categorical: they must not see you. Raymond is in the hands of the Gestapo, so you have become dangerous."

"First of all," I say, "Raymond will never talk; I am absolutely certain of that. You want to know what I did on Wednesday afternoon? I went to see Barbie! So you can imagine how much I agree that I should meet as few friends as possible. It's for their sake, of course, but above all for mine, because I don't want anyone to suspect me of any contact whatsoever with the Resistance." A little bitterly, I add: "But you know, Copeau sees me every day. It's tough to be left alone. After all, those Communist party members you're talking about are old comrades of mine from the youth groups and from the Latin Quarter. We've known each other for ages. They have come to our house many times since 1940; that, too, is contrary to safety!"

I tell him about my interview with Barbie and confide in him that I'm expecting a baby.

"My dear," he says, as he leaves, "you sure must love your man to do such a thing. It was daring—in fact foolhardy! Maybe that's why you'll win! In any case, I'll manage to see you again from time to time. But don't be too critical of our comrades."

He kisses me, which is unexpected.

"You go ahead first." He adds: "Nothing ventured, nothing gained."

My bitterness makes my legs even stronger and I tear home. I know they're right! But aren't unreasonable things also part of the battle?

In the afternoon, with my number one outfit in a bag, I go to Maurice's store and rush into the fitting room. I change quickly, put on a little makeup, and am already at the door when I say: "I'm going back there, Maurice. See you later."

By the time he realizes what I mean, I'm at the trolley station for Bellecour.

This time, when I get to the avenue Berthelot, I don't ask for anything, but pass through the gates with confidence, just nodding to the sentries. I climb the stairs. On the double door there is, indeed, a sign, which I missed the other day: Obersturmführer K. Barbie—no accent on the final e. I knock.

"*Herein.*"

Today he is alone, with a magnificent dog. The door hasn't even closed behind me before he has crossed the office with the dog at his heels: "You again! I have nothing to say to you—get out. Your fiancé is ready for his last cigarette and his last glass of rum, as you say in France," he adds, grinning.

He turns me around—he's stronger than he looks, this guy—and pushes me out, slamming the door in my face.

There! Now, old girl, you've got to clear out of here before he has second thoughts and has you arrested, I say to myself. Once on the sidewalk I go about twenty yards, cross the avenue, and go into a corridor, where I pretend to be adjusting my garter. It all happened so fast that there's no way anyone could be discreetly shadowing me. No one is running after me. Nobody is standing at the gates of the school of health scanning the area. Let's go. I take the rue Pasteur to the cours Gambetta, where I jump on a trolley crossing the Rhône to Bellecour, and then I go down the rue de la Ré to reach the rue Puits-Gaillot. Maurice is in a dither: "There you are! You're really stupid! We'll have to tie you up."

"That's it, Maurice, I won't go again. It's hopeless. He's been sentenced. They're going to kill him. Now I'll have to avenge him. I'll be thirty-one tomorrow. We were supposed to celebrate my birthday at my sister's in Cusset. I'm going there tonight. Try to reach my brother-in-law at his press office in Vichy to tell him I'm on my way. Tell Maria I'll be back tomorrow."

Back at the Perrache station: three weeks ago, we were so happy, coming home from Carqueiranne. You really have to be stupid when you've been burned once to start the whole idiotic game all over again!

Morin-Forestier is indeed en route to London. His wife has been reassured. On the train from Lyon to Vichy, crammed like all trains nowadays—where first-class coaches are reserved for occupation troops and for high Vichy officials—I'm utterly disgusted and revolted. I hate everybody: the travelers in the compartments (five of us squeezed on benches meant for four), the police coming along to check identification cards, and the fellow from the fiscal bureau who arrives first: "Open your baggage."

"I have no baggage."

He calls the identity police: "She has no baggage."

The policeman turns to me: "Why are you traveling?"

I'm outraged: "Here is my identity card, I'll be thirty-one tomorrow. I'm joining my husband at my sister and brother-in-law's in Vichy, to celebrate my birthday. That's not forbidden, is it?"

They are perplexed. Such a tone of voice. A brother-in-law in Vichy! Cops are not exactly daring—one never knows. They leave. The nine other travelers, who haven't budged, all look at me out of the corners of their eyes. In Vichy, my brother-in-law is waiting for me with his bike.

"You sit on the frame," he says. "I'll pedal, the road is almost level; your sister is waiting for us. We'll celebrate as soon as Raymond gets here. Come to think of it, how is he coming?"

I blurt out the truth: "Raymond has been arrested by the Gestapo; they're going to shoot him."

He gets off his bike. "But what are you doing here? Surely you're being followed."

"Relax, they haven't any way to connect him with his family or mine." We keep going, in silence and on foot. When we reach Cusset, my sister immediately senses that something is terribly wrong. So I tell them everything: about June 21, about Barbie, our friends, my pregnancy. She couldn't be sweeter, rallying around me.

"Come—lie down. I'll bring you a bowl of soup. Pierre, just for tonight, why don't you sleep in the girls' room?"

Night comes—with sobs, with despair, and with rebellion. I do not accept my powerlessness. My sister, lying close to me, holds my hand.

"Calm down, Lucie dear. Tomorrow, I'll go to Lyon with you and I'll take Boubou to the children's home at the foot of the Vercors mountains. He'll be in lovely company and well fed. With one less worry you'll be able to think straight."

"I don't want to live if Raymond dies. It's impossible. I'll give you my kid, and then . . ."

In my imagination I already see myself in a suicide attack on the Gestapo, dying in an apotheosis of carnage of German policemen. Why shouldn't I blow up all of them, in the school of health? I know where their leader is and I won't chicken out.

Tuesday, June 29, 1943

What a sad birthday. In Lyon, my sister and I call the children's home in the mountains. Everything is all right. They will take Boubou. We quickly pack his bags; they will leave tomorrow.

A week has already gone by since catastrophe struck. We still have no news of Max. Pascal says that Claudius Petit saw some of them getting off the train at the Paris Gare de Lyon. They had a heavy escort: Lassagne was there, in bad shape, Aubry, Schwartzfeld, and Dugoujon as well. According to him, neither Max, nor Raymond, nor Bruno was with them, but a woman, Mrs. Raisin, Aubry's secretary, was.

Pascal talked to his *résistant* police inspector again. Yesterday, the Gestapo apparently came to get Didot-Hardy at the Antiquaille hospital and took him to the German military hospital at Croix-Rousse. That's a bizarre way of dealing with somebody who tried to escape at Caluire! There are a lot of wounded prisoners—some in casts, others even dying—and they are not entitled to such privileges but are still agonizing in the basement at avenue Berthelot, or in the Montluc cells. We feel less and less comfortable with this Didot-Hardy story. "Next week," Pascal tells me, "Claude Bourdet and Claudius Petit will be in Lyon. We'll discuss the matter together."

I turn this information over in my mind. If Max, Bruno, and Raymond were not transferred to Paris, what became of them? Did they leave by another train? We would have heard about it. We have a permanent lookout in the railroad stations for all the trains going to Paris. Could they have been driven somewhere? Why just the three of them? For Max, that might be understandable. If they identify him, he is too big a catch. He would have to be turned over to the highest level of the Gestapo. But the other two? Yesterday Barbie told me Raymond had been sentenced; Barbie didn't say he was gone. There are only two possibilities: either they are still at Montluc or they are dead. I've got to find out.

By one o'clock I'm back at Montluc with a package for each of them. I also bought—at a very high price—a small box of good peaches. At the guard house I say: "Here are packages for Ermelin, Martel, and Larat. The peaches are for you."

"Thank you, miss, you wait."

Three minutes later, the same soldier, a man with gray hair, his heavy lids concealing his eyes, gives me back the packages and says: "No more packages, miss. Please, don't come here anymore, never again."

He kept the peaches. Bad news? A warning? There wasn't time for him to check the list at the guard house—he just went in, put away the peaches, and came back. After all, these soldiers are not all rotten. Perhaps he saved me from running into real trouble. All right. That leaves the morgue, which isn't far from here. That's where the police often take people who die at Montluc or who are killed in the street. If they are executed near Bron, they're buried on the spot. I ring the bell at the morgue and go inside.

"I'd like to know if you have any bodies that haven't been identified."

"These days there are plenty of those. Are you looking for someone?"

"Yes. May I see them?"

"That's not allowed without a police officer present. But describe the person you're looking for."

How awful! I imagine Raymond lying there, stiff, his chest riddled with bullets but his face intact, his conspirator's moustache disguising his beautiful and so welcoming lips. I feel that describing him is like killing him. It's as if I accepted his death.

"No, madam, there's nobody corresponding to that description. It's forbidden, but I'll show you the only one with a moustache."

We go down some steps to a room where the walls are lined halfway up to the ceiling with big squares of metal. Each one has a handle. He pulls one out, it's the front end of a long box. He shows me a face. How pale is the corpse of this unknown young man! And how I thank him for not being Raymond!

"If you come back again, remember this is a good time of day. Mornings, the police are often here. But in the afternoons they do the interments; they bury them at the Guillotière cemetery. If you still have the man's tobacco ration card, get his ration. I'll take some. Tobacco, not cigarettes."

I have never vomited as much in my life as in that half-mile home. Lying in bed, my ears buzzing, I gradually calm down.

Look, Lucie, you're thirty-one, you've had to face very serious situations before. This time it's worse. Even more reason to fight back. Tomorrow, you'll be alone in this house with Maria. Don't let yourself be cut off from your friends; show them that you are still part of the action, that you share in the fight. They must not get into the habit of thinking of you as a wife who is overwhelmed by what happened, a mother expecting a second child, a weak woman who has to be protected, who has to be spared.

I swear I'll be calm when I see them, and effective at whatever job I'm given. That way, if I manage to think up a rescue operation they'll trust me and help me.

Friday, July 9, 1943

What a day! I have just spent it with my first-year students. We met in front of the Cathedral of Saint-Jean at nine with our picnic baskets. Then for eight hours straight we lived with the Romans. On the Fourvière hills, in the incomplete excavations neglected since 1940, we found the sites of the theater and the circus, remains of sewers and water pipes. We trudged down fifty yards of Roman road and discovered traces of the old forum, the *foro vetere*, which gave the hill its name—Fourvière. The children were pleased with this etymological discovery. I told them that veterans of the Roman legions came here, driven from Vienne by barbarians from the east. "Were things already like that then?" one of the little girls asked.

On these sunny slopes, early dwellers escaped the floods of the Saône and were able to prevail over assailants. We talked about the two possible origins for Lyon's Latin name, Lugdunum: *lug*, solar god, and *lug*, raven. At any rate, it was a Gallic word with a double meaning. Since the raven was the messenger of the sun, we were satisfied with that. Having gobbled up our snack, we took the bus to Francheville. There we went down some narrow paths until we came upon the arches of the aqueduct built under Hadrian to bring water from the hills of the Gier to Lyon. We counted seventy arches in perfect condition, and my students raced from one to the next. I watched them frolic. Twenty times they dashed back like frantic puppies, asked me questions, and took off again. The boldest ones wanted to climb on top of the aqueduct. "Where it's lowest, it's not dangerous!"

I explained that this was a canal where water used to run and that the arches are sometimes higher and sometimes lower because they had to take the land contours into account to obtain an even flow to Lyon. I was so caught up in my passion for teaching that, momentarily, I forgot my situation. When I came back to reality, I asked myself: what am I doing? Could I really forget that the man who is my life is in prison; that he is not alone there, that suffering and humiliation is their lot; that every other day, at the morgue, I see the corpses of young men killed unjustly?

In that landscape where centuries of civilization are accumulated, a woman approached me: her work apron was black cotton, her hair, already gray, was tied in a bun.

"It's a pleasure to see these young ones." She obviously felt like talking. "Look how carefree they are," she said. "I was their age during the Great War. My father was at the front; he never came back. Today, my husband has been 'with them' for more than three years; and now it's my two young boys' turn to leave home. But three men in Germany, that is too much, madam."

I asked her where she was able to send her boys so they could escape compulsory labor service. "They went up into the hills there, above Chazelles. That's where I've been. But they're determined to fight and they're going to join a maquis unit somewhere around Le Puy. That's a lot of worry for a mother, but everybody has to lend a hand if we want to get the job done."

Like me, she listens to the BBC and draws on it for hope. While we were talking, the little girls came back.

"Mrs. Samuel, we're thirsty."

My new friend led us to her house behind a vineyard and a marvelous golden yellow field of colza. She took a huge basket of peaches from her basement. "Go to it, girls, dig in!" A stampede ensued. "Easy, there's enough for everybody."

I was concerned about this pillage and the loss of income for this country woman, at a time when everything is so costly. I offered to pay her, but she refused: "It's really nothing! I only hope somebody will do the same thing for my two guys in the maquis."

In Chaponost, we had to wait an hour for a bus that was packed when it got there. I couldn't separate my flock, but all of us would never have fit on that bus. The driver told me that at five o'clock there was a direct bus for Lyon on the main road, three kilometers from there. So off we went at a good clip, our wooden soles clacking noisily down the pebbled road. Soon we were on the bus, sitting on each other's laps. The other travelers smiled at these lively youngsters. We followed the banks of the Rhône into Lyon. Passing Saint-Paul prison I couldn't help thinking: "Those were the good old days!"

I come home exhausted. Maria is pacing like a caged bear. "I'm bored being alone all day long," she says. I promise to take her soon to see her friend who, like Maria, was liberated from the camp at Gurs and is now near Valençay in the Indre department, staying with some good people who have several children. I don't want to let Maria travel alone, where she runs the risk of a police check, with potentially embarrassing questions. God knows what she might say, even in the best of faith!

Tuesday, July 13, 1943

This is commencement day. The graduating students have done very well in their *baccalauréat* exams. Two of them, Irène Altman and Ginette Favre, come to see me. They have been waiting to receive their diplomas before joining the Resistance. I know their parents, who have been with us ever since 1941. These students know what I think and are proud to be at my side now. I promise I'll help them contact the Resistance but it makes me shudder.

What a miserable commencement! The prizes are pathetic— a few classic books but an ample supply of works by Vichy sympathizers . . .

A professor from the upper school delivers a thoroughly literary address, and the choir sings "Maréchal, nous voilà." [20] Impossible to leave before the end. Professors sign the register only after the end of the ceremony. And without a signature, no salary during the vacation.

Thursday, July 15, 1943

I take Maria to Valençay. Whenever I go there, it's a chance to visit two of my professors, Henri Hauser and Charles Guignebert, who both encouraged me at the Sorbonne, and their wives. These two old couples are full of knowledge, charm, and phi-

20. "Marshal (Pétain), we are with you."

losophy. They load me up with a bundle of things we can't find in Lyon: eggs, sausage, a chicken, and that marvelous goat cheese shaped like a truncated pyramid. Raymond always liked to point out how it broke, how it was conchoidal, a sure sign of quality.

I push on as far as the château. André Chamson is there inspecting his treasures.[21] His job is to oversee the preservation of the Lóuvre's masterpieces far from Paris, in well-protected hideaways. The Venus of Milo apparently is hidden here. It is a splendid château with a bizarre ambience: the owner's wife is German. There are guests and visitors of every sort: foreigners living clandestinely, cultured German officers, Jewish academics. One never knows with whom one is dealing. And in the midst of it all, Chamson is at ease and amusing, with his outrageous jokes.

On my way home I make a detour through Saint-Aignan to visit Paul-Boncour. He is well over seventy, living in a beautiful house on the banks of the Cher. He is a former cabinet member and was for a long time France's representative to the League of Nations. He was one of the few deputies who refused to vote full powers for Pétain, and subsequently retired to the country. But his retirement is interspersed with travel. He goes to Vichy, comes to Lyon. Once, in the fall of 1941, he came to our house. He had been told we were Gaullists and that he could meet interesting people at our home. This little man, quite deaf and with a booming voice and an abundant white mane, was almost always accompanied by his valet, who carried his cape. He terrified all our friends—you could hardly miss him! It had been decided that I should be the one to meet him. In his loud voice, he told me all the Vichy gossip. He was a mine of information; he knew everything about events and people. After meeting him two or three times in Lyon, I managed to persuade him that it would be better for me to see him at his place. This charming man, with his Old World manners, was very happy to play host to a young

21. André Chamson was a writer and former curator of the national museums. During the Second World War, he was in charge of large sections of the Louvre; he succeeded in hiding some of the most famous art treasures in the provinces. Later in the war, he joined the armed Resistance and became a major in the French units under General de Lattre de Tassigny. He is a member of the French Academy.

woman. He asked me to stay overnight, after an exquisite dinner that I alone devoured. He ate like a bird. Staying at his home, I became aware that, at nightfall, his park became a crossing point. There clandestine travelers crossed the Cher, which ran along the demarcation line between the occupied and unoccupied zones. I think he must have known but his deafness was his safeguard. Besides, at least once a week during that winter of 1942–43 he would go to the bridge and present the guard with his permanent pass as a border resident, like a man with a clear conscience.

Now, in the summer of 1943, it has been six months since I last saw him. He hardly goes to Vichy anymore. The total occupation of France wounded him deeply, so he stays home. As usual, he offers me his hospitality. That is a bit hard to accept after my expedition to Valençay. I have all this food in my bag, especially the chicken, ready to cook. How will they survive another day on the train in the heat of summer?

"That's no problem," he says; "my cook surely will find a solution."

She does—she will roast it so that tomorrow it can travel to Lyon without any risk.

In this big house full of books and objets d'art, I spend a wonderful evening. Paul-Boncour remembers his encounters with diplomats and heads of state at the League of Nations in Geneva. I never tire of asking him questions. He has many ideas for after the war. "All nations must be federated. What killed the League of Nations was the absence of both the United States and the USSR," he asserts. In turn, I tell him about the secret departure of certain legislators; the development and organization of the Resistance; and the very serious arrests now known to everybody. I tell him Raymond is in London, and I also tell him that I'm expecting a baby in February. He is deeply moved.

"Now go and rest, my child. When the baby is born, the war will be over and your husband will be back."

What a joke! Raymond back at home . . . When? And from where? How? In what shape?

I always come back to him.

Friday, July 16, 1943

I arrive in Lyon in the afternoon and take the provisions from Valençay to my in-laws. What would I do with all that, alone in a house that no longer functions as a welcoming spot for people coming through or even just as a friendly stopover for our many friends?

My in-laws discreetly express some surprise at not seeing me more often and at my lack of eagerness to join little Jean-Pierre now that classes are over.

I have an obsession: I must find a way to communicate with Raymond if he is still at Montluc and I must find out, if I can, what has become of Max. Both the guard at the gate and interior surveillance are manned by soldiers stationed at barracks in Lyon. It shouldn't be too hard for me to make contact with one of them. These guys, far from their families, are surely frequenting prostitutes. There's a good chance that from time to time they get gonorrhea. It's out of the question for them to consult the garrison medical officer. "Shameful diseases" are only for inferior races! For a German soldier, there is no way out: it's the Russian front if they get caught. Maurice refuses to make inquiries about Lyon doctors who discreetly see such patients.

"For those doctors money is the only thing that counts. I don't trust any of them. If one of them is engaged in an information service, he won't blow his cover to connect you with one of his patients."

So I have to try another approach. I know an official at police headquarters, Robert Cluzan, who passes very useful administrative and economic information on to the Resistance. One of his childhood and school friends is a police commissioner in charge of a crackdown squad that specializes in ferreting out Communists. Cluzan sees him cautiously, and from time to time is able to obtain some information from him. That's how he gets the name of a doctor consulted by German soldiers. I go to see him.

In the filthy waiting room there are two German soldiers and three civilians who look like members of a rogues' gallery. The doctor who comes out to call one of the patients is from the same mold. Maurice was right, it's impossible to trust him. I'm anxious to get out of there. As soon as the doctor opens the door of his office again, I jump up and say: "Doctor, could you come by tonight to see my father? He has lumbago and is confined to his bed; we have train reservations to leave tomorrow on a vacation. It's just around the corner from you."

I leave him a fictitious address and go to see Cluzan to let him know what happened. There are two people at his place and we all share a few slices of mortadella and a piece of bread. They are discussing an emergency strategy: a woman who is my colleague, a physics teacher, lent her apartment to some *résistant* Communist academics over the vacation. They used the place to write and mimeograph some leaflets and clandestine newspapers, which they stored there. When they went this morning to pick up a pack of these, they found German official seals on the door. The problem: if the material is still inside, we have to try to get it out! I join their trio to attempt a salvage operation.

The young woman makes sure the coast is clear. With a wet sponge she neatly soaks and unglues the seals, which she instructs us to put back once the removal is completed. Then she stands watch while we load the machines and stacks of newspapers onto a handcart in the courtyard. Off we go through the street at the rear of the building. Our friend is watching on the front side and we simply forget her. Seeing some uniformed Germans enter the building, she panics. She runs to Cluzan's and finds us around a table eating peaches from a basket. She really lets us have it!

It's not so much our lack of concern that disturbs me; it's my own tendency to get involved in any venture. Until Raymond is rescued, I've got better things to do with my freedom and my resourcefulness. But I know full well that at the next opportunity I'll do it again. Of course, my commitment to the Resistance is the result of a conscious decision. But confronting obstacles in difficult operations is part of the game: what a strange addiction!

We keep up our surveillance at the station. Nobody knows anything about Max. He has disappeared into thin air! The railroad workers tell us that the Germans have ordered ten third-class coaches, with engines fired up, to be placed on a siding at the Gerlan freight depot. This time, a whole train is going to be filled with prisoners. I am one of the lookouts. A railroad employee lets us enter a freight car standing right opposite the waiting train. We remove the wooden slat where the bill of lading is stuck, make large holes in the sheet of paper, and stick it back with glue around its edges. The protective grating in front is back in place. From the outside nobody can see anything. We are on the side where they will arrive, on the loading platform, which doesn't quite reach up to the waiting train. Thus everybody they put aboard that train will go right past us.

We have been waiting for an hour when we see a squad of German soldiers line up on the roadbed alongside the train. Next comes a column of people in civilian clothes. Surely they are Jews. All of them are rather well dressed, with suitcases in their hands as if departing peacefully on a vacation. They climb aboard the train while a sergeant major keeps them moving along, "*Schnell, schnell.*" There are men and women of all ages, even children. Among them I see one of my former students, Jeanine Crémieux. She got married in 1941 and had a baby last spring. She is holding the infant in her left arm and a suitcase in her right hand. The first step is very high above the rocky roadbed. She puts the suitcase on the step and holds on with one hand to the doorjamb, but she can't quite hoist herself up. The sergeant major comes running, hollers, and kicks her in the rear. Losing her balance, she screams as her baby falls to the ground, a pathetic little white wailing heap. I will never know if it was hurt, because my friends pulled me back and grabbed my hand just as I was about to shoot.

Today I know what hate is, real hate, and I swear to myself that these acts will be paid for. I'm struggling to control the nausea that sweeps over me, and I hear Julien noisily vomiting in a corner of the freight car. He has five kids, he is a railroad worker and a member of our *groupe-franc*.

Tonight I stay in Vénissieux to eat supper with my friends. These simple people, workers most of them, often with a past as Communist militants, have taken in people even poorer than themselves despite their own destitution. There are three Hungarians, middle-class Jews from Budapest and refugees from Admiral Horty's brand of anti-Semitism, who have been in France since 1938. In 1939, they volunteered to serve France in the army. After the armistice of June 1940, when the Vichy government wanted to place all foreign volunteers in camps, they ran away and found shelter in French working-class circles. There is also a young Portuguese man in this *groupe-franc*. He is fiercely silent and extraordinarily loyal. He has befriended me, and I know he would follow me to the ends of the earth.

These fifteen young men have accepted the authority of one who is younger than themselves, Serge Ravanel. He is absolutely fearless and has often proved it. We discuss things together for hours on end. This guy is the younger brother I never had, and I'd like to know everything about him and tell him what to think and do. Few people I know have such joie de vivre, such reserves of physical strength, such an ability to decide quickly and act just as fast. He also has a conspiratorial side that irritates me. He speaks in a low voice and always seems to be letting his listener in on some important secret. That's why I feel frustrated when I can't hear what he says to someone else in our group. Here they know me as Catherine, that's all. Only Serge knows my address.

We have had bad news concerning Max. In Fresnes prison, Lassagne was able to communicate with Dugoujon, who sent word to us through a woman friend that Max had been savagely beaten in Lyon and was at death's door with General Delestraint in a Gestapo villa in Neuilly.

Pascal Copeau, on whose shoulder I can cry without restraint when I can't stand it anymore, is the most attentive of friends. He keeps me posted on whatever he finds out about our ongoing drama. We often speak of Hardy; I am convinced he is guilty of betraying us. Pascal tells me that Claude Bourdet isn't sure that Hardy is a traitor. Claudius Petit, on the other hand, with his heart of gold and the scruples of a true believer, is shaken and tends to think he is guilty. As for me, I agree with those of our leaders who have decided to eliminate him because their suspicions are strong enough. But how shall we go about it? He has already been at the German military hospital in Croix-Rousse for four weeks. That injured arm required a lot of careful attention! What preferential treatment! How can we get to him there? We can't even consider any operation that risks sacrificing comrades of the *groupe-franc*. Maybe an accomplice inside the hospital? We must be dreaming. We decide that our only hope is to send a package of poisoned food. We know how precious food is these days, especially in prison. To avoid a hitch—prisoners always share—we have to put something in the package that is only enough for one person: we can put it in a little glass jar. A colleague who is a science professor at the university gives me an aspirin container almost full of cyanide crystals. "Be careful—with that amount you could kill all of Lyon."

I mix it in with some jam in the small glass jar. In no time at all the package is ready, and we drop it off at the hospital reception desk. For days and nights afterward, the idea of what will happen tortures me. It's one thing to decide, but quite another to execute such a decision. Now that I'm sure I have inside me a new promise, a child, life takes on even more value. Even when the man's a dirty rat! Three or four times a week I go to greet the anonymous dead at the morgue. But I wouldn't recognize Didot-Hardy if he showed up—I never saw him.

Wednesday, August 11, 1943

Days are so long now and night comes late. Tonight, I just can't fall asleep. Vergaville was here this afternoon. He is thoughtful, and in his own gruff way he tries to keep my spirits up. Today he told me an incredible story—his way of showing me that anything is possible when it comes to luck.

"Last night, I met Didot-Hardy, a guy who is a friend in the Combat organization. He just had an unbelievable adventure. In June, he was on a train bound for Paris, between Mâcon and Chalon, and he recognized one of his comrades in the company of a German cop. When the train slowed down, he threw his suitcase out the window and jumped out behind it. The suitcase broke open, and he couldn't recover its contents, but he rolled when he hit the ground and got up unhurt. He immediately went back to work for Combat in the railroad service. He described also how he escaped from the place Castellane at Caluire when the Gestapo arrested Moulin, Raymond, and the others. He was lucky that time, too. Unfortunately, he was wounded in the arm while escaping, and the French police caught him and put him in the prisoners' ward at Antiquaille hospital. He was treated there, his arm put in a cast, and then the Germans came to claim him and locked him up in their hospital. After four weeks there, when he realized they were about to remove his cast, he decided to escape. Using the safety pin from the sling around his neck, he succeeded in picking the lock of the iron bars at his window. He jumped from the second floor into the courtyard and went over the outer wall without being seen. He doesn't seem to realize he has to get out of Lyon as fast as possible. He told me Fouché is going to take him to the Creuse and find him a place to hide. What a guy!"

Vergaville, who isn't aware of the decision to eliminate Didot-Hardy, is surprised by my lack of enthusiasm. I don't say anything. Whatever happened to the cyanide?

Lying in bed I can't fall asleep. The rising moon makes the night as bright as it was at twilight. I imagine a thousand horrendous scenarios with that poisoned little pot; and another thousand represented by the dangers of that man's going free.

I absolutely must sleep. My baby, three months in the making, needs to grow in peace and quiet. If I don't fall asleep soon I'll be hungry, and I don't have much to eat. The calcium that the obstetrician prescribed whets my appetite. I can't manage to drink the pint of milk that is distributed to pregnant women. It's already eleven o'clock. I go down to the yard and pick an apple. It's green and sour and irritates my teeth and gums. I eat it in this sweet, gentle summer night. The moon is in its first quarter and so bright that it prevents me from seeing the stars clearly. When we were camping in the Vosges Mountains in June 1939, Raymond and I used to look at the constellations together. Raymond had a soft spot for Cassiopeia. I said to him: "When I go to the Rocky Mountains to do research for my thesis, we'll find each other at night by looking at Cassiopeia!"

"You're forgetting the six-hour time difference."

But tonight, August 11, 1943, we're less than 1,500 yards apart from each other. From his prison cell, can he glimpse the W figure we watched as we made love in the Vosges? I climb back into bed, clinging to my fetish—his pajamas, which still smell like him. I have to restrain myself from howling with suffering and loneliness.

And yet I'm not that isolated. My friends from the Resistance make cautious visits, except one of them, who is a stickler for the safety regulations. I also still see Pierre-the-forger. He knows how determined I am, and he has found a way that might help me.

One of his friends is a young Jewish woman, a refugee from Paris, who provided him with German rubber stamps and passes. She knows a colonel in the Abwehr[22] who used to be in the reserves; he is a specialist in economic problems. His family and this young woman's family were friends years ago, and when he was made head of the Lyon area economic services, she reconnected with him. Of course, he never noticed that she spirited away forms and rubber stamps that enabled Pierre to fabricate passes and other such documents.

He introduced me to the young woman. We hit it off at once. I don't mention escape attempts, I just talk about my anguish as a pregnant fiancée. I want to know the fate of my baby's father. She agrees to introduce me to the colonel. The time of the meeting is set for August 17, at 6 p.m.

August 12–17, 1943

I have plenty to do as I wait out the next five days. Now I need a verifiable address corresponding to the name on my identity

22. The Abwehr, a military secret service, often competed with the Gestapo, to the point of bloody feuds.

card. I must be absolutely transparent if I see my Boche, as Maurice says.

The Gros family, from whom Raymond had rented a secret room, was never bothered after his arrest. They are willing to rent me this room, separate from their living quarters, which has remained unoccupied since June. I take my clothes there, some books and toiletries, and I begin a slow metamorphosis. First the beauty parlor: to bleach my hair a little and to have a permanent on top of that. Woe is me! When they take off the curlers, a lot of my hair remains stuck to them. It was weakened by the bleach, and the heat finished it off. The hairdresser is embarrassed and sells me a wig, a shock of fake hair, which I attach with two tiny clips above my ears. It really gives me quite a different look. With a hat on, the wig is invisible. During the summer, it's not too hard or expensive to look elegant. I have some dresses, which, once ironed, look terrific. To make myself seem taller I put on sandals with extra-thick soles—my transformation is complete.

I try out my new look on Pierre, who is flabbergasted. "My identity card as Barbentane is still good, isn't it, Pierre? But you have to make me a new one because now I have an official residence in Lyon."

"No need to make a new one. All you've got to do is go to the police station in the Jacobin quarter with a residence certificate. They'll make a note of your change of address, put their own stamp on it, and register it in the local records. Then you'll be perfectly okay."

I'm a little reluctant; police stations are not exactly the best place to go these days.

"It won't be dangerous, take my word for it. Then afterward you'll have an identity that is absolutely solid and verifiable."

Tuesday, August 17, 1943

Everything works just the way Pierre said it would. I meet Jacqueline and go with her to visit the German colonel. Both his office and his apartment are on the fifth floor of the Carlton Hotel, which has been requisitioned. In the wheezing hydraulic elevator, with its decorative wrought iron spirals, I wonder what, if anything, I'm going to gain from this new contact, who turns out to be a fat white-haired man—not at all impressive. I explain to him that I'm the fiancée of a prisoner at Montluc.

"He was arrested at a doctor's office, and I'm told it's a very serious matter; I assure you he has done nothing. I really want to know what's become of him, where he is, and how he is."

He promises to find out and to let us know soon. When we arrived, Jacqueline was carrying a parcel; she no longer has it.

"You get nothing for nothing," she tells me. "He likes presents. But because he is head of German economic services he doesn't want to get anything from French people. He's leery of gossip and of denunciation by French suppliers or German inspectors. In that outfit, everybody is afraid of everybody else, and the Gestapo immediately takes an interest in military personnel who have been denounced for one thing or another. "Taking an interest in them" means, depending on their age, a quick sendoff to a concentration camp or the Russian front. So he is careful. His motto is: "Don't give them anything to find fault with in the service.""

I tell Maurice and Pascal about this new possibility.

"Let's see," Pascal says, "but be very careful; he's going to try and make you talk."

"Those guys," Maurice says, "they're scared to death of the Gestapo. They'd even sell their father and mother. So you see— you don't even count!"

I continue the argument: "Jacqueline has been seeing him for a long time; nothing has happened to her, even though he knows she's Jewish."

"Yeah, but she never asked him for anything, did she?"

"How do you know? He knows her name, her address, and she's still here."

"The Germans have their good Jews. That may turn out to be a lightning rod one of these days." Maurice grins.

The next day he brings over a silk scarf: "Here—if you go to see your Boche again, you can give it to him, for his wife."

Another visit to the Carlton. I have wrapped the scarf in a pretty package. The colonel looks gloomy. He tells us that my fiancé is mixed up in a very nasty business. A friend of his who holds an important job at the school of health, Gestapo headquarters, advised him not to get involved. Barbie, the head of the Gestapo, is taking care of it himself. Some of the people arrested in June are already dead. My fiancé is at Montluc; he has been sentenced to death—that's all he can tell us. We recognize that this is not the day to insist. When may we come again to see him?

He is leaving three weeks from now for a few days in Germany with his family: his wife and two daughters.

"Thank you for the scarf."

"If you'd like, colonel, next week I can bring you a piece of silk for your daughters."

We say good-bye—he didn't refuse the offer.

Since I know the way to his apartment at the Carlton, I'll go there by myself from now on. The most urgent thing is to see Copeau and give him the news. Who are the dead whom the Gestapo lieutenant mentioned? We fear the worst for Max. I have to tell Copeau about my new plan, so I describe my two visits. At first he is fearful: "You've got yourself in a fine mess now," he says. "They'll pull a fast one on you, that's for sure."

"No, Pascal, I've considered all that. The old colonel won't take any chances. He's too comfy where he is right now, so he won't do anything that might be compromising for him. He has a friend in the Gestapo. He's the one I must meet. Then I have to be persuasive enough that he will allow me to see Raymond. Maybe he'll know something about Max. Of course, visiting Montluc is out of the question, it's never been done and won't ever be. But what if he could have Raymond come for an interrogation in his office?"

"As for Max," I went on, "we have studied every possible means of escape, and the one that seems most practical is to attack the prison van between Montluc and the health science school. We know the departure times at both ends. We also know that the van moves about without an escort. Our *groupe-franc* is

Lucie Aubrac in front of her Lyon lycée, 1943

German soldiers touring
Montmarte, June 25, 1940

Parisian newsstand filled
with German publications

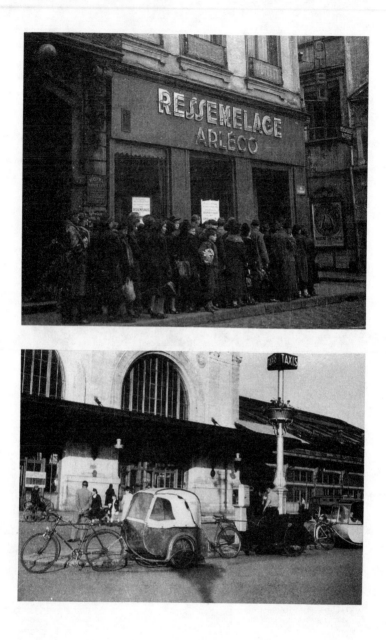

Queue outside a shoe repair shop,
rue Sainte-Catherine, Lyon

Bicycle taxis in front of
the Lyon train station

German troops entering the
French military academy,
July 1940

Lucie Aubrac in 1985

ready to attempt the operation. Serge thinks we'll succeed. I'll go see him and together we'll figure out what we need in the way of men and equipment. It's a question of means. It's going to cost a lot. The colonel can't be bought with plain water. If we up the ante, perhaps he'll persuade his Gestapo friend to meet me."

"Well, my little chickadee, you can always dream!" Pascal says. "After all, this business of yours isn't entirely utopian. I'm going to talk to Bourdet and Claudius Petit about it. Well, here's an advance of 5,000 francs."

That's twice what I make per month as a teacher! This donation is a good omen, and I take it as such.

When I get back to avenue Esquirol, I find a note in my mailbox from the secretary of the lycée: "Mr. Lardanchet wants you to come by his bookstore. He has received a shipment of books that might prove interesting for the history library. A decision regarding possible purchases is urgent." It's strange that the school office would be so zealous during vacation! What's even stranger is that such a suggestion would come from Lardanchet's bookstore! In July, their windows were displaying the latest work by Fabre-Luce, who is pretty Pétainist! He must have a whole lot of books from the Vichy point of view that he wants to unload on the lycée. Anyhow, I risk nothing by going there. After all, my colleagues and I could always forget the books in a closet.

Wednesday, August 25, 1943

The trolley lets me off near the bookstore just a stone's throw from Cordeliers. All of a sudden I remember the roll of film I left at the nearby camera shop on June 15. In the display window, enlarged to an 8 × 12 format, is a superb picture: my father, in his yard, leaning over his grandson, who is crouching in front of a strawberry bed. Underneath the picture, a caption: First amateur photography prize for small format, Mr. Samuel. I'm in a cold sweat. There, in the drawer in that shop, is an envelope with processed photos of Raymond, my parents, his parents, my uncles, the little one, and myself. That is highly explosive! They have to be destroyed immediately. But first, a visit to Lardanchet. I'll attend to this afterward.

In this bookstore, rare books are shelved with recent editions. A man in his forties greets me. He is a bit formal and looks rather severe.

"I'm the history teacher at the Lycée Edgar Quinet. You wished to show me some books that might be of interest for our library."

"Yes, of course, madam; I put them aside. Would you please follow me?"

In the back room he makes me sit down.

"Madam, I used this subterfuge to make contact. The truth is, I have news of your husband."

My heart stops. I mustn't lose my head . . .

"That's impossible, sir. My husband left several months ago, he decided to go to London. I don't know where he is myself. How could you have news of him?"

For the second time in my short life as a married woman I see a man make the same gesture: from his vest pocket, he produces a wedding band.

"Let's say, madam, that a Mr. Ermelin, with whom I've just shared a cell at Montluc for two weeks, has charged me with giving you this wedding band. He told me that he wants you to keep it until he can take it back himself."

He knows Raymond's real name, also his false identity, and he has the ring. It's too cruel. The Germans have already shot him and they are using this go-between to catch me. But inside I rebel. That's impossible! If he were dead, I would have felt it. The back of my head feels fuzzy. I don't want to cry, I don't want to faint. Mr. Lardanchet is distressed and moved.

"Madam, trust me. I'm as credible as Mr. Fauconnet, the lawyer who conveyed this ring to you at an earlier meeting. Your husband told me many things, known only to the two of you. He knew you would be distrustful." And without once stopping to catch his breath, he recites: "After your wedding, on December 14, 1939, you spent a ten-day vacation in Paris, in a hotel on the rue Madame. Your favorite aperitif is a *porto-flip*. Your sister's oldest daughter's name is Martine. For your wedding, your brother-in-law gave you Paul Géraldy's *Toi et Moi*. Your husband can recite *Le Bateau ivre* by heart. Jacques Copeau nick-named your little Boubou. He also told me about the death of a certain goose . . ."

At that, I start laughing uncontrollably and crying at the same time.

"Come, come, are you feeling better now? Do you believe me now? Don't cry anymore."

I must look a mess. I hiccup and look at Lardanchet as if he had dropped from the moon. For two months, I have been trying everything I could think of to find out what had happened to Raymond. Just last night, a German colonel confirmed that he had been sentenced to death, and today, here is a book dealer, a Lyon notable, a specialist in incunabula, a publisher of Catholic newspapers, quietly telling me: "I've spent two weeks with him at Montluc and have his wedding band."

My Raymond, usually so cautious, so careful to protect his family, gave him his ring and my name and told him how to contact me. Either he has lost his head altogether, or he judged his cell mate trustworthy. Naturally, I cling to the latter conclusion. I have to know what happened.

First, Lardanchet published Fabre-Luce's latest work and put it in his display case. But the book contained a rather sharp criticism of the Germans, which didn't escape the censors. They couldn't locate the author, so the Gestapo asked the publisher to justify himself.

"I was very politely received," Lardanchet tells me; "they questioned me with the utmost courtesy, and at 6 p.m. they said: 'We'll continue our conversation tomorrow; we're keeping you overnight.' A car took me to Montluc, I had to sign the register, then I was taken to cell 77, without being searched, by the way. The cell was a small room, seven by eight. Nothing in there except, in a corner, a can whose purpose you can guess. Otherwise empty except for a man who at first glance seemed a little frightening, long-haired, unshaven, with a reddish moustache and pretty disgusting clothes. I didn't want him to think I was scared, so I greeted him, giving my name, 'Paul Lardanchet, book dealer and publisher.' He answered, 'Claude Ermelin, employee.' I explained the reason for my overnight presence in this uncomfortable place. He looked as incredulous as you did just now. He told me: 'I've been here for over a month, alone. I went to see a doctor in Caluire and they arrested me there. The Germans don't believe me. They take me for a terrorist. Four days ago, they took me to an office where they read me a judgment by a military court in Paris, sentencing me to death. I can't believe this is possible.' "

"I was stunned," Lardanchet continues, "to hear of such a miscarriage of justice. I promised him I would talk to the German who had summoned me and who was so correct. He smiled. 'In the meantime,' he said, 'make yourself at home here, I'm going to sleep.' He lay down on the bare floor—no bed, no blanket. I asked: 'What time do they bring dinner?' He laughed loudly at that: 'Tonight's soup has already come and gone. You'll have to wait for tomorrow morning's coffee.' "

Very emotionally, Lardanchet tells me that he still hadn't understood, that he spent the night standing; he forced himself not to use the awful latrine can; he was horrified seeing his companion fall asleep without worrying about the legions of bedbugs running all over him. The next morning, ready to leave, he refused the blackish liquid served in a filthy metal cup. Nothing happened. At noon Raymond ate the ration Lardanchet was unable to swallow.

The book dealer's wife, who knew about the summons he had received, obtained permission to bring him his meals. He shared them with Raymond.

"I found him to be a very congenial companion. He asked me a lot of questions about my profession as a book dealer; about publishing, about the big bookstores in Paris and Strasbourg that he used to visit. I was dumbfounded the day he confessed to me: 'Now I'm sure you're not an informer, you're an honest-to-goodness book dealer. What a funny situation you're in here; you haven't participated in any Resistance activity.' I ended up living just the way he did, sleeping on the bare floor in my clothes, carrying out the latrine can every morning before washing at the faucet in the courtyard. My wife kept feeding us; your husband appreciated that a lot. She also brought us some books. Your husband has a soft spot for the Pléiade editions. There is so much text in such a small volume. Little by little he told me very personal details about the two of you and your family. I realized why when he said to me: 'They're not going to keep you here long, this prison stay is to teach you a lesson. I'm going to entrust you with my wedding band.' He took it out of the padding of his jacket. 'I'm also entrusting you with what I hold dearest in the world: my wife and our son. Here is her name, you can contact her through the lycée where she teaches. Find a trick—she won't believe you—then you can tell her the little anecdotes I've related to you these past few days.' I prayed to God with all my soul, madam, that he grant me freedom so that I might merit your husband's trust. When I told my wife all that, we wept together in the presence of so much serenity, courage, and faith."

Leaving Lardanchet, I wonder whether this loyal, dutiful man has any idea how much hope he has given me. With my two wedding bands, having retrieved the photos next door (as a prize, Raymond had won free processing and printing, even the enlarged picture), I walk home to the place des Jacobins. I feel so light, so light. I feel like the air today is unusually clear, that all the passersby are beautiful, and I feel like singing. I'm wearing Raymond's wedding band as a pendant around my neck, with a medal from my first communion that I found at my parents', and a piece of amber and some trinkets said to bring good luck. My own ring is on my finger; it's white gold. I know how to forestall any questions: "It's a ring I wear for cover. Being pregnant, I want to look married."

Mrs. Gros immediately sends the envelope of photos to an old friend of hers in Mâcon, who will keep them for me. These pictures evoke such happy memories that I don't have the heart to destroy them.

Monday, August 30, 1943

Maurice can find me anything! He gives me six yards of superb satin. It's perhaps a little too green, a little too shiny. "It certainly isn't a fashionable color, so it ought to please the colonel," Maurice says.

Let's hope he's there. I never saw such a slow elevator, you'd think I weigh a ton! I knock at his apartment door.

"Herein."

He is there. A young soldier is handing him some papers to be signed.

"Sit down, miss. I'll see you in a moment."

The young soldier leaves quickly; he probably envies his boss's good fortune. Why else would an elegant young woman wearing makeup visit the apartment of an old German colonel?

I show him the heavy silks and he is delighted. I tell him that although I'm engaged to Ermelin, I'm not asking for any favors for him. The only thing I would like is to see him just once before he is executed.

"I'm expecting a baby. It's awful, you know. I implore you, colonel, ask your friend to let me see him. I promise you I'll know how to behave. I won't make a scene, I promise."

Three times I repeat my promise. The old colonel is quite moved. Now it is his turn to promise. He will see his friend, and before leaving for Freiburg he will try—on humanitarian grounds, he says—to arrange that meeting for me.

"Come see me the day before I leave. If you could find me some cigars, that would be nice."

I feel I have a chance of getting what I want. It's a question of time. They won't kill him before I get a chance to see him, will they? For the first time I enter the gate of the morgue without trepidation. Today, no dead from Montluc . . .

For the first time, too, I do not vomit on the way home. I have now been pregnant for three and a half months, and I can write my parents about it and tell my in-laws. I have two pregnancy ration cards—one in my own name with a certificate from Dr. Eparvier, who helped bring Jean-Pierre into this world; another one in the name of Guillaine de Barbentane, certified by the maternity unit at the Hôtel-Dieu. I take my alloted cans of condensed milk and pass them on to the social services of our movement. They are very convenient for parcels sent to prisoners. Julien's wife can use the additional ration coupons. Julien is a member of the *groupe-franc*; they have five kids and their small budget doesn't allow them to buy on the black market. When I go to get the condensed milk, I buy three balls of soft yellow wool and start on a layette. "Nobody dresses babies in yellow," a friend tells me when she sees me knitting. I stick to my guns: "You have to start sometime; it's like everything else— nothing ventured, nothing gained."

Tuesday, August 31, 1943

I start my day with a visit to Pierre-the-forger. We have a deep, close friendship. He was indirectly responsible for my contact with the German colonel at the Carlton Hotel. I want to tell him about my visits to that man and describe how I bribed him. It may help others. But this morning I find Pierre, ordinarily so serene, deeply upset: his brother, the departmental head of Libération in the Haute-Loire, has been arrested. The militia chased him down along with three other *résistants* on their way back from monitoring operations among the maquis. Some of the men are said to be wounded, nothing more is known to date.

I'm going to see what I can find out. I have kept in touch with a guard at Saint-Paul prison; he helped us after the arrest in March. I can easily look up his wife and little daughter, and through him, within twenty-four hours I'll know in which prison these four *résistants* are being held. Cluzan's friend, the police commissioner, can tell me whether they were turned over to the Germans.

I have mostly bad news when I return to Pierre. All four have been interrogated by the Gestapo in Saint-Etienne. Two of them were wounded by bullets during the arrest and two were so badly roughed up that the Gestapo has transferred them to the hospital and placed them under the responsibility of the French police.

Like Pierre, I immediately think of how well our operation at the Antiquaille hospital went in May, leading to the escape of our three secret army comrades. We could do it again in Saint-Etienne.

Ravanel, whom I met at noon, agrees. He will put the same things at my disposal that we used in May: three cars and a determined crew.

I have come to know the men of the *groupe-franc* much better now. From time to time I have a drink with them. I also regularly visit them in their garage, and they take me out to dinner near Vienne, at Chifflot's. This afternoon I tell them of the plan and am surprised that they immediately approve. We work out together how the operation is to be set up: they will come to Saint-Etienne only to carry out the project. It's up to me to make all the preparations. We have to work fast: except for Hardy, no prisoner of the Gestapo ever stays at the hospital for any length of time.

Wednesday, September 1, 1943

A former colleague of mine from Strasbourg lives in Saint-Etienne. After an exhausting three-hour trip in a crowded bus surrounded by packages of all sorts, whose odors, mixed with those of sweat and a poorly regulated exhaust system, are unbearable, I arrive at his place. However, I no longer have the uncontrollable nausea I had in the first few months. The little three-month-old promise is still discreet because of my height and wide hips. A more ample chest, a little arch to my back, and a dazzling complexion are the only indications of this promise . . .

My colleague disappoints me and I'm eager to leave him. This man from Franche-Comté, son of a Communard, libertarian, poet, and bon vivant, in the course of three years has turned into a shriveled, bent old man who is barely clean and terribly embittered. His vigorous language, which used to resemble that of Marcel Aymé, has degenerated into a filthy stream, more like Céline.[23] I am stunned and depressed. The young woman who shared his joyous epicureanism in Strasbourg is there. She is blond and well-groomed, and her connections assure him a comfortable life.

"I've never been either jealous or possessive," he says, offering

23. Marcel Aymé (1902–67) was a novelist and dramatist of a satirical bent. Céline is the pen name of Louis-Ferdinand Destouches (1894–1961), a physician-turned-novelist. His masterpiece, *Voyage to the End of the Night* (1932), was followed by virulently anti-Semitic books and pamphlets. During the Second World War, Céline became an outright fascist, siding with the Nazi cause almost until the liberation of France. He fled to Germany, where he sought refuge together with members of the Vichy government, and then went to Denmark. After the war he was allowed to return to France, where he resumed practicing medicine.

114

me a cup of good coffee and nice golden-brown butter cookies. It's no use telling them of my plans to attempt to contact our comrades who are being held in the hospital. He is so indifferent and disillusioned that he would make fun of me. And as for her, my confidences might earn some more cookies! So I tell them Raymond is in London.

"It's full of kikes over there," he says; "besides, de Gaulle is a Jewish name; you realize that place-names are Jewish names."

I laughingly reply that in that case the de Gaulle family didn't arrive in France yesterday, for it's been quite some time since France was called Gaul—with a single l. He has a nasty grin: "You, too, are one of them?"

My heart is heavy, but I have to protect myself. "I have sued for divorce on grounds of desertion, but I'm not all that secure. My maiden name is Bernard."

"That's an old Teutonic name," he asserts with authority. "Bern is the bear. It came from up north and from the mountains, all sorts of places where Semites don't go! But why did you come here?"

I tell him I felt like seeing him, hoping he might fill me in on my chances of finding a job at the lycée in the fall. "After my divorce I'd like to make a new start."

He smiles: "That's easy. I'm ending my teaching career on December 1; I've been appointed superintendent of schools. I'll save my position for you."

I thank him. "What luck! Should I look for an apartment right away?"

He assures me he will do that and we part. His eye looks brighter than when I came. How is it possible that an intelligent man could stoop to such sectarian idiocy?

My hospital problem is far from resolved. I return to Lyon. Tomorrow I'll come back.

I ask Dr. Riva for a white gown and a stethoscope.

"Are you kidding?" he says. "Look at my size and yours. But I'll get them for you at the Institut Pasteur. Come along."

So I'm going to have to commute every day between Lyon and Saint-Etienne. It takes six hours by bus. I find a train that takes only an hour—much better—and then a ramshackle trolley that stops at the hospital. I know few places as depressing as the long streets of Saint-Etienne. Low houses, one or two stories high, with two stone steps to the sidewalk, dirty walls, wooden shutters with peeling paint—everything is black: the ground, the walls, and the doors. At the windows, white macramé curtains are dazzling in the midst of all that desolation. How can anyone live in these houses and raise children there?

I walk into the hospital as if perfectly at home, with my canvas bag slung over my arm, and I get to the toilets without being stopped. I slip on the white gown and put the stethoscope around my neck, then with total self-confidence I walk toward one of the general medical wards. A nurse greets me and shows no sign of surprise. Everything is going fine. Ten beds to this ward. I go up to one of them, where an old woman lies dozing. At the foot of the bed I pick up the medical chart, note the temperature curve, the date of admission, the diagnosis, the frequency and the name of the medications. Thus, if necessary, I will be familiar with these charts. For this first morning, I limit myself to one walk up and down the corridors.

Day by day, the staff grows accustomed to seeing me there. On the third day I locate the section on the second floor where our buddies are being kept.

Saturday, September 4, 1943

I see a doctor enter the prison section of the hospital; he is followed by two interns and a male nurse. He stays there for almost an hour. As they are leaving, the nurse stops to light a cigarette. I walk up to him and say: "Can I have a light?"

We both stop walking while I slowly take out a cigarette from my purse and light it just as slowly. By now the three others are way ahead of us.

"Are they in such bad shape?"

"Oh," he answers, "two of them have to be operated on, but we drag the process out as long as we can because afterward, the Gestapo will take them back. It's wretched!"

He hurries off to rejoin the group. I turn on my heels as if I have something urgent to attend to. As I pass by two policemen who saw me talking to the nurse, I mumble: "They forgot to take number three's blood pressure again."

And without further explanation I enter the room. I pause, just long enough to read the name—Germain—on the chart, and I whisper: "Tell Pierre's brother that I'll be back tomorrow." I go out and the policemen wave. When I return in the afternoon, two other cops are there.

"How's this assignment? Not too boring?"

These two are not talkative. I'd rather do the escape operation in the afternoon, when there's more traffic from visitors and fewer medical teams. The four men are expecting me. I note the names written on the charts at the foot of each bed; those are their prisoner identities, therefore the names known to the Gestapo, the ones we'll have to use when we demand these patients from the administration. My stethoscope provides a good excuse to lean over each man's chest and back.

"We'll come tomorrow or the day after as if taking you off for a Gestapo interrogation. Play your part well, but don't overdo it!"

At the groupe-franc garage in Lyon, we know that at the hospital four men must be counting the hours. We prepare the expedition. Pierre-the-forger has spoken to a surgeon, who will operate on his brother. He has a bullet in his buttock; it appears not to have touched any vital organ or bone. I memorized the chart and the X-ray report. The other wounded man will be cared for by the doctor who looks after the members of the groupe-franc. We will take the two others directly to a maquis in the Ain department, without passing through Lyon.

Monday, September 6, 1943

I made a precise map of the hospital, showing the access to the prison section. My friends carefully study this map and rehearse their roles. Then we leave in three cars, black Citroëns, the kind used by the Gestapo and the police. The license plates are faked; German stickers are on the windshield and the rear window, well in sight. There are seven of us counting me.

My part consists merely of going ahead as a scout toward the room where the prisoners are. One of the cars stops in front of the entrance gate, two enter the courtyard, and two supposed Gestapo agents demand that the hospital director surrender the four prisoners. Suddenly, at the entrance to the prison section where I'm waiting, I am astonished to see two stretcher bearers and a doctor run in. They dash into the room and come back with Pierre's brother lying on the rolling stretcher. At this point my team arrives, with the hospital director, who is saying, "You can see, gentlemen, this man is going to the operating room." Then he turns to me: "He was prepared this morning, wasn't he, doctor?"

"Stop, I want all four prisoners, that's an order!" says the one with the German accent. He prods Pierre's brother to make him get off the stretcher. "Go and get dressed quickly." He conspicuously draws an enormous Mauser.

I disappear into the toilet. With the hastily rolled up white gown in my purse, I go out to the sidewalk and signal the other car: All goes well. I walk as far as the next corner, to the place where they are to pick me up.

Here come the three Citroëns. I get into the back of the third one.

"We've got to drive fast," Christophe says; "the French cops didn't stir when we first arrived, but when we finished loading, I saw one of them go over to the phone in the hall."

Leaving Saint-Etienne, we stop for a moment to coordinate our next move. We won't take the national road—Rive-de-Gier has a big team of GMS, the Mobile Security Groups, which were created to beef up the gendarmerie. Those guys are tough and well armed. We're going to take the mountain roads and come back to Lyon from the north. So we take off at top speed. I'm sitting next to one of the liberated men, a Pole who, in his own country, had fought against the Pilsudski dictatorship. In 1939 he enrolled in the Foreign Legion and now is joining a maquis in the Haute-Loire department. He was caught, interrogated, and tortured with hideous brutality. Even after a week in the hospital, his face looks frightening—no front teeth, swollen ears, his skin bruised in every color, and a bandaged eye. The doctor said there was a chance they could save the eye.

Sprawled on my lap, he lets go for a moment: "Free! It's hard to believe. They sure gave it to me! Anything rather than letting myself be caught again. Excuse me, comrade, but it's human, you know, after what I've been through!" He doesn't know how to end his emotional outburst, so he adds: "You did a swell job!" I think of the other prisoner, over there in his cell at Montluc. Will he pay us the same compliment someday?

Brindas, Craponne, Quincieux, Dardilly. Tearing down the bad roads of the monts Dore, we bounce along in the back seat of our Citroën. In Dardilly, we stop. I trade my passenger for Pierre's brother. We separate from two of the cars, which take off in different directions. My back aches, cramping painfully, though sometimes it's okay. By the time we reach Pierre's family, I am sweating profusely. Everybody is happy. The surgeon has prepared the dining room table to operate on his patient. He looks at me oddly: "What's wrong with you?"

"I think it was that trip in the back of the Citroën. Every now and then my back hurts so much I could scream."

"She's not going to pull a miscarriage on us, is she?" he says. He sends for some ice at the corner café, makes me lie down, and gives me a shot. Everybody is standing around me. I'm not feeling so hot. In a little less than an hour, the pain goes away.

"Now I'll get on with extracting that bullet. I prefer that to a miscarriage at the end of the third month!"

Me, too! I don't budge. The ice is freezing my stomach; it feels like my skin is contracting and I hear the conversation in the next room as if I were wrapped in cotton.

"This is amazing! The bullet stuck in the muscle as if it had no force! Could it have been shot from some distance?"

Drowsily I remember what my buddies say—that the last few bullets in a round shot from a Sten practically dribble onto the toes of the person shooting. Allowing, of course, for exaggeration, that must be the explanation. On the verge of sleep I think: the Boches don't have any Stens! But yes they do. Unfortunately, they sometimes swipe ours.

Wednesday, September 8, 1943

Here I am again at the Carlton, at the German colonel's. He welcomes us, my cigars and me, with a smile. He saw his friend, who is willing to meet me on Friday afternoon at three. He tells me his name and how to get in touch with him, advising me to go directly to his office without asking anyone how to get there, and without leaving a card with my name. I hug him briefly when I wish him bon voyage.

The eighth of September is definitely a great day. Pascal, whom I meet at the end of the day, is almost as excited as I am. "I'm just back from Paris. Nobody knows anything specific about Max," he tells me. "I saw Bernard; he is extremely worried about what may happen to Raymond. When I told him you were organizing his rescue, he immediately said: 'She will succeed; she is tenacious; it's a matter of time and money. We must help her as much as possible.'"

Pascal hands me a parcel the size of a book.

"What is this?"

He puts his arm around my shoulders. "This may be Raymond's freedom. It contains 350,000 francs in five-thousand-franc notes. You need a lot of money, Lucie; the guys in the *groupe-franc* need equipment, new hiding places, and also some money for themselves. Many of them lead completely illegal lives. Bernard was emphatic: we are not to skimp. Use it; if there is any left over you can return it to me."

Dear Bernard! He is the very soul of our movement. In 1940 nobody would have guessed that one day he would become the wise and effective leader of a great resistance movement. We met in October 1940. I had gone to Clermont-Ferrand when the University of Strasbourg, to which I had belonged administratively as a teacher, retreated there from Alsace. After his escape from the POW camp, Raymond and I renounced our plan to go to the United States, deciding instead to move to Lyon, in the unoccupied zone. Before we could do that, I had to get my papers in order with the university administration after the turmoil of a summer that brought debacle, defeat, and armistice. I wanted a position as a teacher in Lyon, which the Strasbourg administration granted without difficulty, and I made use of my day in Clermont-Ferrand to renew contact with my Strasbourg colleagues.

I met Jean Cavaillès, who had been demobilized after a daring escape from Belgium. We were on exactly the same wavelength about everything that was important then: Vichy, the Nazis. "Come have lunch with me," he said; "I'll introduce you to some interesting people."

At the restaurant, I was introduced to Mr. Spanien, the attorney representing Léon Blum, who was then imprisoned at Riom.[24] There was also a startling person, with both the gait and the stature of Don Quixote, very tall, very gaunt with marked features, an aquiline nose and thin lips. He was about forty years old, and his hair, thinning at the temples, was otherwise thick, black, and curly with a few gray strands. His large fine hands, delicate and well kept, struck me at once. We all listened to Spanien, who described Blum's prison situation: his trial was imminent. I don't remember how our conversation about Vichy began. Cavaillès whispered to me: "I've only known this journalist for a short while; his name is Emmanuel d'Astier de la Vigerie; he is a naval officer now, but before the war he wrote for two weeklies, Lu and Vu.

For me, the name de la Vigerie evoked the name of an archbishop from Algiers who, around 1890, in the course of a luncheon with the admiral of the French fleet, had proposed a toast to the Third Republic. It was an indirect way for the Church to acknowledge this government. I asked d'Astier if he was from the same family. My question surprised him: how did I know of this man? I told him I had my degree in history and lived in Lyon. When Spanien left, d'Astier told us of his attempts to establish a nucleus of opposition on the Côte d'Azur against the occupiers, along with René Lefèvre

24. Léon Blum (1872–1950), the Socialist leader and literary figure, headed the government of the Popular Front in 1936, combining Socialists, Communists, and Radicals.

and Corniglion-Molinier. They had created what he called "the last column."[25] He explained to us: "We have to use every means available to prevent Vichy from helping the conquering forces." They had already sabotaged a locomotive that was leaving for Italy. "Above all," said d'Astier, "we have to inform people. Nobody knows anything. The political newspapers have been suspended or scuttled. Information in the other papers is censored; as for the radio, it's in Vichy's hands in the southern zone and in the Germans' in the north." All three of us agreed. We needed to know as much as possible about Vichy and the Germans and get the news out. But how were we to go about it?

Cavaillès confided that he had already made contact with the local paper, *La Montagne*, edited by an old radical Freemason, Alexandre Varenne. His neutrality was guaranteed. He would allow us to use his machines and to steal several pounds of paper. Printers traditionally lean to the left, and one of the journalists, Rochon, was already in league with them. "Fantastic!" d'Astier exclaimed, "then we're on the right track! We'll write short leaflets—simple, forceful, and to the point." How would we get them distributed? We each set forth our ideas: we'd mobilize our personal friends, our colleagues, and acquaintances we felt sure about for transportation and distribution. And what about money? We'd start with our own contributions. "Through Spanien," d'Astier added, "I met a rich man: his name is Zéraffa. He is Jewish and he was a militant in antiracist movements before the war. I'm certain he will help finance the undertaking."

D'Astier knew the Mediterranean coast from Nice to Marseille, Cavaillès knew the Auvergne and Toulouse, and I was familiar with the Rhône-Alpes region. That made three regions already where we could anchor our efforts. D'Astier had never been to Lyon. He came without delay. When he arrived

25. René Lefèvre was a film star; Corniglion-Molinier was a pioneer of early aviation. "Last Column" was a takeoff on the infamous Nazi fifth column, consisting of German soldiers disguised as nuns, who were smuggled into neutral Holland in 1940, where they contributed to the success of the Nazi attack.

at our house on the rue Pierre Corneille, Raymond, to whom I had spoken of our plans, was determined to sound him out before committing himself.

D'Astier, who soon adopted the name Bernard, was astoundingly seductive. He had innumerable ways of ingratiating himself: culture, poetry, travel, the people he knew, the interest he showed in whomever he was talking to. All these approaches worked equally well. People as different as Maurice Cuvillon, Yvon Morandat, and Raymond were quickly won over. Each one felt he suddenly had a new friend. And that was true.

Before 1939 his friends saw d'Astier as a dilettante, a lazy man, with an eighteenth-century roué's indifference. But in the Resistance we discovered quite another man: earnest, courageous, impassioned, staunch in his friendship, one who listened to the opinions of those around him. Bernard, the lover of poetry who chose passwords from Apollinaire and Valéry, had become a responsible politician and a first-rate organizer.

Right from the start, our movement consisted of a group of deeply united friends. We met at our home, or at the Martin-Chauffiers', despite all security rules. Our friendship was such that we believed we could protect one another, that we were invulnerable. And as long as we were together, nothing ever happened to us.

Until this spring of 1943, I had had the good fortune to see us as a couple, our baby, and our friends all remain intact. Today, the couple is apart, our little boy is far away, at the foot of the Vercors Mountains, hidden away with other children. And our friends—nobody comes to the house anymore. I set up meetings through my cousin Maurice. I have no right to endanger the safety of those who are still free. It is true, our rules were less rigorous than those of the Communists: didn't we accept members of the Communist party into our movement after an escape that set in motion a lengthy, detailed investigation in their organization?

As more time passed, the more efficient the German police and Vichy became, and the more we were obliged by elementary prudence to practice utmost caution. Whenever there was an arrest, we had to change the mailboxes, the passwords, organize new hiding places, find new refuges, switch liaison agents, change our people's identities and even their appearances.

As for me, I considered myself totally safe. That's just my temperament. I have never believed bad news, never accepted the worst; that's perhaps a primitive way to exorcise misfortune, but it's also a great advantage that makes you a winner, come what may. But while I was sure I was invulnerable, the others had the right to doubt that this was true. So I ended up accepting their distance and their cautious behavior. This didn't apply to everyone. Some of them took risks: Maurice, Raymond's cousin, whom I saw every day; Vergaville, the friend from way before the war, who stopped by the house every time he passed through Lyon; Pierre-the-forger, who had changed nothing in his clandestine operation that I knew of; Ravanel and the *groupe-franc* from Libération, whose partner I was in their raids, now my accomplices in my endeavor to save Raymond. Nor did it apply to Pascal Copeau, who regularly followed all my efforts and who told me each time, in his beautiful deep voice: "You know, you scare me, Lucie. How can I be so dumb as to keep seeing you? Come, let's go have a drink before they put us in the cooler."

Besides these people there were three men in positions of responsibility in other movements who gave me the invaluable gift of their presence several times: Claude Bourdet of Combat, who was uneasy about the equivocal role of Didot-Hardy; Claudius Petit of Franc-Tireur, so totally good and warmhearted; and Georges Marrane, who, braving all the strict regulations of the Communist party, had introduced more flexibility about cautiousness into the National Front. Twice he arranged the most unbelievable rendezvous with me. I never dared tell him that I knew all along about his clandestine lodgings in Lyon!

Now I'm waiting for Friday, September 10, the day of my appointment with that Gestapo lieutenant. I have a plan. In French law, there is a marriage clause called *mariage in extremis*, which permits an engaged couple to marry if either of them is at death's door. In general, these marriages are performed to legitimate an expected child that might otherwise be born without a father. Under our law, there are even post mortem marriages, a procedure used particularly during war. If a soldier is killed in battle and has made known his intent to marry, a young girl, especially if she is pregnant, can suddenly wind up simultaneously married and a war widow.

What interests *me* is marriage in extremis.

Friday, September 10, 1943

I have no difficulty finding the office that the Carlton colonel told me about. Now here I am, face to face with a uniformed German officer—tall, plain, dark haired, forty to fifty years of age. He looks austere, a bit stiff. He receives me politely, even courteously, nothing at all like Barbie's brutality. I show him my identity card. He examines it but takes no notes. Then I tell my story again: Claude Ermelin, our meeting on the Côte d'Azur in May, love at first sight, my weakness, a hitch: pregnancy. He is willing to assume his responsibilities. We decided to get married quickly. We are legally of age and don't need parental consent to marry; we will tell them later. But then the tragedy: on June 21, in Caluire, at Dr. Dugoujon's he was arrested. Patients and *résistants* alike were loaded up and taken away. I have heard nothing of him since that day. The colonel told me that he is actually a *résistant*, that his name is Vallet, and that he has been sentenced to die.

The officer doesn't say a word. He listens, with his hands flat on the desk. I have to keep going:

"Sir, I come from an officer's family. I know what order and discipline mean. I'm not here to beg for mercy for this man. But I'm expecting his child. For my family's sake and for society's, I absolutely cannot be an unwed mother. And this child is entitled to have a father. In French law there is an article permitting marriage on the eve of death. It's called marriage in extremis. Since you have sentenced him to death, please grant me the possibility of marrying under these circumstances. My child will then be born the son of Mr. and Mrs. Vallet—since you say that is his real name."

He had not expected this; he is completely dumbfounded. In rather decent French he tells me that if he is speaking slowly, it's because he is deeply moved and doesn't know what to say to me.

"Come back on Tuesday at the same time; I will have had time to think over your problem."

I add—just to see what happens—a sort of provocation: "Do you want to introduce me to the chief of police? I could present my case to him."

He jumps up: "Oh, no. I'll do nothing of the sort and you are not to go see him; you would be arrested immediately." Then he informs me that an envoy from General de Gaulle was involved in this matter. He died more than a month ago. Things are just starting to be forgotten. He adds: "I've told you much too much. Come back on Tuesday."

When I report this to Maurice, I add that I don't think Raymond is in any danger before Tuesday. The police lieutenant told me things were settling down. If that hadn't been the case, he probably wouldn't have received me.

"You can never trust those guys," Maurice concludes, distrustful. "We'll try to get hold of Copeau at once. Even though we aren't sure it's important that we circulate the news that Max died a month ago."

September 10–12, 1943

I spend the weekend quietly. The villa on the avenue Esquirol already looks like an abandoned house, with dust on the furniture. I busy myself putting my class texts in order. As I do every summer, I destroy the course notes I had prepared for the previous school year. When I first started teaching I promised myself to prepare a fresh course every year.

Last summer, Raymond had said laughingly: "The death of Henri IV and the battle of Austerlitz always have the same dates." Yes, but my students are not the same. Neither are the circumstances, and I don't want to get in a rut. I file away the documents

I use to teach history and geography. It feels like I still lead a normal life with a certain future. In my heart of hearts, I do realize that whatever Raymond's lot, nothing will be the same at the beginning of the new school year. Nevertheless, I have to act as if everything will remain as it is. I'm going to order my ration of coal and get some tobacco for the morgue employee and wine for the guys in the *groupe-franc*.

Monday, September 13, 1943

I have a long talk with Serge tonight. He's in charge of using a small part of the fortune that Pascal handed to me. He's distributing a sort of monthly pay to the members of the group who are without any means.

All that money! I never saw so much at once. I hide it carefully in my lodgings at the place des Jacobins and try to sleep peacefully. Through the open window, the full moon lights my room. I follow its bright course from east to west for a little while, but I fall asleep when its rays stop at my windowsill—once the moon is high up in the sky I can no longer see it from my bed.

Tuesday, September 14, 1943

Maurice and I have lunch together. He is determined to go and reconnoiter around the school of health before I have my next appointment. We will meet at 2:45 on the Claude-Bernard quay, near the Gallieni bridge.

At the appointed hour he reappears and gives me the green light: "Just the same, watch out for yourself. I'll wait for you at the place des Jacobins. Don't give me too many white hairs!"

When I reach the avenue Berthelot, everything seems quiet. From a side street next to the school of health, two black Citroëns burst out. Where are they going so fast? What spying or denunciation has put an end to the activities of some group of *résistants* today? And what if my Gestapo man is part of this expedition? No—he is in his office.

As soon as I close the door, he begins speaking: he has found out that French law does indeed authorize this kind of marriage.

He acknowledges my great dignity, but he adds, with a combination of seriousness and good humor, that I should have thought about my respectability a little sooner. He understands what I'm trying to do. But what guarantee do I have that my fiancé will behave in the same manner? With these terrorists, nothing is ever certain.

"He deceived you about who he is; he probably no longer cares about you, you were just someone who passed through his life."

"Go and ask him; you can see him, can't you?"

"He won't trust me; I saw the record of his interrogation, he always denied everything, he'll say he doesn't know you."

Now it's my turn to play ball.

"In that case, let me confront him face to face. It will be painful for me, but I'm ready to do anything to get married. Sir, I felt such great passion for this man and I still love him, he's the father of my child. I will be brave enough to see him again, I will know how not to lose my head; all I want is for him to accept the marriage."

For the longest time he keeps silent, and I can feel he is shaken. He begins to look through some papers on his desk, leafs through a notebook, checks a date, and finally says:

"Come back next Tuesday at the same time. I'll have him brought to my office—unless something happens in the meantime," he adds rather abruptly.

"Thank you, sir, I will be on time. I'll go and rest with some friends in the countryside; this is going to seem like a long week."

Almost three weeks ago, I was in despair, stepping out onto this same sidewalk along the avenue Berthelot. But today, new hope gives me the same desire to cry out. I don't want to remember his last sentence. I have the means to rescue Raymond and my plan is becoming clearer. I can't miss a beat. Still—be cautious, don't leave in a hurry, stop in a corridor, do the garter trick. The Gallieni bridge. The trolley to the Hôtel-Dieu. Then down the busy streets in the center of town to the place des Jacobins. Maurice is sitting there on a bench. He gets up and walks toward Terreaux. I follow him. He is walking slowly, so I understand and pass him. He catches up with me near the town hall.

"Everything is okay, let's go to the store."

I can hardly control myself. In the tiny back room I kiss him passionately.

"Hey, come on now, come on! What would Raymond say?"

"I'll see Raymond next Tuesday. We have one week to prepare the raid on the van while he's in it. We've got to get hold of Ravanel at once. We're winning, Maurice."

My cautious cousin, as happens whenever he is moved, begins to perspire, to blush, and can't keep still. We hurry off to the garage. I ask the guy in charge to tell Ravanel to come see me at home tonight if possible. In any case, I won't budge tomorrow, Wednesday. Then we dine together, Maurice and I, on the place Morand.

"I'm going home, Maurice. No need to see me home tonight. It's my lucky day."

By ten Serge still hasn't come. He won't come tonight. I'm going to bed. The full moon shines on my bed. My grandmother used to say that it was a face and that its expression was an omen. In truth, it's looking at me! It winks at me as I stretch out. I hold in my arms, as I do every night, the pajamas that Raymond left behind on the morning of June 21. What is happening? My stomach quivers. A contraction? Sort of a big movement from one hip to the other. It's the baby, moving for the first time! The other day, when I told the doctor I was certain I'd conceived on May 14, he reminded me that the first child stirs at about four and a half months, but that the second one moves earlier, often before four months of gestation. I cry with joy. She is there, really alive, my little girl to be, this Catherine who is helping me to save her daddy. Because I'm sure to have a girl. Raymond, with whom I talk every night—it's my evening prayer, that monologue when I tell him about my day!—Raymond will be near me in just one week to enjoy our victory.

Wednesday, September 15, 1943

We spend the morning with Serge, elaborating our operation. We agree right away on the time of day: late afternoon, on the return trip to Montluc. I will have seen Raymond in the afternoon, and he will know to expect something; we, on the other hand, will be certain he is in that van. We will have to renew all the surveillance we did around the prison in June when we tried to save Max. Starting this afternoon, Serge is going to give the members of the group their assignments: to make sure the pickup truck still leaves in the morning and returns at night; to verify that there is no special protection in front or in back of it; to be sure it follows the same itinerary every day.

Thursday, September 16, 1943

We have two days to observe everything, two days during which I am the busybody, pedaling my bike up and down the boulevard des Hirondelles.

This Thursday night, I meet with the group in the back room of a friendly café in Vénissieux. We all report our observations. Serge takes down everything. We run through it all again, and then we work out the strategy of the operation. Serge has drawn a sketch tracing the van's itinerary. It leaves the school of health, drives up the avenue Berthelot, turns left at a right angle onto the boulevard des Hirondelles. Then it goes along the tracks, which are in a gully that goes from Perrache to Brotteaux. Along this stretch there are two bridges: one at the end of the rue de la Guillotière, the other on the cours Gambetta. We have to make our move before these two bridges. The cars will be on a perpendicular street and will block the path of the van. The attack must be swift, and the evacuation, too. Lardanchet, to whom Raymond described his visits to the Gestapo, told me that the prisoners were handcuffed two by two. Therefore, Raymond will be attached to another prisoner. We have to find cutting pliers, something stronger than simple wire cutters. At the railroad tool shed we ought to be able to find long-handled pliers capable of breaking the steel rings of the handcuffs.

A car will immediately take Raymond to a hideout, which I have to find quickly. One of the guys suggests that he could drive the German pickup truck with its load to Bron and dump it in the underbrush, once the prisoners have been liberated.

"No," Serge says, "we're not going to use that vehicle. We're

130

going to buy another van to take all the other prisoners. No matter how much it costs, we've got to find one by Saturday. We need time to check it out in our garage, transform its exterior, and paint on the license numbers corresponding to the fake papers that Pierre will deliver to us. That will take two days. Sunday, at the end of the day, Daniel, Lucie, and I will inspect the location and adjust our tactics accordingly." We decide to meet, all of us, on Monday night, here in Vénissieux.

Friday, September 17, 1943

Years later, when I tell my children about the German occupation and the Resistance, my most tenacious memory will be that impression of having spent my life waiting: for the end of the curfew in the morning, to have coupons stamped for food distribution, to exchange one's ration cards every month, for a pass—everything means waiting. On the sidewalk in front of the stores, at the trolley stop, on station platforms, at town hall desks. In addition, for us, in our clandestine lives, there are other long waits: for a liaison agent, for a friend coming from afar, for the arrival of illegal newspapers, for the start of a military action—the fabric of daily life riddled with dangers. And I am waiting for the afternoon of the twenty-first, waiting for Raymond, and expecting a BABY! Fortunately, I will be very busy during these four days.

This Friday I've got to do two important things. First, find a hiding place for Raymond. But I try to work out another possibility as well. Since I will see Raymond, I will give him something he can use to make himself ill, ill enough to be transferred to a hospital in the event the escape attempt should fail. I'm going to see Dr. Riva and lay out my plan. Can he procure, in a harmless form, something that would make a prisoner very ill? Something that causes him to catch an infectious disease, for example. The Germans are very afraid of that and would perhaps send the contagious person to the hospital. Dr. Riva has exactly what I need: the German health services have sent specimens of Argentinian meat that their physicians judge responsible for a great epidemic of dysentery to the laboratory of the Institut Pasteur, for analysis and identification of the dangerous element. Dr. Riva took a culture from these epidemic agents.

"It's a form of typhus virus," he tells me. "How are you going to administer it to your prisoner? I can't inoculate a piece of meat. I've got an idea. Try to get a small package of hard candies wrapped in transparent paper without any inscription, so they won't think it contains a message, and bring it to me."

I run to La Marquise de Sévigné, the confectionery store, where I don't need any ration coupons, to buy some sour balls wrapped in cellophane. The doctor inoculates about ten candies with a syringe, carefully rewraps each one, and warns me to be extremely cautious when handling these small biological weapons.

Second task: find a place for Raymond. Rather than an apartment, rather than outside Lyon, it seems to me the best place once again is a hospital. The public hospitals are under the supervision of every police organization, so I can't count on any of them. For half a second I think of the private hospital where I gave birth, and whose director is a *résistant*. Unfortunately, it's a maternity! I now remember that Simone Martin-Chauffier went to see her daughter, Claudie, after she was operated on in a private Lyon hospital. Knowing Simone, she must have gotten chummy with the surgeon. She is quite intuitive and surely has a good sense of his politics. Our Bernard is staying with them at the moment. They live in a large house with many doors in and out, in Collonges. Maurice Cuvillon goes there every day to get his instructions from Bernard. Through Copeau I have asked him to arrange a rendezvous: I want to meet Bernard on the Saône embankment, on the road to Saint-Rambert. I think it's better and more effective if Bernard asks Simone to meet the surgeon in order to get a room in his hospital for the evening of the twenty-first.

I have arranged that rendezvous for this Friday in the early evening. It's a time when people come to stroll on the banks of the Saône to enjoy the late summer, so we won't be noticed. When I get there, it's Simone who is waiting for me. She explains: "It isn't wise for Bernard to walk around when it's still light; his picture has been widely distributed and he is so easy to recognize. It would be silly to have both of you arrested, all the more so as he has to leave tonight . . ."

I lash out furiously. She listens to my fierce, wounding words with a little smile.

"You don't mean any of that," she says. "What was so important that you had to tell Bernard?"

I calm down. "I wanted him to plead my case with you, Simone! A while ago, Claudie was at the hospital in Lyon; you know the director well, you must have sounded him out. Someone has to ask him to reserve a room for a patient, on the night of the twenty-first. It's a patient who requires the utmost discretion. It's Raymond, whom we are trying to liberate. Simone! Your surgeon has to agree. But tell him as little as possible. Of course, Raymond will require a private room; he will look like a genuine mummy under his bandages, and only one nurse, handpicked, will come anywhere near him."

She looks at me and doesn't seem too astounded. How should she let me know what happens when she speaks to him?

"We'll meet in front of where they post the news at *Le Nouvelliste*, Sunday at noon. It has to work. Tell him also that if nobody comes Tuesday night, he can consider the room unoccupied."

Simone takes my arm. Since I came this far, I can easily accompany her home. She thinks it will be funny to see the expression on their faces when Bernard and her husband, Louis, see me. Proudly, I refuse: "See you on Sunday, my dear; do explain to them that I understand what safety rules are for."

I can't help it, I am deeply vexed by Bernard's legitimate caution, and I let them know it.

Sunday, September 19, 1943

In front of the newspaper building, Simone barely stops to whisper. "It's all right."

I meet Serge and Daniel at six-thirty on the boulevard des Hirondelles. We walk up and down the street several times; it goes slightly uphill before reaching the crossroads where the rue de la Guillotière meets the boulevard. The pickup is bound to slow down. I will be standing on the bridge, and when I see the truck enter the boulevard I'll raise my umbrella. At that moment the other cars will pull out into position, one in front of the pickup, the other behind it; on the other side of the bridge will be a car with its engine running, to evacuate Raymond, and a van to take the other prisoners. The whole operation must not last more than five minutes at the most. Serge times it: our first car stops in the middle of the road; its passengers execute the driver and the soldier sitting in the front seat of the blocked pickup; the other car takes care of the soldiers who are inside. As soon as Raymond appears, one of our guys will cut his handcuffs and lead him to the car standing by; I will have rushed to it and be sitting inside. The other prisoners will be taken away in our panel truck. We immediately head off in two different directions—the hospital for Raymond, Bron and the woods for the others.

Rain is beginning to fall and the boulevard is soon deserted. The tobacco factory is closed on Sundays, and only an occasional trolley goes by. We arrange with Serge to reconnoiter again the next evening before the whole group meets in Vénissieux.

Tuesday, September 21, 1943

I come home alone. The operation failed, or rather, was never even attempted. I had no problem being at the Gestapo lieutenant's office at three o'clock. He received me almost ceremoniously.

We talk about my family. I tell him that my father belonged to the Black Cadre at Saumur, the military academy for mounted officers; that he was an incomparable horseman; that I have two brothers who are still adolescents. He is quite relaxed and says he will have my fiancé brought in; the interview will be short and he hopes I get what I want. He calls a soldier in the corridor, gives him an order. Ten minutes later, the door opens; Raymond is flanked by two soldiers. One of them takes off his handcuffs; afterward both of them leave the room.

My poor Raymond! He is dirty, his clothes no longer have any shape, he has lost a frightful amount of weight, his hair is dull and lank, he is poorly shaved. A bizarre moustache covers his lips, a moustache black at its tips but mostly red. The dye that made us laugh so much in Carqueiranne was good stuff! In other circumstances the results would have caused great hilarity. I can see that my presence shocks him. The German keeps him standing and asks him whether he knows me. Raymond: "No, I never saw this lady."

"You can see, miss, what I've told you was true: these people have neither faith nor morality."

He takes my hand and kisses it—something he has never done before—and leads me to a chair. The idiot! He couldn't have done better if he'd tried to make Raymond understand that I am not under arrest! I get up again and walk toward Raymond, beginning my speech: "I know that your real name is François Vallet. Don't be surprised at my using the polite form of address—I spoke to Claude Ermelin in the familiar form. I've come to ask you to keep your promise and to confirm in front of this lieutenant your desire to marry me. I'm expecting your child."

Raymond doesn't have to make an effort to show great emotion. He is pale, his nose is pinched, and his eyes mist over. He swallows hard. He looks me straight in the eye. He has understood.

"Of course I stand by my word; I'm really sorry to have put you in such a difficult situation."

He is very unsteady. I ask: "Where can he sit down?" The curt response: "That's not allowed for prisoners!"

I talk and talk and talk. I ask a thousand questions about his situation, his comfort, his hygiene.

"That's enough," the lieutenant says, "you've got your promise, miss. Get your papers together and apply at the office of vital statistics for permission to register your marriage in my office."

"Sir, I have a few hard candies here; may I give them to him? Look, there are just about ten left in this package."

He says yes as he opens the door. Then the two soldiers, handcuffs, departure, repeating in reverse what happened half an hour ago. Then my love is gone after a long exchange of looks, meaning: "Did you understand, Raymond?"—"Yes, Lucie, I got it."

What an ordeal! I collapse on a chair.

And now the other man addresses me in a monologue: "How could you ever have let yourself be deceived by that man? You saw—he didn't even salute me, not coming in or going out. He never once looked at me. He hates me—they are all the same, all of them—there is no humanity in them."

That's the last straw! This character, whom I had almost started to like, has the nerve to talk of humanity in such terms. What a boor! To show that he was in charge, he kissed my hand, showed some regard for me, while my brave Raymond could only take it and keep silent. I am upset, and I remind this officer that Mr. Vallet must be ill, that he doesn't look good and has lost a lot of weight. Then I add, while thanking him very politely, that I will let him know through the colonel at the Carlton as soon as I have the marriage license.

I can't afford to jeopardize my position, so I extend my hand to him, forcing myself to smile.

Two hours to go before I'm to meet my buddies. I take the trolley to have a cup of broth on the place Bellecour. Then I go home to change and go to the rendezvous with my umbrella. The whole team is in place. Each one has an assigned position. I stand on the bridge; it's not raining, but I open my umbrella anyway when I see the pickup truck turn onto the boulevard des Hirondelles.

Nothing happens. Our timing was bad. The pickup goes much faster than we thought, and our cars had no chance to get into position. The pickup heads off to Montluc at a fast clip. The tarpaulin is rolled up in the back, and I glimpse two rows of men sitting along the sides of the van. At the very end of the bench, two German soldiers face the prisoners, with submachine guns pointed at them.

We go to Chifflot's, the friendly café, with Alphonse and Daniel. I'm very disappointed, discouraged, near tears. Daniel says: "In the end, it was lucky we didn't try anything today. You saw how the soldiers are positioned. They would have shot everybody on that truck immediately if we had attacked. We've got to revise our tactics."

He's right. It would have been shortsighted to say the least if we had let them all be shot while trying to save them! I have less trouble eating now. But how quiet my house is tonight and how large the bed is! Luckily I am not alone. As soon as I stretch out, the baby unfolds, turns over, cuddles up, and finds a good place to spend the night.

Wednesday, September 22, 1943

This morning I don't feel beaten. To be sure, the escape was a failure, but I don't consider it a defeat. We have to seriously rethink our plans, and I must not let go of my German contacts. The Carlton colonel will return any day now from his furlough in Germany. Soon I can see him again. These days Boches will probably be much less understanding. The day before yesterday, after the capitulation of the Italians and Mussolini's internment, General Badoglio called on the Italians to fight side by side with the Allies against the Nazis. The retort has been swift. This morning a German commando operation abducted Mussolini, whom the Italian resistance had arrested, and now he is completely in the hands of the Nazis. Vichy radio is announcing the "realignment" of Italy in communiqué after communiqué. The entire Mediterranean coast from Tuscany to Marseille is a restricted zone. The Italian resistance, which had dropped its cover after the September 8 surrender by Badoglio, has been decimated. All the prisons in northern Italy are filled and under the control of Gestapo and Feldgendarmerie, who are far from gentle with their former allies.

In France, the GMS and the Milice are instituting an ever-greater repression. Jews are the target of ferocious persecution on the Côte d'Azur. Vichy has issued a decree forbidding Jews to live within five miles of big cities—a clever way to arrest large numbers of them immediately before they can take any safety precautions. In Grenoble the Milice went to the maternity hospital, where they arrested a young Austrian woman who had given birth three days earlier. Everywhere, denunciations abound.

In Lyon, few of my comrades from the winter of 1940–41 are left. Some of them disappeared: sent to prison or deported or else shot. The leaders who are still free are in Paris, integrated into the higher echelons of the Resistance. Others are scattered in various regions. I see Serge Ravanel, Vergaville, our cousin Maurice, and from time to time Pascal Copeau, who comes to Lyon most frequently. D'Astier is in Paris, Simone Martin-Chauffier left the very night we last met. She took the night train to be in Paris to celebrate her son Jean's birthday. I heard today that he was arrested the same day. Stupidly, I gather, somewhere he should never have been.

Friday, September 24, 1943

Every day I force myself to go to the morgue, bringing the accommodating guard his tobacco. I alerted an intern and two nurses at Grange-Blanche to be on the lookout for arrivals in the section for infectious diseases. If a patient with typhoid arrives from Montluc, we will have to play shrewdly to get him out of the hospital, because our Gestapo trick is too well known. Still— with some luck! After a week, nobody has been hospitalized. But Dr. Riva told me that the incubation time was short. We have to wait and wait . . .

Saturday, September 25, 1943

Back at the Carlton. The colonel is there, very happy with his stay in Germany but not at all optimistic about the outcome of the war. This man who could be my father is anxious about everything. He fears the result of Allied bombings for his family. His own future is uncertain; if things go badly in Italy, maybe they'll send reserve officers there. He has no delusions about the outcome of the war but would much prefer to finish his war service in Lyon! I tell him about my visits with his Gestapo friend, and ask for advice: how can I thank him for allowing me to see my fiancé and authorizing my marriage?

"I'll take care of it," he says. "If you can get me a case of Cognac, I will discreetly pass it on to him."

I promise to find two cases; he will have his own, too.

Later on, I tell Maurice about this conversation.

"These men are voracious! I'll find it for you—it's just a question of money. You can take it there in two trips. It's heavy:

six bottles, that's twenty pounds. Soon they'll want the Eiffel Tower!"

I say to Maurice: "But that's not all. My story has to sound credible. Do you know of a notary who could draw up the marriage contract for me?"

Maurice moans: "What have you cooked up this time?"

"Let me go through with it, Maurice; I want to do a really good job of this marriage, organize it in two stages. First we sign the contract. The actual wedding another day—in case we botch the escape again."

"My poor Lucie, you're out of your mind. How on earth do you think he'll fall for it?"

I reply that it's worth a try—"nothing ventured, nothing gained." At the end of the week, I'll pay another visit to my Gestapo man.

Tuesday, September 28, 1943

My Gestapo man doesn't seem surprised to see me—he is even polite. I pretend to be completely at ease with him. Like the colonel, I speak of the events in Italy without taking sides. And I talk about the First World War, which my father, who was an infantry major, had often described to me.

"Ah, miss," the lieutenant sighs, walking toward the window opening onto the avenue, "that war was a clean and honest war! Come here and look! Of the five people passing on that sidewalk, two are terrorists, two are scared, and the fifth is an informer. In Lyon, you can't be sure of anything! There are traps everywhere. Even far from the front you risk your life. You can never anticipate where an attack may come from."

What can I say?

"There must surely have been a resistance movement against French military occupation in the Ruhr in 1918. It's a question of patriotism that you, a military man, can understand."

"Terrorists are not military men, miss; they know nothing about patriotism—they are Jews, Communists, and in the less serious cases, weaklings and fanatics. They don't wage war openly; they kill in the dark!"

139

I stick my neck out, replying that they hardly have a choice, those Jews and Communists.

"You kill them just because they are Jews and Communists. Since the Montoire encounter between Hitler and Pétain, the French no longer have the option of fighting in the open; and since the occupation of France in November 1942, a French army no longer exists."

His face becomes less friendly. I'd better make up for that insolent remark because I have to ask him for something.

"Sir, all these problems are beyond me. Here I am pregnant by a man whom you call a terrorist and whom I still love. I can't be responsible for his acts; besides, he denies everything. I am submitting to your law, no matter how harsh it may be. All I want is to get married. I'm in the process of having a marriage contract prepared by a notary. Mr. Vallet must accept it and sign it."

"What's that about a contract?"

"I spoke to you of my family. We have some property, my child will be my heir. Mr. Vallet has been sentenced to death. I know nothing of his family. I don't want them to be able, someday, to claim part of my fortune. The notary will draw up a contract establishing judicial separation of property."

The final blow! My Boche is thunderstruck.

"Ah, the French, they think of everything. We are right when we say they are Cartesians and rationalists. To think of the distant future when your present circumstances and your own future are so uncertain! Everything depends on me, miss, don't you forget it, for now and perhaps for a long time to come."

"I know, sir, that's why I'm informing you of all the steps I'm taking, since you were so kind to listen to me and understand my situation."

He is stunned and shakes his head like a dazed boxer.

"Never mind, you are strong; one can see you come from a long line of military men."

I leave him to his stupefaction, saying good-bye and thank you and that I will have the necessary papers very soon. I have a sort of regular route now, and I calmly leave the school of health building. I'm certain nobody other than his friend the colonel knows about our meetings.

But I still take the usual precautions leaving the area, and later I visit Dr. Riva. When we found out that the section for contagious diseases hadn't admitted anyone, the doctor began to wonder whether Raymond had survived the typhoid candy. After today's visit to the Gestapo, I am certain that, though he took the candies, Raymond is still at Montluc.

"What happened, doctor? I know Raymond; he ate those candies. Twice already he has gone the illness route so he could get to the hospital. Tell me the truth. You were afraid, weren't you? You didn't inject those candies!"

"No, not at all, I would have told you if I hadn't wanted to do it. But I think I see now what must have happened. I've thought about it a lot. Those candies are made of grape sugar, which is not very stable and ferments easily. To prevent the fermentation, the makers add an antiseptic agent. That can kill or at least diminish the strength of the virus. It's stupid, but there it is."

I won't give up on the idea of getting Raymond transferred to the hospital, so I ask him to think of some other means. It has to look like he has an infectious disease that the Germans are afraid of so they'll be likely to put him in isolation. The good doctor thinks hard. He knows all about Raymond's health, his tendency to allergies. He goes into a regular lecture, for my benefit, on anaphylactic shock: a simple injection with ant serum or contact with nettles could make him break out in huge welts. Apparently, it's spectacular. But how can we get Raymond to brush against nettles or be bitten by an ant? The doctor has an idea. "I'll inject a bar of soap with formic acid. When your husband washes, his skin will come in contact with the acid and he'll develop a rash."

The soap one obtains with ration coupons is a small greenish parallelepiped, as much clay as real soap. Using a hypodermic needle, the doctor injects the bar with two cubic centimeters of formic acid. Now we have to get it to the prisoner. There's no question of delivering the parcel myself. One of my colleagues is spending her summer working for National Aid, a Vichy organization, making up parcels for war prisoners. I don't know what her political ideas are, but she might know one of the Red Cross volunteers who distribute packages to those interned in Lyon prisons. She gives me the names of two lady "patronnesses." I call on one of them, under my real name, in my capacity as a professor and with my colleague's recommendation. I volunteer my assistance and am well received. I will help put clothes and food into boxes. A large number of these boxes are anonymous. Some have a name and a cell number.

I put my soap into one of these and write on the label "Ermelin, Claude, cell 77," then I throw the whole thing into a huge basket destined for Montluc. I promise to come back to help with the next packing in a week, if my pregnancy goes well. This time it's going to succeed!

When I deliver the first case of Cognac to the Carlton Hotel, the colonel has heard what I said to his friend, who apparently thinks I'm inhuman. The colonel worries: did anyone see me come up here with a box? I reassure him and promise a second delivery soon, as agreed.

Thursday, September 30, 1943

Serge Ravanel literally kidnapped me this morning. "Come along, I'm taking you to Mâcon. A passenger train left the Brotteaux station this morning with two carloads of prisoners from Montluc. We're going as fast as we can to Mâcon. There we'll find out if the train is taking the main line, in which case there will be a derailment in the vicinity of Sennecey. If the train is rerouted to the Bresse area via Saint-Amour, we'll try to hook up with our comrades in Cuiseaux in time. Your husband may be part of the convoy. We have to try something."

Serge has a real hot rod, a red convertible Torpedo. Sitting next to him, I at first am exhilarated by the speed, but after being shaken by the jolts I don't feel so great. Serge drives fast and hard. He's right. We look too eccentric for anyone to be suspicious. On the other hand, I have a baby who doesn't like the ride at all, and I don't want to need ice on my stomach again. I ask Serge to slow down. As soon as we arrive in Mâcon, I install myself in the bar of the Champs-Elysées Hotel while Serge is inquiring about the train. He comes back disappointed. The train went through Bresse. Behind the locomotive there was a flatcar with antiaircraft guns and another one at the rear of the train. According to our intelligence, there were no ordinary travelers on that train. Apart from the two coaches with prisoners from Montluc, and all the other coaches were full of Italian soldiers in uniform: prisoners or volunteers?

The maquis groups in Cluny blew up the main track at Sennecey-le-Grand: a freight train derailed and a tank car caught fire. The ties burned; it will be at least two days before traffic can be resumed. The place will be swarming with cops of all kinds, and there is no dearth of informers in these parts. We're not going to stick around.

On the road back we think it over. In my view, Raymond is not on that train, for two reasons. He was notified of his death sentence in Lyon, therefore he will be executed in Lyon. Second reason: if the Gestapo lieutenant got his Cognac, his involvement with his friend the colonel will encourage him to sit on his prisoner—if I may put it that way—and contrive to prolong the situation. Being optimistic, Serge is of the same opinion. We discuss the best way to tackle our second escape attempt to ensure its success. On September 21 we learned one thing: in case of an attack, the guards inside the truck will machine-gun the prisoners first. Therefore we must not make any abrupt move that would put them on the alert. We know from experience that the pickup truck goes too fast for us to catch it if we wait until we see it coming. So the best thing would be to drive down the avenue and come alongside the truck on the boulevard des Hirondelles. Going at the same speed, if we aimed at the driver and the guard on the front seat, we wouldn't miss them, but the noise of the shots would alert the guards in the rear, who would then shoot their passengers.

Conclusion: we must equip ourselves with silencers. I had read in detective stories about gangsters and killers putting silencers on their weapons. I always thought that was science fiction.

"Not at all," Serge tells me, "such a thing exists." He methodically describes this gadget to me and explains why it muffles the sound of a detonation. I understand, but we don't have any such device. Where can we find one? Serge knows they are produced in Switzerland, and even more or less openly sold there, but one has to find a supplier and a way to contact him. We make a quick decision: I will go to Switzerland. With the help of our friends the Lyon railroad workers, I will make the proper connections at Annemasse and successfully cross the border! That's how many Jewish families get there.

"Easy, now," Serge says. "We have to think it through. First, make sure we can get the item we want. Border crossing has become very difficult. Ever since their about-face, the Italians no longer patrol. The Germans control the whole Swiss frontier night and day, with dogs."

I agree—indeed, before attempting the crossing we have to be sure we can get a silencer. At least one is absolutely indispensable; two would be terrific.

Who is going to believe us when one of these days—if we ever come out of this alive—we tell them that nothing seemed impossible to us; that a deep complicity united a history professor with the railroad workers in Vénissieux; that some Swiss citizens, although their country was neutral, took great risks to help *résistants* and the Resistance in their neighbor country?

Monday, October 4, 1943

Three days, no more! I found the channel to Switzerland. Swiss customs officials will take charge of me at Annemasse, at the station. I will approach them and they will hand me two boxes containing silencers. Of course, I will have to pay; it's expensive, but I have the money. Pascal gave it to me so I could make the best use of it to save Raymond.

The first of October fell on a Friday. That was the first day of school. Since I was excused from the second session of the *baccalauréat*, I started today, October 4. When I signed the record book on July 13, I never thought I would see my school again or that my professional life would resume as always. I have the same schedule as last year, but with some new faces in the different classes. My colleagues have not changed. The young professor of German is missing; I saw her on June 21 as she was waiting in front of the lycée when I left for the dinner planned with Max. Nobody knows anything about her. Where is she? Arrested? In hiding? Shot? Freedom and life are precarious now, in the fall of 1943 . . .

I like the ambience in a class when you first meet new students. I spend the first day of school meeting with students, filling out forms, giving advice, explaining the program. Special vouchers, which the professor has to sign, enable the students to buy notebooks, pencils, and textbooks. The academic year is starting without a hitch.

I announce to my students that I am expecting a baby. That immediately creates an amazing bond. I am no longer just a professor; I am also a mother. In February I will be absent for three weeks; that's the legal maternity leave, but I assure them I will make up the lost time.

At noon, instead of returning to my empty house, I go with some colleagues to a restaurant on the place Morand. Those ration coupons are a headache! We have to turn in whatever corresponds to our meal: two ounces of bread; a third of an ounce of fat, an ounce of cold cuts. Only grapes and a few vegetables are sold freely. We all talk about our holidays and practical matters: food, winter clothing. We trade thrifty recipes. Someone even suggests an omelet without eggs. It's crazy! These restrictions, this advice about how to finagle a meal—it all conspires to direct everyone's thoughts and efforts toward the most down-to-earth facts of daily life. After all, my colleagues may also have a double life that I know nothing about, with a path through the underground as secret as my own.

As usual, at the end of the day I stop at Maurice's store and tell him of my impending trip to Annemasse. "I'll leave on Thursday. If I can't make the round trip in one day, I'll stay over since I have no classes on Friday."

"I'm coming along," Maurice says; "that's settled. If there's a hitch, at least I can come back to tell people here."

I gladly accept. I dislike being alone so long on those nightmarish trains.

Wednesday, October 6, 1943

This afternoon we went to see the notary who lives next door to the store. Maurice made an appointment yesterday morning. What a performance! Sitting next to me, Maurice is visibly nervous. His face is red, his eyes are popping out, and he is sweating. I don't look at him. I'm afraid I couldn't keep a straight face, since I'm in the midst of an act that leaves the notary speechless. I show him my identity card: Miss Guillaine de Barbentane, born on June 27, 1912, at Blanzy, residing at 3, place des Jacobins. I explain that I intend to marry a man who is in Montluc prison, condemned to death, and that I must have a marriage contract capable of safeguarding my rights.

The notary, finally able to speak, asks me if I envisage a "marriage in extremis"; in that case the contract could be signed just before the execution, at the same time as the marriage certificate. I answer that he has understood, but that I must present the document to the German authorities at the earliest possible moment so they can determine the date of the wedding and the contract signing. After that, we review the list of my family's properties, and my own. Has the future spouse any private means? I don't know, I don't even know his exact vital statistics. The notary, again perplexed, asks me if I have given the matter sufficient thought. I say yes, and I leave him a deposit toward his fees. We make an appointment for October 13, at four-thirty.

We don't say a word as we descend the dark staircase and pass through a narrow corridor, which gave no warning of the rather plush office we have just left. Not until the next street, out of sight of the notary's window, do we explode into bursts of laughter. We laugh so hard that tears come to our eyes. Maurice starts coughing and has trouble catching his breath. To celebrate, my cousin invites me to Brazier's restaurant. I have a delicious poule au pot and an enormous piece of apple tart. Maurice negotiates the purchase, for a hefty price, of sandwiches for tomorrow's trip: ham, cheese, apples, and grapes. A royal treat!

Thursday, October 7, 1943

The trip to Annemasse goes smoothly. We arrive at three. The police screening on the French side is no problem. "Where are you going?"—"Nowhere. We are waiting for our old aunt who lives in Lussy, to take her to Lyon. I wish she'd get here soon. We'd like to take the earliest possible return train."

Maurice will stay in the waiting room while I watch for the arrival of the bus. We talk to each other, natural as can be, as if this were just a little jaunt between Lyon and Annemasse.

At the exit, near the toilets, a railroad worker is waiting for me. I have the Nazi magazine *Signal* in my hand. He lets me into the baggage room and then escorts me through a turnstile marked "Service." To the Swiss customs official he says: "Here's that lady who forgot two packages in the train from Lausanne. I caught up with her at the French exit."

The customs official says "Ah, yes," and takes me to his office. I give him two thousand francs, the price of the silencers, and he hands me two rather heavy packages, wrapped in brown paper, no larger than two small shoe boxes. Each one is labeled: square nails for blacksmith. Twenty minutes later, the same turnstile spits me out again into the baggage room on the French side. I go back past the toilets and meet Maurice in the waiting room.

"Our aunt wasn't on the bus, but I found some nails at the hardware store, they were a real bargain. When are we leaving? I'm in a hurry."

"And what about me?" Maurice answers. "I'm all sweaty."

There is a train leaving for Lyon at 4:45. We easily find seats, and our two packages go in the baggage rack above us with the remains of our picnic lunch. Before the train starts to move, four gendarmes climb aboard and plant themselves in front of the doors at both ends of the coach. Few people are on this train. What do they want? We lean on the handrails of the windows, in the corridor, watching them. The train moves slowly along the border; at the grade crossings, armed German soldiers are posted with dogs and motor vehicles. I can't stand it any longer. I walk up to the gendarmes.

147

"Surely nobody's likely to risk slipping into Switzerland these days, in this area, with all that surveillance?"

"You think not?" one of them answers. "In fact, nobody goes by road now; all attempts are made from the train. Whenever it slows down, people jump off and get to the other side. We'll stay on the train as far as Saint-Julien. We go back and forth here, so we know every yard of the trip and nobody can jump off because we're blocking the doors."

I say that it takes courage to jump from a moving train.

"Yeah, some get killed. And once on the ground, they still have to cross the road; sometimes they run right into the patrol."

All of a sudden I realize that an hour ago I was in Switzerland, under the protection of a Swiss customs official; I could have remained in a neutral country. Laughing, I tell Maurice.

"It's true," he says, "you've got to be crazy to return voluntarily to this shithole . . ."

For me, this shithole, as Maurice calls it, means my buddies—all our preparations designed to lead to Raymond's liberation. So I come back gladly. Afterward, we'll see.

Night falls little by little. There is no light on the train. In Ambérieu, a police inspection without any problems. We eat the remaining sandwiches in the blue gleam of the little night light above the compartment door. A conductor passes to check that all the curtains are drawn over the windows. The train is moving so slowly that we are sure to reach the Perrache station after curfew. We don't dare ask for a pass to get home. One has to answer too many questions.

We know what nights are like. Groups of Milice and German patrols, often drunk and wild, are the masters of the street. If you're lucky, they just rob you, but they also rape and kill, sure of their impunity!

We arrive twenty minutes before the curfew. I won't have time to get to the avenue Esquirol. There is no systematic inspection at the station exit. With our little brown packages under our arms—I still have *Signal* in my hand—we run to catch the last trolley to the place Morand. Maurice is now staying at the apartment on the rue Pierre Corneille where Raymond and I started our Lyon life in September 1940. It's only a few minutes away.

We can't just rush up to the apartment on the second floor without any precautions. We walk past the door. Everything seems quiet, so we go up to the third floor, jangling our keys. Maurice tiptoes down again and listens at his door. Not a sound. He goes in and comes back up to get me with my two packages. We draw the curtains before putting on the light; we drink some coffee substitute, which certainly won't keep us awake. I am so tired!

"Take the bed," Maurice says. "You need the rest. I'll give you some of my pajamas; I'll manage on an armchair in the dining room."

I fall asleep at once, but am soon awakened by an odd noise. The light is on in the dining room, and Maurice, who cannot go to sleep, is moving chairs around to find space on the floor.

"Listen, Maurice, this is a big bed; Raymond and I both used to sleep in it. Get in. At least we both will have a bit of sleep for what's left of the night."

With my nose in the pillow, I turn to the wall and begin to doze off. My cousin still hasn't turned off the lamp. I roll over.

"What are you doing? Turn out the light and go to sleep."

Awkwardly propped up on his elbow, half-reclining at the far edge of the bed, he looks at me, sighing: "Can you imagine? Sleeping with the wife of my first cousin! Who will ever believe nothing happened? I've always been good to the ladies who shared my bed."

I'm fed up with his soul-searching.

"Tell that to Raymond after we get him out. I'm tired, put out the light and go to sleep."

His good, loyal face, so expressive, lights up with a smile: "All right, Lucie, but you must admit it's a funny situation."

"It's more so than you think, Maurice. My baby doesn't like me to be on my side. You stay on your side, I need some space, I sleep flat on my back. Good night, or rather, good what's left of the night."

Friday, October 8, 1943

When I take the silencers to the guys of the groupe-franc, I get a delirious welcome. Everyone wants to touch them and attach

149

them to the barrels of the submachine guns. A little practice in the back of the garage convinces us of their effectiveness. They make no more noise than a light knock at the door. But at the same time, we notice that the weapon's firepower is much diminished and that you have to shoot from very close range. We have perfected the tactics outlined with Ravanel on the way back from Mâcon: one of our cars will drive at the same speed as the German pickup truck; while moving, the marksman will aim at the driver and his neighbor. It has to be a complete success—we won't have a second try. Without the noise of shots, there's a chance that the guards in the back of the pickup will think it's a mechanical problem—but just one chance.

The guys decide to start training immediately. In some quiet spot in the country, far from Lyon, we have to learn how to shoot at a moving target while we ourselves are moving. We're not rich in ammunition, so we mustn't waste any; a thirty-round clip represents a fortune. Since I'm free, I accompany them. We have as much fun as kids and are very pleased with ourselves. We finish the evening at Chifflot's, where I wolf down potatoes with bacon. Along with my buddies I also down our wine ration for the whole month, which I had passed on to them; afterward, Christophe takes me to Grange-Blanche. I go the rest of the way on foot. I feel heavy, I ate and drank too much—the baby doesn't like that. When I'm in bed, it takes baby a good half-hour to calm down. Tonight everything's reeling a bit. In my daily report to Raymond's pajamas, I very seriously explain that things are going fine, that our operation will be launched soon, that I have Saturday class tomorrow morning at eight o'clock, that I'll get up early to prepare. Then I sleep like a rock.

Wednesday, October 13, 1943

The notary hands me an outline of the contract. He has had time to think it over and is visibly terrified. He will, he tells me, in no event come to Gestapo headquarters to attend the signing of the contract. He will find out if the presence of the registrar, who has to be there to legitimize the marriage, is considered sufficient to authenticate the signatures on the contract. "In an exceptional situation," he says, "the conventions can be bent a little." He asks me to specify to the German authorities "that he knows me only as a client and is not at all interested in politics."

Thursday, October 14, 1943

I went to the seventh arrondissement town hall to pick up the form to publish the banns; at three, here I am again in the office of the German lieutenant. By now, we are old acquaintances. He invites me to sit down, without a word about the case of Cognac. (Could that rascal, the colonel, have kept it all for himself?) I show him the outline of the contract. To show me how well informed he is he holds forth at length on the Napoleonic Code. I spread the form from town hall on his desk.

"I don't have the vital statistics on the father of my child. You say his name is Vallet. Do you have his date and place of birth?"

This punctilious approach irritates him.

"Ah, you French! I will never understand your reverence for laws. Do you realize, miss, that I did you a great favor by permitting you to see that bandit? And you are talking about law, when it is a question of life and death for him! This has really become long and awkward for me. I yielded to compassion too quickly. Well, I will get the information." He takes his engagement book from his desk.

"Come see me on Tuesday. I will have the vital statistics. Well—no—people are going to start noticing your visits—come on Thursday the twenty-first at three o'clock, with your contract to be signed. I will have Ermelin brought here. My boss will be in Paris that day."

My heart beats loudly. Is it possible that he doesn't hear it?

"Thank you, sir; I, too, am eager to get this over with. Will you permit me, to show my gratitude, to have a friend send you a case of Champagne?"

He doesn't answer; I assume that he accepts. So my two scoundrels have already shared my earlier gifts. If that weren't so, he would have protested. He shows me to the door of his office and kisses my hand. "Good-bye, miss, see you on Thursday the twenty-first at three."

Anyone who noticed my coming and going to the Gestapo would think I'm either an informer or the good fortune of one of these gentlemen. Neither of these assumptions is pleasing. Well—the hell with caution! I'm going straight to the colonel at the Carlton. After all, that's the best precaution. I scrupulously report to him all the steps I've taken. He knows, moreover, all the episodes of the novel I've spun—from the German side, of course. How could men their age allow themselves to be taken in by a young woman who tells them such an unbelievable story? When I say I intend to send a case of Champagne to his friend, his eyes light up with such obvious envy that I promise him the same gift. In my heart of hearts I hope this will be the last expense made on their account.

Friday, October 15, 1943

Wait for the twenty-first! I will have spent this whole summer waiting. But now the goal is near, and I'm confident of success. Serge and the guys in the group are just as impatient as I am. They keep on with their lives to the rhythm of underground activities, such as sabotaging high tension pylons and railroad tracks; Serge has to make inspections and keep in contact with the maquis and other leaders of the secret army in the Rhône-Alpes region: R.1, as we call it. Serge is indefatigable in his activity, always up hill and down dale; his audacity is unheard of, he goes everywhere and has a knack for persuading and enthusing everyone he talks to. He's so sure and energetic, he always has a thousand plans underway. How can we fail with him on our side?

Sunday, October 17, 1943

I saw Serge again. Everything is going well. The group is ready to act; our equipment and cars are in good order so they will function without a hitch. Serge has to be away from Lyon and won't be back until Wednesday. That's when we'll hold our last "conference," as he puts it. Maurice has been busy finding a hideout for Raymond. A prominent young couple from Lyon, childhood friends of his, agreed without hesitation to take in this "cousin" Maurice has described: having escaped from a prison camp, he has to be sheltered for a while before continuing on to England. So Mr. and Mrs. Nicolas, well-known silk merchants in the Lyon market, have invited Maurice, the said cousin, and his wife to dinner on Thursday night.

Monday, October 18, 1943

A great day in class. Time flies. For first-year students, the academic year begins with ancient history. Names that make you dream: Mesopotamia, Babylon, Nebuchadnezzar, Abraham, the Temple in Jerusalem, the Hebrews, Moses, and Mount Sinai. The little Jewish girls in the class light up when they hear these names, which doesn't happen often! Today, we discuss how the Hebrews were the first people in antiquity to abandon totems, idols, and multiple gods, to believe in one god. He is not particularly loving, this god! But the tablets of law transmitted to Moses are a series of commands that all my little Catholic girls have learned at catechism, so they can make their first communion this year. My young students recognize each other as equals in the identity of a faith that originated with the nomad shepherds of the desert, was passed on to the sedentary agricultural populations of the Fertile Crescent, and so forth up to the Western world.

With the seniors we study the great powers of the world. I began a series of classes on the metal industries of the United States and the USSR. No need to inflate the statistics (from 1938–39, since we don't have any more recent information) for the whole class to understand that, in 1943, industrial power is on the side of the Allies.

During recess in the faculty lounge, my colleague who teaches French is raising Cain. All the works of Anatole France, Erkmann-Chatrian, Zola, and Bergson have been withdrawn from the upper school library. This colleague surely will be willing to do me a favor when asked.

The day is not over: a circular is passed around in all classes. We have to initial it so that we won't be able to say we haven't read it. The movie theaters in Lyon are going to show the anti-Semitic propaganda film *Le Juif Suss*, produced by the Nazis. To prepare the students before they see it, the minister of education asks that we take them to the traveling exhibit on racial characteristics, which will open tomorrow at what used to be the labor exchange. This government circular concerns all history, literature, and natural science teachers. In the faculty lounge, the ones who protest the loudest are probably those least involved in the underground. Nobody would understand if I didn't protest, too, given my name and my outspokenness. There are moments when silence is no longer prudence but simply cowardice, and I propose writing a short letter to the principal: "The teachers of history and literature, whose duty it is to convey to their students, in addition to culture, a taste for freedom and for tolerance, wish to state that they consider it unworthy of their mission to take their classes to such an exhibit."

Out of eleven colleagues, five of us sign it. Five out of eleven! The others say that they agree with us, but suggest not tackling the problem head on. "Let's get medical certificates to be absent," they say. Four colleagues follow that advice. That's nine out of eleven. Not too bad! The other two—just beginning their careers—are still in awe of the school administration. My profession conducts itself pretty well; if only all of France were like that!

At night, I prepare my classes for the next day. The house is quiet, too quiet. The winter time, German time, as we say, two hours behind the sun, makes night fall fast. It's a full moon, rising early. When I go to bed, with all the lights out, my curtains and window open, the moon is still there, lighting up my room like last month, before the failed attempt. The moon enables me to make out, under my windows, Serge Ravanel's silhouette. He is calling me softly from the sidewalk. I go down to open the door. He is pale, perspiring, and dirty, and his coat is torn.

"Where did you come from?"

"I'm wounded. The German Feldgendarmerie surrounded us in the house where we were meeting in the Ain department. I was lucky and got away."

Five or six *résistants* were discussing measures to be taken regarding the secret army when the house was surrounded and they were taken prisoner. The German gendarmes divided up responsibility for guarding them. Serge was on the second floor, in a room with a German who had searched him without finding his second pistol, concealed in his pants, next to his genitals. After an hour, the surveillance became less strict, and Serge grabbed his pistol by the barrel, clobbered the guard over the head, jumped out the window, and landed on a glass roof, which caused a frightful noise when it broke. Without stopping to worry about the commotion, he ran to a nearby riverbed and hid as fast as he could in the brush. A bullet struck him in the arm and penetrated his biceps. He began to run a fever but was able to get as far as Lyon. He intends to go to the apartment of the "cheese merchant" who sheltered him after he got out of Antiquaille hospital, arriving there before the curfew. I will meet him there tomorrow night.

Tuesday, October 19, 1943

After class I went to see Serge. Our physician friend tended to him. He disinfected the many cuts that Serge suffered, besides the wound caused by the bullet. Serge is in a bad way, with a high fever and an incipient infection. His participation in Thursday's raid is out of the question. I go to the garage to tell the group, who are somewhat distraught and suggest postponing the whole venture. This is terrible as far as I'm concerned. I use all the means at my disposal: persuasion, anger, and contempt.

"Who wants to chicken out? Everything is ready. Daniel is an excellent marksman and he's fast. There won't be another opportunity. Nobody's forcing anyone who doesn't want to go. As for me, I'll go with anyone who's game. We have a real chance: it's been announced everywhere that on Thursday night there will be a lecture by a German race theorist, Professor Grimm. The whole police force will concentrate around the auditorium where he's going to speak, in the center of Lyon. This time, we're sure to win."

The guys look at one another. Alphonse is the first to speak: "I'll go."—"Me, too," says Daniel. José adds: "We'll all go. There are thirteen of us; counting you, fourteen."

I correct him: "We'll be fifteen; Maurice is coming with us. He's the one who will take Raymond away as soon as he's free. Tomorrow after school we'll go with the drivers to inspect the area for the last time. Rendezvous here at five-thirty. We'll choose the best place near the school of health for seeing when the gates open. Then we can start the cars as soon as the paddy wagon shows its nose. We'll let it pass us. On the boulevard des Hirondelles we'll catch up with it and shoot. Behind us, the two other cars will stop; the guys will take up their positions to cut down the guards who get out of the pickup. José's car will then pick up Maurice and Raymond as soon as the handcuffs tying him to another prisoner are cut. Then you will carry off all the other prisoners in our van, driven by Février. You'll take them to Vancia; there they'll be set free after we get them equipped with what they need to resume their lives as free men. Christophe will drive the car I'll be in. Next to him, Daniel, with his Sten gun and the silencer. Behind them, Julien and me, also armed. The prison van won't make a smooth stop. We'll have to get out of the car right away and duck behind our car, because we'll probably be the closest to the guards jumping from the rear and we can pick them off. They have to be cut down before they have time to realize what's happening and to shoot. It all has to go very quickly. Speed will make success possible. Now, remember! At six it's dark; we mustn't shoot in every direction and hit the wrong targets. Daniel, the whole thing rests on you. Don't miss them! We'll talk about all this tomorrow night. We're having dinner together, aren't we? I'll manage to find something good. How's that?"

"It's a deal," Daniel answers for all of them. The tall, quiet boy whom we call Février, always so meticulous in his manners, accompanies me part of the way home. As he leaves me, his serious face lights up and he says, smiling: "Catherine, everything will be fine; you can count on the guys."

I hate returning to this lonely house. On the façade a rose bush climbs up either side of the stained-glass window, spreading big roses that don't smell; they are pale yellow, heavy and stupid. The flowers I love are down on the ground—the last petunias, bent over the long, anemic stems of an exuberant mass of marigolds. The moon shines on them, its white light punctuating the dark earth with the marigolds' orange and yellow and the light purple corollas of the petunias. No one is there to welcome me; I open the door, enter the darkness, feeling how automatic all my gestures are. I draw the curtains, then turn on the lights. Before going to bed, I prepare a suitcase that has to be taken, tomorrow, to the Nicolases' apartment—some underwear and shirts, a suit, shoes to replace the rags Raymond has been wearing for four months. Pajamas, a towel, and a toiletry case; in these times of dearth, even hotels don't provide towels or soap, so we are in the habit of carrying them with us in our baggage. As for me, back in September I deposited a trunk at a friend's house, with my winter clothes, a bit of layette, and a case of costume jewelry— some bronze, some ceramic, necklaces, rings, and earrings, all things I adore.

Wednesday, October 20, 1943

I tied the suitcase on the baggage rack of my bicycle, which I leave at Maurice's at rue Pierre Corneille. When school is over, he will bring me a sausage, a lot of paté, and—he hopes—a bottle of booze for the evening meal with our buddies. He doesn't yet have the Champagne for "my" Germans, but produces two boxes of cigars.

"This will keep them happy," he says. "If we succeed tomorrow, they'll never see the Champagne." Maurice thinks of everything; being superstitious, he says "if"—something I refuse to consider.

As always when I am in class, I forget all outside worries. This must be what is called "an educational vocation." This afternoon at 1:45, before classes resume, a note from the principal summons me to her office. The five of us who signed yesterday's protest now find ourselves facing the principal. Her warning is brief and threatening:

"Ladies, I'm obliged to forward your protest to the superintendent of schools, who sent me the governmental convocation that you refuse to obey. Last year you refused to parade in the stadium with your students, giving the Olympic salute, on the pretext that it resembled the Nazi salute. The superintendent called you in at that time and surely noted it in his files. You have to expect some trouble."

Not worried in the least, we leave the office. In November 1942 the superintendent made his feelings clear to us: "Your principal's reports are filed in my records. As long as she considers me the obligatory stage in the government hierarchy, you don't risk anything. She is too respectful of authority to sidestep or go over my head."

From two to five, three hours of classes without any problems. My second-year students and I had a good laugh: half of the students didn't understand how the moon, while both rotating and revolving around the Earth, could always offer the same face to Earth dwellers. We acted it out in pantomime: one student was the earth, rotating on its axis, another the moon with its dual motion, and a third one the sun. It all ended in giddiness and general confusion.

At five-thirty, five of us are checking out the exact locations for our cars the next day. My comrades have already decided to come out of the street perpendicular to the avenue Berthelot to follow the German truck when it leaves the school of health. The car that is going to pass us found a discreet parking place before the turn onto the boulevard des Hirondelles. For the other two cars it's very simple. After the curve our van will start to follow, and the Citroën earmarked for Raymond will take up position right behind the tobacco factory.

"It works, you guys, I'm completely confident now. I found something good to eat for tonight, all we need now is bread and wine."

"We'll take care of that," Chevalier says.

When we arrive at the restaurant in Vénissieux, the proprietor is busy skinning two rabbits in her yard. They are freshly killed; the entrails and the skin, which she is turning inside out like a stocking, steam in the twilight of this rather chilly night.

She says it will take a little less than an hour to cook the stew. My buddies drink an apéritif, actually an ersatz Pernod. I loathe its cheap smell. The café is closed, with the iron gate pulled down. The marble table is quickly set for dinner. We start out very well with sausage, pâté and a potato salad to make the bread go further. As I sip a young Beaujolais, I ask where the rabbits came from. "Don't ask any questions," Daniel says. These guys are no choirboys, as Vergaville has told me . . .

The men take out their knives and methodically cut square pieces of bread that they cover with pâté, eating mouthful after mouthful. They certainly have big appetites! The rabbit stew appears. I have never eaten such tough rabbit. At first we all chew conscientiously. We had so anticipated this feast, a rabbit stew.

Finally, someone explodes: "Hey, patronne! Your rabbits aren't cooked."

The cook retorts: "They'll never be any more tender; the meat is much too fresh. You all were in such a hurry, you almost wanted them cooked alive."

She is mollified when I tell her the sauce is exquisite. I distribute the cigars that Maurice had intended for my German contacts. All around me the excitement is palpable, my comrades are happy and exuberant. The air is becoming unbreathable. They draw on their cigars with such eagerness that it is obvious they have never smoked any before. I want to get home early. "It's my knightly vigil, my eve of combat; if I'm not made a knight tomorrow, I never will be." They don't understand a word I say. So now I have to explain the rules of knighthood to them.

Daniel bursts out laughing: "Tomorrow you'll see some good work done with our machine guns for swords and lances!"

When I leave, I urge them to be cautious. "Don't hang around too late; above all, don't let anyone spot you. If even one of you gets caught, we're screwed. Keep a good watch on the garage. I'll come by in the morning."

Thursday, October 21, 1943

I leave my house early. The sun is rising in a blue sky and the marigolds are heavy with dew. Behind me I hear the muffled thump of a falling apple. I feel like this is good-bye to the little house that I am abandoning forever. I leave as if in a dream. Something is going to happen that will change my life. In July 1914, when my father went off to war, leaving his vineyard, his wife, and his little girls, was he in the same frame of mind? Mobilization suddenly forces people to break with their whole past and environment. Perhaps that's how it is when one joins a religious order. I remember the sense of renunciation I felt at the ceremony when my cousin took the veil. I was fourteen then.

As I close the door, I wonder whether the house has a memory. Does it remember the two of us, our happiness? And the relaxed times our welcome provided all those *résistants*, old friends and more recent ones? And our address! How many people had it? "You're going to Lyon, so stop at Lucie Bernard's and Raymond Samuel's; they belong to one of the movements. They'll help you, and there's always room at their place." Every Christmas I decorate a tree. Three Christmases since the summer of 1940, with small gifts and simple cards, which I give to anyone who happens to be there then. You should have seen the surprise of these rough men, committed to underground combat—their emotion and their gratitude. A little warmth, a breath of normal life in the midst of all the dangers and anonymity. I always managed to have a few provisions around so I could improvise a meal. All the reserves I had built up as if it would be a normal winter for me are being left behind today, in the basement. Maria, who returns tomorrow from her summer in the Indre department, will find them.

The real house of a real family, like one in peacetime, is no more. A house that gave people in hiding the memory of stability and the urge to regain it. A real house where, since the spring of 1941, our comrades had watched our happy little boy be born and grow up. He was the only child in our world of lonely people. He was there like a promise of the return to happiness and security.

The only baggage I carry is an old tapestry bag that my mother-in-law embroidered for me last winter. It contains what remains of the money Pascal Copeau entrusted to me, a few pipes, the last tobacco ration, and a small flask of rum. I imagine Raymond rediscovering the slow gestures his beautiful hands will make filling his first pipe as a free man. I will leave this bag at the house of an aunt where I can get it after the operation. Maurice is going to pick me up there so we can join Raymond, because I must stay with the group to the very end, when we all disperse.

Walking toward the trolley terminus, I pass the morgue. I will no longer go to look at corpses—the guardian can no longer expect his tip of tobacco every ten days. It's autumn; the birch trees on the square are beginning to drop their leaves, small golden disks, they flutter, glide down, and slowly, slowly fall. Following one of those leaves with my eyes, I make a bet. "If I have time to count to twenty before it touches the ground, it's going to work tonight!" Every time I try, I win. Then I go to see Ravanel at his "cheese merchant's." Fidgety and feverish, he can't keep still on the couch where he is supposed to be resting. He is so angry not to be able to join us today that he can't stop talking about caution and risks. I kiss him with all the depth of my friendship and promise to succeed even without his help. My morning is very busy. I go to my in-laws' place on the rue des Charmettes to give them a hug. They have no idea what is going on and firmly believe their son is in London. My young sister-in-law, Ginette, accompanies me on the way out. She knows what's up and shows no sign of worry. I think she trusts me; after all, twice already I have gotten her brother out of trouble. She will take my bag to our aunt's house. I also make her repeat our little boy's address, as a precaution for the future, but I'm sure it's unnecessary.

I meet my comrades at the garage. Two of them are in the process of replacing the right front door of our Citroën. They have removed the window, which didn't slide down completely inside the door; that would have made it difficult to steady the submachine gun aimed at the German driver. I can't help giving more advice: "Daniel, we drive side by side; you get your weapon out, you steady it, you aim, and you shoot: right on target and fast. You did practice, you timed it?"

"Don't worry, Catherine, I know my Sten gun by heart. I've tried it out in the same conditions. After sixteen rounds it shows some wear, the silencer takes away some strength, but it's a good machine. The first three shots will be bull's-eyes. Don't worry— it's as good as done!"

I stand there, feeling a little heavy. I'm in my sixth month. The smell of the oil and the gasoline turns my stomach. I stay there, unable to leave. These boys are so ready for tonight. They realize they are engaged in a difficult and even dangerous task. Several of them have wives and children. They know they are going to liberate a man who was one of the leaders of the secret army. I told them, long ago, that he is my husband. They know the strength of my love, my determination, my will to prevail. More than anything else, they are grateful for my assuming, despite my pregnancy, the same risks they faced over the past months, and being there tonight with them, fighting with them, fighting just like all the others in the group. Our feeling of unity, of esteem, is total—that's why desertion is impossible. I leave them quite simply: "See you tonight, you guys, each one at his place, after five-thirty." At the garage door, I turn around for a last wave. Under the blue light, filtered by the glass roof with its blue-painted panes, five men watch me leave. My last memory: Alphonse slams shut the windowless door of the Citroën while José and Février slowly wipe their hands on a greasy rag.

I'm hungry. In the center of town I buy, without ration coupons, a cookie described as a macaroon. I nibble on it as I walk— it tastes like a mixture of sand and bran. It's a fine autumn day. On the sidewalk, wooden soles clatter rhythmically; their thickness makes the women's silhouettes—already heightened by the built-up curly hairdos on top of their heads—even taller. There are lines outside all the stores. Each day the quest for food in exchange for coupons starts all over again. How removed I feel from these everyday problems! Today my own quest has quite another object. Among the women waiting in these lines may be the mother or the sister of one of the boys at whose side I will be fighting tonight. I can imagine tomorrow's conversation in these lines: "The Resistance attacked a German truck full of prisoners just outside Montluc."

I imagine shoulders straightening, glances becoming livelier, unexpressed jubilation: the invincible Gestapo bit the dust. I wonder to myself how many dead Germans we will have to our credit. At Mrs. Gros's on the place des Jacobins I change clothes. Then I have a cup of bouillon and a sausage with some cabbage at the restaurant next door. For the last time I go off to play the part of the young girl seduced. I walk up the avenue Berthelot from the Gallieni bridge. I'm amazed that I'm not nervous. Action is the best tranquilizer.

Raymond is already standing in the lieutenant's office when I enter. The officer has taken precautions to avoid my being seen by the soldiers escorting the prisoner. I bet he sends me away first. It's the usual ceremony: he welcomes me with the utmost courtesy, pretends not to see Raymond, addresses him with contempt, hands me a paper with the date and place of birth of François Vallet, looks at us while we examine the contract, which Raymond accepts at once, and says to me: "This is all, right? Don't come back without an appointment. Let me know through my friend at the Carlton, and wait until he says you are to come."

I can clearly see he is scared. Is there gossip among his subordinates? Maybe his boss has detected something? I don't know. In any case, he is nervous. He opens the door of his office, looks out into the corridor, and says: "Go now. Good-bye, miss," this time without kissing my hand.

I was barely able to talk to Raymond. He risked only a quick wink when I looked at him while the other peeked into the corridor. So he did understand.

Halfway downstairs my legs fail! All of a sudden I hear someone running behind me. It flashes through my mind that Raymond understood nothing, that he is trying to escape on his own from that office. Then a big devil of a young soldier, his arms overflowing with dossiers, rushes past me, taking the steps two at a time to cross the courtyard and disappear in the building at the back. Whew!

On my way out I go directly to the town hall of the arrondissement; I enter the office of vital statistics and deposit a form requesting the posting of the banns. Maybe the lieutenant had me shadowed? Maybe he is watching my coming and going to see what I do? As I leave the town hall, Maurice, my guardian

163

angel, precedes me, then lets me pass him just before the trolley station. I enter the Marquise de Sévigné tearoom and order a hot chocolate. It's a concoction of cocoa husks sweetened with saccharine. It's hot and has the vague aroma of chocolate. I feel like ordering another but resist the temptation. With this baby beginning its sixth month, my bladder gives me problems. I must not drink too much liquid. That would be the height of irony, to be obsessed by a terrible need to pee later on when we go into action. Now it's time to take off my nice suit, to wash off my makeup. I have some difficulty climbing the six flights to Mrs. Gros's apartment; she is not home. I leave her a note to say good-bye. This room, which was Ermelin's hideout before becoming the official residence of Miss de Barbentane, retains few traces of our presence. It will have been a dressing room. Tonight our successive moltings, Raymond's and mine, will bear fruit: we're going to be metamorphosed . . .

How well I know these streets, the embankments, the trolleys, the bridges of Lyon. At five-twenty I step off the trolley on the rue Jean-Macé. At five-thirty I'm seated in the rear of the Citroën, behind the driver. Let's hope the gates of the school of health open quickly and we don't attract attention by staying parked for a long time. At five minutes to six the last act begins: as a curtain raiser, two German soldiers come out to direct the very sparse traffic on the avenue Berthelot. Christophe starts the car. The gate opens, here comes the pickup truck, appearing from a street perpendicular to the avenue. It follows the avenue and accelerates. We follow. None of us speak. Daniel holds the submachine gun on his knees. I am holding the pistol tightly in my hand. We turn sharp left, now we're on the boulevard des Hirondelles.

I say to Christophe: "Our turn."

He accelerates. We pull up next to the driver's cab. Daniel shoots—no noise of any detonation can be heard.

Then something amazing happens: the German van just slows down and stops without a jolt at the curb. "You missed them," Christophe says. But as we climb out through the left-hand doors to take cover behind our car, we see the German driver slump over the wheel while his neighbor slides on top of him. The guards in the back, surprised by this unexpected stop, jump down with weapons in hand. Our men have already taken up position behind their car; the quicker of the two guards somersaults and disappears into the railroad gully. Within two minutes we have emptied our clips, and so have the Germans. But they are dead. By the glow of our headlights, in the midst of the fighting, I see Raymond jump out with another man linked to him. I scream: "Watch out—the one in the raincoat is Raymond."

"Shit!" says Lyonnet, turning his Sten gun away. "I've hit him."

Maurice calls out to Raymond, cuts his handcuffs with the special pliers, and they take off in the third Citroën toward the planned refuge. Meanwhile, our buddies transfer the remaining prisoners to our van.

At six the tobacco factory workers are let out. The headlights of the German truck are still on, and by their light, from behind my Citroën, I see a lot of workers dive for cover on the road. All except one with a bicycle, which he holds by the handlebar so it is up on its back wheel, apparently trying to shield his face with the front wheel. A bag of potatoes falls off his baggage rack. He hesitates, goes back, picks it up—a ludicrous episode in the play we are performing.

I yell: "Let's get out of here now, fast."

In the car, next to me, Chevalier is bleeding. He is conscious and coherent, but he took a bullet in the mouth. We have to get him to our doctor, who was alerted beforehand.

I thought the show was over, but it's not time to lower the curtain yet. The doctor has Chevalier sit astride a chair, with his head and arms leaning on the chair back. He unbuttons the collar of his shirt.

"You're lucky," the doctor says. "Look. The bullet went out the back. Since you can move, it means nothing vital has been touched. I've got to evacuate all that blood forming a big hematoma, then we can disinfect. Christophe, hold the basin."

The doctor begins to press and the blood flows.

"Daniel, take over for me," says Christophe, white as a sheet, and he goes to vomit in the toilet. A minute later, Daniel is in the same condition.

"It's your turn," the doctor says, handing the basin to me.

Once the wound is thoroughly cleaned and bandaged, the

doctor says to Chevalier, who hasn't flinched: "I'm giving you a tetanus shot, just to be on the safe side."

Our buddy, who has been absolutely mute, with his mouth open, ever since leaving the boulevard des Hirondelles, finds his voice again: "Oh, no! I don't like shots."

How dearly I love my three terrorists! They risk their lives, are ready to accept any dare, but are terrified by the sight of blood or a needle. We all laugh about it.

We must leave quickly now. I want to reach my aunt's in time for Maurice to take me to Raymond. At the rue de la Martinière I leave them. They too are in a hurry to return the Citroën to the garage. At nine o'clock at night the city is blanketed by all available police. Loudspeakers announce the curfew for ten. It's not healthy to hang around the streets tonight.

As I walk up the stairs to the fourth floor, where my aunt lives, I begin to feel the fatigue produced by this eventful day. My aunt is waiting for me on the landing. I haven't reached the last step when she welcomes me with the words: "My poor child!" I don't know how I ever make it to an armchair inside the apartment. I think: "Raymond has been fatally injured." I'm ready to faint. She comforts me with a glass of spirits and reassures me. She only meant to say how hard it seemed for me to walk up the stairs and that I looked exhausted.

Maurice is anxious to take me to Raymond. We quickly head toward the Croix-Rousse cable car. I take my tapestry bag and the presents for Raymond with me. The Nicolases are perfect. They welcomed Raymond, tended to his wound, and left him in his room with plenty of hot water. Going upstairs, Maurice says: "You'll see, he has a tiny wound, it's really nothing," and he adds, laughing: "A little bullet hole right in the middle of his cheek."

They leave me alone with Raymond, who is in the process of finishing a thorough wash. He has gotten rid of the dirt accumulated over four months by scrubbing again and again. There he stands, almost naked, very thin and pale. In the small of his back, where it is hard for him to see in the mirror, there is a gray scab, evidence of his stay with the Gestapo. There is a dressing on his cheek, underneath his jaw, along his neck, another dressing.

"I really got through by the skin of my teeth. The bullet that entered the cheek came out on a slant by my neck. It left a trail as long as my finger. Even if you had killed me, I think I would have died happy just knowing I had escaped the Nazis."

We can't stop looking at each other.

"But, look, it's true—you're pregnant! In less than four months we'll have another child!"

Just as I imagined it, he has slowly filled one of his pipes and smokes as he walks up and down. He can't chew with his wound, so I eat everything on the tray that Mrs. Nicolas has left in the room. I'm sleepy, but I want to listen to what he is saying. After all, he has four months of silence to recover. He talks on and on, smoking and drinking the rum in the little bottle. I'm sleepy and doze off to the sound of his voice.

I open one eye when I feel the soft touch of his lips on my stomach and a lukewarm moisture. Is he crying? No. His wounds are bleeding from all the talking; the dressing on his cheek is all red, completely soaked with blood. We don't wake our hosts. I fall asleep next to a man who looks a lot like an Easter egg, with a towel tied around his head.

Friday, October 22, 1943

Mrs. Nicolas brings us breakfast in the room. A pretty blond woman, she is very discreet and apparently calm but looks a bit nonplussed by the presence of these two characters. She senses that the situation does not quite conform to the explanations that our cousin gave her. I can imagine the amazement of this young couple last night when Maurice delivered Raymond, bleeding, unkempt, and filthy. He must have looked weird for an escaped prisoner of war whom they were to shelter for a few days!

Even people who are not terribly well informed would easily connect his fresh bullet wound with yesterday's shooting, plus the severe measures taken by the Germans all over town. The Nicolases have small children, whom we must not endanger. They are decent people, sharing our ideas, to be sure, but their hospitality is above all guided by friendship. They are not committed to our dangerous games and anyhow have not been warned of the risks they run. For the first time, Raymond and I are not merely people in hiding; we have become genuine bombs. Anyone near us risks being blown up. Raymond, even more than I, is aware of that.

"We mustn't stay here; it would be terrible for them if something went wrong."

"We're not going to stay. But, you know, we're not taking any risks." I remind him that our guardian angel, Maurice, is part of this Lyon world—a world considered cold but one in which friendship is sacred. In his name one can ask for almost any favor and it will be done. Also, everything has been planned; we will make a second stop outside Lyon. Mrs. Nicolas tells us that Dr. Joie is coming to get us shortly. The third stage will coincide with the next full moon, somewhere on the banks of the Saône: departure for London.

Shortly thereafter Maurice escorts his friend Dr. Joie to the rue Coste, where we are. He loudly rejoices over our success yesterday: "During the scuffle I lost my keys. I only noticed it when I got home last night. Thinking it over, I was sure they were on the ground on the boulevard des Hirondelles. I went back there this morning and found them."

I am angry: "Idiot! To risk your life for some keys."

"What do you mean, risk my life? That's not where the Germans expect us to be. You should see the train stations and the main exit roads in Lyon this morning."

Despite the caduceus displayed on the doctor's car we feel uneasy.

"Don't worry, I know all the roads; we'll be outside Lyon before you know it."

Dr. Joie's parents run a quiet clinic in a large park in Pollionnay. As far as the staff is concerned, Raymond's physical condition is such that a rest with his wife nearby is required. What are these bandages on the cheek and under the right jaw? Infected boils that the doctor insists on examining and tending himself. So here we are, together in a quiet room on the second floor, with a large window opening onto the garden.

Raymond is tired, irritable, nervous, always on the alert.

"I want them to bring me a gun. During those four months at

Montluc I saw only too well what those Germans can do to a man. I will never let myself be taken again! And neither will you be taken alive!"

As long as that blasted gun isn't here yet, I'm all right. But when he gets it, God knows what might happen. Meanwhile, he demands a thick rope.

"Tonight I'll attach it to the windowsill; if anything happens during the night, we can hide in the garden."

I can just imagine myself, with a baby beginning to stir, sliding down that rope. But for now it's better for me to keep quiet; later on, we'll see, God willing. Pascal Copeau—our Salard—arrives two days later, escorted by Maurice. He really likes us. Day after day he followed my efforts, my tricks, the steps I took to succeed in freeing Raymond. His friendship is precious to us; but he also comes because he needs to find out whether Raymond is the only one, besides Dr. Dugoujon's maid and his honest-to-goodness patients, who escaped the Gestapo's claws after the arrest on June 21. Bernard has left for London and won't return to France. De Gaulle wants to entrust him with an important position in the government led by the general in Algiers.

"I'm replacing him," Pascal says. "It's not just an interim post like last summer; it's permanent."

He asks Raymond to tell him at length about the arrest on June 21 and the behavior of everyone arrested then. As far as Raymond is concerned, Hardy's guilt is established beyond any doubt. He doesn't understand why the man was even present at the meeting. The day before, in the Tête-d'Or park, Max had mentioned only Aubry. That very first night in the basement of the military's school of health, Raymond also learned that Hardy had escaped while people were being pushed into the Gestapo cars.

"Everybody was handcuffed, even the patients, except that man . . ."

Copeau interrupts him: "We know all that. The witnesses in Caluire told us about it the next day. Tell me about Max. What do you know of his fate?"

"Max and I were to meet Colonel Schwartzfeld on the place Carnot, above the cable cars. He wasn't on time and we had to wait for him about twenty minutes. Because of our delay, Dr. Dugoujon's maid let us into the waiting room with the patients. I congratulated Max on how seriously he prepared his meetings. What could be better than consultation day at the office of a doctor known to be a peaceable man with moderate ideas, a good Catholic? 'That's not all,' Max said, 'to cover myself, I have a letter of introduction from a physician to his colleague.' We were still congratulating ourselves when the German police broke in with an enormous hullabaloo.

"We heard them shouting on the second floor. Dr. Dugoujon, in his white coat, came out of his office: 'What's going on here?' They pushed him brutally into the waiting room: 'Everybody stand up, face the wall, arms over your head.' I put my pipe down on the mantelpiece and obeyed the orders, standing next to Max. We added our loud protests to those of the patients. Nothing doing. While they were watching the yard and searching the doctor's desk, Max got a chance to say to me: 'In my right-hand pocket there are two small sheets of paper; grab them and eat them. My name is Martel.'

"I answered him: 'And I'm Ermelin, repatriated from Tunisia, in April.'

"It was the first time I ever ate paper. My mouth was all dry, and it was hard to swallow the stuff. A German guarded the door with his submachine gun pointing into the waiting room. We heard someone rushing down the stairs. There were orders shouted in German, a few shots could be heard outside, then the noise of car doors slamming. Then Germans in plainclothes came in and handcuffed everybody. They didn't keep us there long, but herded us quickly into Citroëns waiting outside, and we left for the avenue Berthelot."

"Did you stay with Max?" Pascal asked.

"Yes," he answered. "They didn't pay special attention to either him or me. We remained together in the basement; they took off our handcuffs and did likewise for the doctor and his patients. We were sitting on the floor, watched by a sentry. We spoke very little because we couldn't be sure one of the doctor's patients wasn't an informer. Anyway, that day, there was no interrogation for us. That night they put handcuffs on us again and took us by car to Montluc. On arrival, after they freed our hands, they made us write our name, religion, and profession in the register. I'd like to find that page again, after the war. Then we were separated and I found myself alone in cell 77 in a space only six by nine feet. There was nothing, absolutely nothing except a can in a corner and a concrete shelf in a corner at eye level."

"And about Max, what else do you know?"

"I saw him again two more times. My cell was right opposite the staircase. As soon as I heard anyone walking, I rushed to the peephole. Two days after our arrest I saw him go by, in the morning; he had obviously not been worked over yet. I didn't see him come back, but the next morning he came down the stairs, supported by two soldiers and in very bad shape. His face was all swollen; I even wondered how he could stand up. That's all. I never saw him again. The same day, I ran into Aubry. The Boche soldier who was escorting me on latrine duty shoved me away when he saw us talking to each other. Aubry was stripped to the waist; his back was completely black—I mean bruised black. He said to me: 'It's tough, you know; I couldn't take it. I talked a little.' I didn't get a chance to answer and find out more; the German soldier separated us."

Pascal, sitting on the bed with his elbows on his knees, his head in his hand, is filled with dismay. "Poor Max, you'll see, they killed him, which confirms what Lucie found out. He must have sweated blood to be in the condition you describe. And afterward, Raymond, tell me what happened to you."

"Lucie must have told you that I tried to let you know. She brought me that bundle of clean clothes on the twenty-second of June, and I saw that she had wrapped the socks in a piece of newspaper. There was a crossword puzzle that someone had started to solve, with words scribbled and circled and certain definitions underlined. I wrote in Léonie as a feminine first name, underlining it."

"What an odd idea," Pascal exclaims. "What did that mean?"

"I was sure Lucie would understand. When I was at Saint-Paul, I was in the habit of walking back and forth, if you could call it that, in my cell. In order not to gesticulate while talking, I held the button on my jacket with my left hand, so my buddies baptized me Napoléon. You see: Napoléon, Léon, Léonie—Léon nie, from the verb 'nier,' to deny."

"Only you two would put together something like that!"

"I understood at once that Raymond wanted me to know he would never talk. I trusted him, and I was right to refuse to give up my legal existence and my teaching."

"There was another definition," Raymond continued, "that I put to good use. It was 'modern physicist.' I wrote 'Maxwell,' and I erased everything around it, thinking the 'well' would not escape Lucie's attention."

"That definition, too, I got right away—remember, I talked to you about it, Pascal, on the twenty-third, when we met Commissioner Henry."

"Unfortunately, I didn't receive any more parcels, so I couldn't let you know about the rapid change in our situation."

Pascal fills our glasses with the white wine he brought and turns again to Raymond, his beautiful, optimistic voice now dull and muffled.

"Try to tell what happened to you," he says.

"I was interrogated on the fourth day and every day after that for a whole week. It was always the same ceremony. In the morning, the guards went down the corridors opening cell doors, shouting 'Interrogation!' We left by truck, with the other prisoners, for the basement of the school of health. Any hope of escaping en route was quickly abandoned. We were seated on benches, along the sides of the truck, handcuffed two by two. And at the back end by the exit, two or three soldiers held their submachine guns pointed inside. They think they are so strong that they can't imagine an attack from outside. Inside that truck there were fifteen to twenty guys of all ages, all types. Some really messed up, with swollen faces and blotches of caked blood on their clothes and their hands. The first time you see these men, you think: 'They've really been through the mill! What's going to happen to me?' And then, when you've had your turn at the experience, these repeated trips are more and more traumatizing. So you adopt the same absent look, the same impassivity. That's the only way to stand it once you've tasted Nazi methods.

"In the basement, they took off the handcuffs connecting us

two by two; then they put on individual ones for interrogation. While waiting to be called in, we sat on the floor without anything to eat or drink, without being allowed to speak to our neighbors, and with a special security system to go to the toilet. The soldiers guarding us never moved; they called on others to escort us there.

"The first time I went upstairs to the office of the Gestapo chief, I firmly believed my alibi was going to stick, so I went in without much fear.

"There was a large desk and, behind it, a blondish man of medium height, about my age. At his feet, a big dog. Near the door, next to a small table, a young woman in uniform—what we call a 'gray mouse'—smartly dressed, well made-up. Standing there in front of the desk, I decided to forget I was dirty, unshaven, without a tie, and wearing rumpled clothes. Since my arrest in March on the rue de l'Hôtel-de-Ville, I know one has to maintain one's dignity, above all, in spite of appearances. I had the vague impression of having already seen this guy somewhere—maybe simply because he was the one yelling so loudly at the doctor's on Monday afternoon. He started firing questions at me right away: 'We have identified Jean Moulin, your Max, the envoy of General de Gaulle, your de Gaulle. Here I have'—he was thumbing through about fifteen typewritten pages—'the statements and confessions of the men arrested at Caluire. You were with Max, you arrived at the doctor's office with him. What was your function? Who is your leader? Whom are you commanding? Where is Bernard? Where is Charvet?'

"He made me sit astride a chair, with the chair back supporting my shackled arms. I began to speak: 'Sir, I don't understand any of your questions; I went to consult the doctor and had the bad luck to be caught up in something I know nothing about.' He got up as I spoke and started walking slowly around the room, playing with a sort of horsewhip, which he bent between his hands, then tapped up and down his legs. All of a sudden, with no warning, wham! he gave me a vicious blow on the shoulders. 'You pig! I've broken guys tougher than you. Your so-called buddies talked! Talk—it's in your own interest, you'll end up doing it anyway!' As he shouted he hit me again repeatedly. After a while,

173

he went to the door and called the soldiers in the corridor, giving them orders in German. As they came in, he was standing near the young German woman, smiling at her, relaxed. They grabbed me by my arms and brutally marched me to the basement. That was all for the first day.

"Oh, that basement was awful! There were some guys who still hadn't been touched and others who were unconscious. Some men were moaning, but some like me just clenched their teeth after this foretaste of what they had to expect.

"You know, Pascal, I still haven't figured out which is worse— the pain of the blows? the humiliation of being chained and beaten? But that day it was anger that was dominant. It helps. That night the truck went back to Montluc with its load of prisoners. I looked at my traveling companions, those messed up and those who weren't. You're going to think I must be a little crazy, but it made me feel better. I said to myself: All these guys are against the occupiers. The Gestapo arrests some every day and interrogates them—and how!—every day. That means we still have relief forces—we're winning. But for the Boches it's just the daily routine. Handcuff people, take off their handcuffs, put them on again, off again, escort prisoners, lock them up in their cells. And the next day, start all over again: roll call, handcuffs, paddy wagon, basement.

"Locked up in cell 77, I was in a stupor of hunger and thirst because I got back too late for the evening meal. I was sleepy. But how can you find a good spot on a cement floor when your back hurts so much?"

"You didn't have a bed—not even a straw mattress?" I ask Raymond.

Raymond: "Nothing, no bed, no straw mattress, nothing but four walls, a cement floor, and, in a corner, the latrine bucket. The next day, having swallowed the blackish morning 'coffee' with a piece of moldy bread and emptied the latrine bucket, I didn't even have time to reach the row of cold-water faucets in the courtyard to wash a little. Roll call: 'Ermelin, *schnell, schnell, komm, komm*, interrogation.' This trip, I was less cocky than the day before. I had no more illusions about my defense system and wondered what was going to happen. It wasn't exactly original.

The same policeman, the chief, as indicated by the sign on his door—Obersturmführer Barbie—started right in with his brutality; the same girl, the same dog. The same chair and the same position. He struck me again and again until finally I fainted. I fell on the floor and he woke me up by kicking my ribs. It's strange: one kind of pain puts you to sleep, another one wakes you up."

"Like in the old song," Pascal says. "But there it's love that wakes you.[26] Come now, drink a little and don't fall asleep."

Good old Pascal tries to lighten the atmosphere a bit. I clench my teeth, feeling close to nausea. Raymond continues: "It was always the same ritual: 'Talk. Who is your leader? What do you do? Whom do you obey? Dirty pig! (That was his favorite epithet.) Where is Bernard? Where is Charvet? Look here—see this testimony—I know everything! Poor idiot! Aubry spilled the beans. And the others confirmed it and filled in the gaps.' As for Aubry, I knew he had talked since he himself had warned me, but I was convinced he'd said nothing essential. And if this guy said 'the others,' without saying who specifically, that was proof he didn't know much. He would hit me and shout: 'Ermelin, that's not your name!' Suddenly, I was scared and thought: they've found out, Lucie's going to be caught!

"Then he said, 'Your name is François Vallet, and you were in Saint-Paul prison. The French police, they're all idiots. They let you go. That won't happen again, here!' Then I realized why, the day before, I had had the impression of déjà vu. We had been brought before him, at the end of March, at the Hotel Terminus. He was the one who had said, in German, to his colleagues, without knowing that Valrimont understood: 'We're wasting our time with these guys, they're poor jerks, not even equipped to handle a business deal of any real scope. They're just shit; let's send them back to the French.' Remembering that, I thought: If we fooled you once, you bastard, maybe I can do it again! And if you think my name is Vallet, you have no idea I'm Jewish. You want me to believe the others talked. But I know they didn't. All

26. The song goes: "Le bon vin m'endort, l'amour me réveille encore" (Good wine puts me to sleep; love will wake me again).

those people who used to come to my house, like Lassagne and Dugoujon—they said nothing. Now it's my turn to hold out!

"All that time he just kept beating me and swearing: 'You dog, you pig! Ah, we've got all of you. None of you are going to get away!' I fainted several times. Oh, Lucie, don't cry. It's really a privilege to pass out. It gives you a reprieve between blows. You don't feel anything or hear anything anymore. Of course, he's still the stronger one, but at the same time there's nothing he can do against this temporary absence. He has to say to himself, 'Let's hope he snaps out of it . . .' Perhaps some day this kind of torturer will find a physician who can tell him how far he can go without a risk. Once it took me longer than usual to recover. Opening one eye, I saw my executioner and his 'gray mouse' frightfully busy . . . These sessions obviously aroused them. When I was able to utter a word, I limited myself to saying: 'I know nothing, I'm not informed of anything, I'm just unlucky. First I was arrested for black marketeering, and now I'm caught up in something far worse.' "

"Raymond, you never directly answered his questions?"

"I believe that didn't really matter to him. He screamed, struck me, hollered. Obviously he enjoyed it, and the girl, too. I thought that ultimately his prime concern was to show his strength and to humiliate people. That guy is not normal; he's sadistic. A real policeman doesn't act like that. He had his own special refinements. Once he stood beside me—this was the worst of all—and rhythmically punctuated his questions with constant blows at the base of my skull. Not just slaps to the face, not ordinary blows; little regular shocks over a long period of time. Torture that drives you crazy but doesn't make you faint. You reach a point where everything looks blue, you think your eyes are going to pop out, and your head weighs a ton. That little game went on for ten days at least. After that, no more anything. I remained alone in cell 77 until the end of July. Then I was taken by car to a Gestapo office on the avenue Berthelot. There an officer read me a sentence by a military court in Paris condemning me to death. From then on I had plenty to keep my mind busy. How would they do it? I imagined the soldier in his glory, as in some *image d'Epinal*, where he faces the firing squad and falls shouting 'Vive la France!' That was my dream. But I knew the reality. Alone in a cell, kneeling in a corner, facing the wall, you wait for the bullet in the back of your head while the killer calmly takes his time preparing it . . . Under my hat band I had concealed a razor blade I'd found near the faucets in the prison courtyard. I wondered: Will I have time to do it?"

"Enough, Raymond, stop it!"

I can't listen to his monologue any longer, seeing how agitated and pale he is, ready to faint again, reliving these horrors.

"Quiet now. We won. And we're expecting a new child."

I take his hand and put it on my stomach, where, having caught my passion, my baby is kicking and rolling around like a kitten turning circles to find the best position for a peaceful sleep.

Tuesday, November 2, 1943

Pascal and Maurice are the only ones who know of our refuge in Pollionnay. In this resting place the days unfold quietly. Little by little Raymond recovers. His back no longer aches. He still has awful nightmares and sometimes wakes up moaning, sometimes with both fists out in front of him. His injuries are healing well. Because of where we are it's difficult to leave the wounds open to the air. In a pinch, the smaller hollow on his cheek could be taken to be the crater left by a boil, but the furrow underneath his jaw in no way fits such a description. The skin around it is red and rolled back—pretty disturbing. I wonder whether the passage of time will erase the scars.

Pascal brought Raymond the pistol he asked for. He won't let go of it. He takes it apart, oils it, checks the mechanism, puts the cartridge clip back in, and puts a bullet in the barrel. At night he slips it under his pillow.

The doctor advised me: "It's better if he falls asleep before you; then you take away the gun. He hasn't yet quite regained his equilibrium. I don't like the idea of waking up suddenly to loud bangs in this silent clinic. And watch out! If he is hallucinating, you are the nearest target."

So I have to stay awake and not fall asleep when he does. During the four long months of separation I worked hard to find a rhythm of sleeping as regular as possible. As soon as I knew for sure I was pregnant, I wanted to give the little girl—I was sure I was going to have a girl—all the advantages of a calm pregnancy. In bed at night I trained myself to relax systematically, and I could fall sound asleep quickly and sleep the night through. And now I have to stay awake!

I am so sleepy! My baby, too. As soon as I stretch out, baby seeks a comfortable position, sticking an elbow or a knee up under my skin. Then my stomach becomes round again, my baby dozes off and tempts me to sleep, too. How painful it is not to sleep when you're sleepy. Still, I manage to take the gun away every night. When he wakes up, Raymond doesn't take offense. He knows he's still weak, and the way he allows himself to trust me is a magnificent gift.

This morning—we've been here almost two weeks—Pascal and Maurice arrive with an odd look on their faces. Something serious must surely have happened. Maurice looks at me and says: "You asked me to send Ginette to your house on the avenue Esquirol to pick up a suitcase full of clothes for Raymond and yourself. Last night she came to my house, completely beside herself. 'Maurice, the Gestapo are at Raymond and Lucie's! This morning I went to their house, by bicycle; I leaned the bike against the wall, on the sidewalk, and rang the bell. Maria came to open it as if nothing were the matter, but inside there were two men. "German police," they said, "show us your papers." I had my purse under my arm, so I had to show them. After that, how could I deny being Lucie's sister-in-law? She's the one they're after. From what I understood they haven't connected Ermelin and Samuel. When they questioned Maria, she told them what Lucie had confided to her in secret, that her husband left France to join de Gaulle several months ago. One of the policemen went to the phone to have a car sent to pick me up. The other made me sit down in the dining room. Maria made me a cup of herb tea. The window was open, and when he went to the kitchen I got up and jumped out the window, got to my bike, and dashed home to warn my parents. "Get out at once; the Gestapo took my purse with my papers and our address." They left immediately to stay with friends in Lyon. I'm going to stay with Martha, who will keep me for a while at the day care center she directs. Then she'll help me leave town. I'll get away. Please, Maurice, take care of my parents. Here's the address.' "

We're still in shock, speechless. Then Raymond asks: "What can we do?"

"Nothing at all," Pascal replies; "just keep quiet. Do you think your relatives need money?"

"No," Maurice says, "not for the time being; as long as we are here, all of us, the family sticks together."

At night, after dinner, Raymond and I discuss all this at length. How did the Gestapo pick up our trail?

"After that successful raid," Raymond says, "the Germans must have been furious. Their prestige has suffered and they no longer are invulnerable; they cannot let this failure of theirs go unavenged. They must have made an enormous effort to find out where the attack came from. You can bet that the German captain who had me come from Montluc to meet you didn't mention the part he played in all that. Obviously he said nothing. He's much better off in Lyon than on the Russian front."

I say: "They didn't arrest any men from the groupe-franc; first of all, none of them would have talked, but above all, none of them would have let himself get caught. They are always together, several of them, so there would have been a major scuffle and Maurice would have heard about it."

"Could they have recaptured one of those other guys you got out?" Raymond wonders. "Weren't there three or four who had evidently just been arrested?"

"We had a van," I say, "which took them out of Lyon and didn't release them until the next morning."

"There must have been one who didn't understand anything," Raymond guesses. "Since he had been arrested at random, it would have seemed natural to him to return home. During the night the men probably talked about you, which made an impression, and he told the Boches everything when they rearrested him. At any rate, this is the result—it's you they're looking for. You'd do best to keep quiet."

I shrug my shoulders. "I don't see what else I could do. I think they must have realized there were some big fish in the catch.

Maurice told us there were two leaders of the MOI,[27] who left at once for a maquis unit in the Ain department, and there was also a representative from the MUR from Savoy."

"I hope my parents thought of taking along the identity cards I gave them last February," Raymond says. "I'm worried about them. My family is too well known in Lyon. It would take only one racist to denounce them."

Thursday, November 4, 1943

One hard blow after another! Today, Maurice, our indefatigable Maurice, who is so calmly courageous, who in his straightforward manner accomplishes the boldest operations, who knows everybody in Lyon, who is trusted by everybody—Maurice arrives and immediately starts: "Another dirty blow!"

"My parents?"

"No, for the moment they are safely sheltered. But I'm going to have to persuade them to leave Lyon, what with all those Milice roving everywhere. I'm extremely uneasy. You know the technique of the Miliciens: they track down wealthy Jews and arrest them, without a warrant, of course. Then they brutalize them to extort money, jewelry, and property from them. After that they either shoot them down in a ditch or hand them over to the Germans, who, naturally, will congratulate them."

I interrupt him: "Wait a minute, Maurice. Do you know of any specific cases in Lyon?"

"Of course I do, and I also happen to know several of the Lyon hooligans who signed up for the Milice; they are strategically placed to identify local Jewish families. They know their city well enough to quickly find the addresses of any newcomers."

"And don't the French authorities intervene?"

"The cops dread the Miliciens. The one they call 'Twisted Mug' and Touvier, that chief from Chambéry, are more powerful than they are.[28] A Lyon police commissioner has just experienced this

27. The Main-d'oeuvre immigrée (Immigrant Manpower) was composed largely of foreigners of Jewish extraction who had fled Nazi persecution.
28. Touvier was head of the Lyon Milice. As described by Lucie Aubrac, he was

for himself. He had sent Touvier packing over a bank safe that the latter wanted to have opened. But the bank demanded that a police official be present. The police commissioner now is a prisoner at Montluc, together with the bank's vice-president."

I'm listening with only one ear. There's something that doesn't sound right. Why is Maurice so talkative, giving so many details? He surely has very bad news to tell. It must be pretty bad for him to put off telling us for so long.

"What did you really come to tell us, Maurice? Let's have it."

He finally spits it out, his eyes wide, his voice high: "I'm not going to beat around the bush. They know where Boubou is."

We look at each other in dismay. What? I feel my heart beating wildly in my throat. Raymond grits his teeth. His face is the color of the dressing on his cheek.

Maurice quickly adds: "I got hold of Daniel. The three of them have gone to get him."

But what happened? I don't understand. After Raymond's arrest in June, I had to be completely available. As for teaching, it was the end of the school year; the graduating students were having their review period, so there were few hours of classes. Having a small child, I was excused from the *baccalauréat* examining board. Of course I immediately sought a safe refuge for my kid—in the Vercors Mountains, a children's home at a marvelous site, away from the main roads, with a good milk supply. It was already sheltering a few Jewish boys whose parents were in the Resistance. My sister took Boubou there at the end of June. When she got back, she told us she had an excellent impression of the place and the headmistress had promised to send news regularly through a discreet channel.

"In this one unusual instance," Maurice says, "the headmistress wrote to your avenue Esquirol address. She needed

---

less a political than criminal ally of the Nazis. His "death," announced in 1972, was a mere ploy to escape arrest. He finally was arrested in May 1989, after having been sheltered in a series of conservative monasteries. See Laurent Greilsamer and Daniel Schneidermann, *Un certain Monsieur Paul: L'affaire Touvier* (Paris, 1989: Fayard) and Claude Moniquet, *Touvier: Un Milicien à l'ombre de l'Eglise* (Paris, 1989: Olivier Orban).

to have immediate parental authorization for the BCG vaccine, which had been advised for the area where Boubou is. Naturally, the German policeman read the letter. 'We've got her!' he said. 'We'll get her with the kid.' Maria heard him say it. She adores the child. She was cooking for these two men. She went out the door, shouting to them: 'There's no salt left; I have to go get some quick. I'll be back in five minutes.' She ran to the trolley terminus at Grange-Blanche, knowing that I regularly pass by there. Luckily, she saw me and told me everything. At the garage, the men were ready in seconds. They left at once, well armed, I can tell you. They'll be there tomorrow around noon. I arranged a rendezvous with them on the hill behind the cemetery. Now we can't do anything but wait until tomorrow. I'll come to let you know. I've got to go now. A friend of mine is leaving for Paris with Marguerite. I want to give them some food; they'll make packages for people at Fresnes prison. I'm worried about Freddy (Dugoujon). He's only just recovered from his lung ailment. Fresnes isn't exactly a sanatorium. As for Ginette, don't fret—she left for the Isère department with some Girl Scout friends who took her under their wing. I don't know any more details, but at least we can rest easy about her."

He sees how depressed we are, and though he's in a hurry to leave, he adds: "Look, you two, it's going to work—you'll see, Lucie, it will be all right. After all, dammit, I could have waited for those guys to come back before telling you, but you're both strong enough to know everything straight out."

What Maurice doesn't see is that as soon as the door closes behind him, our courage consists mainly of crying in each other's arms for a long time.

"What are we going to do, Raymond? What shall we do?"

"You think we have to go there if they get the kid? I know them, those brutes; it won't do any good. It would be even worse for him. Anyway, we'd all be killed—him as well as us. There's only one solution: if they take him, we'll kill ourselves. That way, maybe he'll have a chance of being spared."

"But how are we going to do it—and where? We can't do it here. Do you realize what a mess it would be for Dr. Joie and everybody around him? We'll have to find a place that wouldn't compromise anybody, and then the Gestapo would have to know in order for the kid to benefit from it."

Knock, knock—the almost six months of life taps on my stomach. What becomes of that hope in all of this?

"Touch it, Raymond—our little girl is stirring. You'll see, we'll all get out of this, and tomorrow night Boubou will be the one to put his hand on my stomach to say hello to the baby."

"There will be room enough for my hand, too," Raymond says, attempting a wan smile.

So we try to act like everything's fine. At the dinner table we don't tell anybody about our anguish. The Joies sense that something has happened. They do everything to help us relax. After dinner that night the doctor gives each of us a sleeping pill: "Don't be afraid to take it; it's not dangerous for the baby. You'll have a good night and feel better tomorrow."

Back in our room, we look at the two pills. Why take them? Sleep doesn't matter. What's the point of a good night's sleep when we're being crucified by this threat we face? Raymond opens the window and we throw the pills out. He doesn't attach the rope he has tied there every other night so we could escape into the garden. He leaves the gun in his coat pocket. We feel we are between parentheses. There was a "before" but we can't speak of an "after." We don't dare talk to each other. Finally I say: "If it hadn't worked, they would have told us."

"On the contrary," Raymond says. "No one ever wants to be the bearer of bad news."

Stretched out like two recumbent effigies, we start on the longest night of our lives. It's a night of agony. I lie still, I wait, I listen to Raymond's breathing. It's not a sleeper's breathing. Next to me, the wounded, bruised, anxious man has suddenly become my strong companion, the protector of my life, of my lives. He puts my head on his shoulder: "Rest, my Lucette, let yourself go; you're making our second child. It's there, our baby is there. And tomorrow we'll have our little boy, too."

Now we're in total harmony: one calm so the other will be calm. One has hope and says so, so the other won't despair. We thank each other for the experience of knowing such love, a love few people will ever experience. And we are still speaking of this love as day breaks. We whisper as if to avert a fate that we know has already been irrevocably determined.

Friday, November 5, 1943

As I did for Raymond's escape, I will myself to be a winner. On September 21, when we couldn't go through with the attack on the paddy wagon, I told the team as spunkily as possible: "Bah, it's just a rehearsal. Next time it'll work like a charm." And after Raymond was freed I asked him: "Weren't you terribly disappointed to find yourself in your cell that night when you hoped we'd try something?" He answered: "I told myself it's like fishing. Lucie saw the fish. She cast her line; next time she'll strike and pull me out of here."

But for Jean-Pierre, there can be no next time. It was yesterday or never. The minutes pass slowly. If Maurice comes, I have to be the first to know. So I frequently go to the toilet, which is between the staircase and our room. I leave the door ajar. As I return from one of my trips, Raymond announces deadpan: "I'm going to smoke my pipe in the hall."

He has the same idea but his solution is more elegant. We look at each other and stay in the room, hand in hand, with the door open.

Somebody is running up the stairs. We've won! Even before I see Maurice come in, I sob with joy.

"Hey—this is no time to cry," he says, "come with me to get your kid. I don't want the other men to know where you are. We've had enough trouble as it is without implicating them more than necessary."

I go with him and race toward the Citroën parked under the hazelnut trees along the road. The three guys are strolling around nearby keeping an eye on the surroundings. I reach the car. Inside Jean-Pierre is kneeling on the seat and playing with a hand grenade on the back shelf. He's holding it by its ring! I'm horror stricken! He's playing with death! I wave at him. He answers with his free hand. Then, with my hands held very high, I act out the puppet song: "Ainsi font, font, font les petites marionettes . . ." A perfect mimic, he puts down the hand grenade and

184

joyously waves his little hands above his head. Maurice adroitly removes him from the car while I faint dead away on the side of the road. Coming to, I see all four of them leaning over me and hear them yelling at each other about the best way to bring me around. Never mind security! Their Catherine is lying on the ground, and they feel powerless.

"It's all right, you guys. Next time don't leave weapons around in a car with a kid."

"We don't do jobs like this every day," Daniel says. "I hope it's the first and last time. The headmistress wasn't exactly keen about handing your son over to us. The fact is, we had to kidnap him. So, as for his clothes and toys, forget it."

I kiss each of them as hard as I can. Now they are embarrassed and moved—kissing isn't one of our habits.

"Well," Maurice says, "you've hung around here long enough. Be careful on the way back, you guys. I'll take these two to Raymond."

His father silently embraces Jean-Pierre, who says, very calmly: "Are we going to say hello to the sea and to the shells?"

For him, being back with his papa and mama means the three of us taking a trip together. The way we did six months ago, when we spent ten days in the sun at Carqueiranne.

Maurice says: "I'm leaving. I've got to explain the kid's presence to the doctor. It wasn't exactly part of the original plan. See you tomorrow."

An hour later the doctor joins us in our room: "Come and get a mattress for the child to sleep on. We'll bring you your meals here. Try to keep him busy so he doesn't get too noisy. I'd also like your husband to refrain from walking with the child in the park. It might appear unusual to both patients and personnel. The nurses are already asking questions about your being here, saying things like: 'We can look after him perfectly well if he is seriously ill. Ordinarily, convalescents don't bring their wives.' I told them that you were related to my wife and that I couldn't very well refuse you."

I understand perfectly. Not that they suspect us of being in hiding. In these times of hardship, stupid jealousy is enough to make people resentful. "Why her and not the others?"

I promise our greatest discretion to this courageous man, who quite simply is risking his life and those of his family by hiding us. But only one thing matters today: we have our child—near us, with us. At night I bathe him in the sink in our room. He's never seemed so beautiful, so perfectly shaped, his flesh so firm and his skin so young and soft. My precious! I move my hands gently and slowly to wash him. Then I tenderly kiss him all over, and then kiss him some more—passionately. He purrs with pleasure.

"Leave me a little, too," Raymond says. Tonight he is calm, almost cheerful. Worn out but peaceful, amid the silence of the clinic, we all three fall asleep, and for the first time sleep overtakes us all at the same time. The glow of the little orange night light above the door illuminates a reunited family.

Saturday, November 6, 1943

You can't keep a child in a hospital room. Last night Maurice hadn't wanted to tell us; today he announces that he has found a family where we can board Jean-Pierre as long as we are in Pollionnay. The parents of the manager of the daycare center where Ginette, Raymond's sister, is hiding will take him. So once again our family is separated.

Since d'Astier's departure for London, Pascal Copeau, who has taken his place as leader of Libération, has much more authority in the committee directing the actions of the MUR.

He comes to see us whenever he can, any time of day. He always brings something—a book, a nice bottle, a pouch of tobacco for Raymond's pipe. His presence means more than the solidarity of the *résistant*, more even than friendship; it radiates an extraordinary warmth, and he also conveys news from our friends and from the various movements.

He also is the one who will determine our future, and he comes to discuss it with us. D'Astier, who has recently been made commissioner for domestic affairs in the provisional government in Algiers, wants Raymond there with him. He would have to go through London, where they have agreed to transfer him at the earliest possible moment. As for me, a woman, the problem is different. After my adventures, with my little boy and my pregnancy, everybody wants me to be hidden away permanently, and the farther away the better. Everyone knows what would happen to me if I were caught. Many people fear the repercussions of my possible arrest. I know far too many things, dating from the fall of 1940 when Libération was established. I know too many people at every level. Many who are well known, some of them sought by the Germans; many heads of sections in the various services; many of the liaison people in the provinces. In other words, I have become very dangerous!

Claudius Petit and Claude Bourdet, friends who have been extremely thoughtful, especially after Caluire, providing me with the financial means to organize Raymond's escape, agree with Pascal. Obviously I have to leave at the same time as Raymond, as soon as possible, with our son.

"You must realize," Pascal says, "that this is less obvious to those in London. After all, this is war, and there are many women and children in danger in France. This is no time to fill scarce planes with refugees. Of course, it's a different matter when it's a question of sheltering an agent's family so that his mind remains free for his work and no pressure can be exerted on him if he's captured. We've had an idea: de Gaulle and the government in Algiers have proclaimed that French women are henceforth full citizens. We've decided to name Lucie representative of the domestic Resistance with a seat in the Advisory Assembly. You'll shake them up a little, all those survivors of the Third Republic who are among us. After all, you're not just a revolutionary; you are also a university *agrégée* and a history teacher; you're married and a mother; you're of Burgundian Catholic extraction. What more could they want?"

Raymond is obviously happy with this solution and proud to see his wife being honored.

Quite moved, just to say something, I ask: "Is that what they'll want? When they see a woman show up, one who is about to give birth in February, they'll say: This is not serious."

"We are the ones who want it, and we're the ones on the spot!" Pascal exclaims, quite cynical for once. "They're just our travel agents. Yes, you're pregnant, it's beginning to show, my dear.

Well, they'll have to understand that entering the Resistance is nothing like taking the veil—and that for us life goes on. Just the same, once you're over there, look out and behave yourself. Louis Martin-Chauffier is telling everybody that despite your prim look you are even more foul-mouthed than he is, with his air of a Benedictine monk. Careful! Nothing is decided yet. We're waiting for a reply. We need two-and-a-half seats. In your condition, we can't just put you on a Lysander plane. But they're beginning to use twin-engine planes. Even with the mail, there are easily ten seats on each of those, with no guarantees as to comfort, punctuality, or safety. There will be a full moon on the thirteenth. Therefore, the operations will start on the eighth or tenth and will be staggered through the sixteenth, maybe the seventeenth. I would very much like you to be part of this batch. We've seen enough of you, and you're not exactly easy to camouflage with your demands as lovers."

He pours the last round of wine, the last drop in my glass: "The old saying's right: a baby this year. This one is on its way!"

"In my family, they say: cuckolded or hanged . . . Do we have to choose?"

"For me, there's only one choice. You can get over being cuckolded," he says, with his big, deep laugh, getting up to leave. "See you soon, kids; go on loving each other."

Sunday, November 7, 1943

We are no longer responsible adults. I am no longer a teacher, respected in her classes, or a housewife concerned with provisions. Together we had organized and directed our lives, and now all of a sudden we are dependent, taken care of like abandoned children or handicapped people who need protection. People are "taking care of us." And we don't know who they are or how it is done.

"This afternoon," Maurice says, "we'll come to say good-bye to you, Pascal and I. A car will take you close to the airstrip from which you're to depart."

"Who are we going to stay with, while waiting?"

188

"I don't know, and I don't want to know. Starting today, I'm out of it . . . "

"Where are we going?" Raymond insists.

"I don't know anything about it."

"Is it far? Raymond is not entirely well yet, and they're looking for him."

"You, too, are in danger, Lucie, and easy to recognize. I don't know the details of your departure. But when they put someone on a plane, you know, it's serious business, and every precaution is taken. All I can tell you is: be ready."

"How about my parents?" Raymond asks.

"I saw them; for the time being they have a small, discreet apartment; they don't want to leave Lyon. Your mother sees her sister every day. They firmly believe that you're in London and that Lucie has joined you, or is about to, with the kid. My own parents are near Aix. With them, I was able to be tough. They at least realized the Milice could find them, very quickly, and I settled them far from the immediate danger. I don't believe they're at risk."

"And Yvon, in his prisoner-of-war camp; who will take care of him?"

"For the moment, your parents still send him parcels. They are distributed by the Vichy prisoners' service, where some of our people work. There's no way the Gestapo could make that connection. As far as you are concerned, he must believe what your parents told him in their letters. All things considered, I'd really prefer that your parents were out of Lyon. I hope you at least are on the right track. Now, good-bye. We'll see each other after the war."

Maurice, my heart's brother, I hug and kiss him and can't let go. "Okay, that's enough. After all, we may be together again even sooner than we think," he says, extricating himself from my embrace, his eyes wet.

I owe him so much! Back in 1940 he joined our adventure without the slightest hesitation. He is devilishly skillful at managing any situation whatsoever. In August 1940 he even successfully escaped from a column of prisoners of war being marched to Germany. He just picked up a wheelbarrow that happened to be on the shoulder of the road as if this were perfectly normal. Then followed in step with the soldiers for a while before turning off into a farmyard without the German sentries on either side of the convoy seeming suspicious in the least. Maurice's support proved extremely valuable. He always knew how to find available lodgings; how to convince the wives of his friends who were prisoners of war to rent out all or part of their apartment or to temporarily house a *résistant* on the run.

In Lyon, he knew the lawyers, the doctors, the business people we could count on. He was welcome in all the small cafés—where one could eat sausages while drinking a carafe of Mâcon white at a reasonable price, as long as you were with him. He was the one who found a garage for rent to hide cars and assure the upkeep of cars and equipment for our *groupe-franc*; he also located a tank of airplane fuel one night near the Bron airfield and found out when it wasn't under guard. Our group had greatly benefited from this tip and we were amply supplied with fuel after adapting the carburetors in our Citroëns' engines.

Like me, he had participated in many raids and arranged many contacts, without having any more specific responsibilities than I had. His friends called him careless. But he didn't get caught any more than I did, probably because we both had a good nose for danger and committed ourselves to action only when we were sure to win. My Maurice, with his priceless Lyon accent, his unique way of telling a story while mimicking all the action, and his lively face, with features that would usually be described as Semitic. He belonged to a Lyon society that was distant and secretive toward strangers. But within this society, there was complete discretion and brotherly support. We saw the proof of that in Nicolas, the "silk man" on the rue Coste, and Joie, the physician of Pollionnay.

After lunch Pascal arrives, as agreed. "Now, kids, we're off! You're going away like a nice, normal little family, with your suitcases, for a vacation in the country."

"We don't have a suitcase, and hardly anything to put in one."

He opens the door. Outside is a leather suitcase. "Here's one— my gift to you. I don't want it anymore. It weighs as much as a dead donkey, it's as heavy empty as full. But since you'll be traveling by car and by plane, the weight doesn't matter. I'm sorry, the company didn't entrust me with your tickets, or tell me the date and place of the flight. There will be a message on the radio one of these days to alert you."

To make the departure less emotional, he keeps joking about the tickets and the seat reservations as though this were a normal cruise. And finally: "Over there, you'll explain exactly what's happening here; that there are police of all shapes and sizes ravaging the cities; that the ranks of the maquis are swelling and training; that it's urgent to send weapons. Tell them to hurry up with their landing before we all get arrested. How are we going to know when you have that baby in February, Lucie? It's also a little bit our baby, all of ours."

"No problem, I already told Maurice. On February 20, for Ginette's birthday, there will be a 'personal message' on the BBC. Boubou will announce the birth."

"And what if it hasn't arrived yet?"

"I counted carefully, she'll be born by the twelfth at the latest. I'm positive I conceived on May 14."

A quick good-bye to our hosts. We barely have time to thank them. "For what?" the doctor asks.

Pascal opens the door of the Citroën. We three hug tightly for a long time. The men have tears in their eyes, and I start crying in earnest, while Jean-Pierre delights only in the certainty of leaving in this car, seated between his papa and mama. We leave behind us our friends, our parents, all our buddies in the Resistance. And Lyon, where we arrived in September of 1940, where every December 14 for three years we have celebrated wedding anniversaries. It's hard to leave all that.

I don't know the driver. Next to him sits a silent blond young man who gives him directions. We follow the Beaujolais roads, through vineyards displaying their glorious autumn colors. These are all the landscapes of my childhood. I know all the roads and paths; I can name all the hamlets. Every steeple is a memory: first communions and weddings in my family; nearly every cemetery has a tomb that I saw opened to receive the lowered coffin of a relative.

On my left, the rock of Solutré, where my Grandmother Vincent took me to watch the Americans who were digging under the white pebbles and the red clay for traces of prehistory. Perhaps the beginning of my taste for archaeology? That's where I had my first chewing gum. "Spit it out," my grandmother said, "it glues your bowels together."

A little farther on is the rock of Vergisson, with its legend of the "pharamine beast," which visited wives when their husbands were away too long and tore out the tongues of chatterboxes and slanderers. A remnant of the fear of the wolf hiding in the wild bushes and brambles on the ridge. Halfway up the slope is the clearly defined line where the well-tended vines begin, surrounding the villages of pretty pale stone houses where life used to be so merry.

In this season, after the grape harvest, the vineyards are deserted; it is the time to taste the new wine. Suddenly, in this car, with these unknown men, I believe I realize fully why we got into this unusual situation. All my roots are here. This land, with its past, its traditions, its inhabitants who work on it and afterward sleep below it, is something I don't want to lose. Our gaiety, our freedom, our pleasures, our way of life, the welcome my uncles, wine-tasting cups in hand, extend to passersby from the doorway to their cellar. It's just not possible all that could disappear. A dull and quavering state of mind, servility camouflaged beneath a punitive morality—that's Pétain and Vichy. But it's not France! And the pilfering conquerors full of arrogance who load freight trains with human beings of all ages, of all races, in addition to the Communist workers and the priests who hid Jewish children—they will never be our allies, and we refuse to let them become our masters.

"Raymond, look at this countryside, the harmony of it. We can't lose all this!"

"There is no price too high to pay for the right to preserve it," Raymond says.

I'm worried. Are they going to leave us in this area, where many people know us and everyone thinks Raymond has been in London for a long time? The car changes direction, arrives at Crèches, and crosses the Saône over the Arciat bridge. As a child, I came here with my winegrowing family for a Sunday fish fry. Water scared these land people. None of them knew how to swim. It would never have crossed their minds to show themselves barechested in swimming trunks. Only foreigners on vacation bathed in the Saône. "They'll catch their death," my grandmother used to say. That's where I saw my first corpse, a young man who had drowned. He had been fishing on the river bank and lost his footing while casting his line. A boatman had found him and hauled him up on land.

The road, here on the left bank, crosses still-green meadows with thick hedges. A few stands of poplars break the monotony of the landscape. On this side of the Saône is the region called the Bresse. The houses, scattered throughout the countryside, are built of clay blocks, long and low, with large sloping roofs which, farther to the south, protrude well beyond the walls. That's where the corn harvest is dried, hung from the rafters. How I would like a good plateful of gaudes now, that thick gruel of corn, with cold milk poured over it. When I was a child, that was the meal you ate when times were lean. Because of the color of that dish, my family, like everybody in fact, calls people from Bresse "yellow bellies."

Pont-de-Vaux. In front of the Hotel des Voyageurs, as night falls, a handsome dark-haired young man with the sweetest smile in the world, a pipe in his hand, is waiting for us: "Come with me."

We cross a small square to steps that lead to a large, beautiful house. A door opens even before we have climbed the steps. "Come in, little ones, and get some rest."

In front of us stands a man with his outstretched hands wide open, like the traveler in Courbet's painting The Encounter. This warm and cordial man reminds us of Gambetta and Jaurès.[29] He has the same stature, the same beard, and as we will soon discover, the same way of speaking.

---

29. Léon Gambetta (1838–82), French statesman, was instrumental in the consolidation of the Third Republic. Jean Jaurès was a Socialist leader whose assassination on the eve of the First World War contributed to reducing Socialist opposition to the war.

"Let me introduce myself: Jean Favier, and this is my wife and my daughter. Now, Charles-Henri (that's how we learn the name of the man with the pipe), how many stars does this one have?"

We are taken aback. What do stars have to do with us?

Charles-Henri smiles: "He's the one who took in General de Lattre after his escape, and who took care of his stay here until his departure."

I ask him how he knows all that.

"I might as well tell you. I'm in charge of air operations in this sector. So you'll be under my wing until your departure, like the general was. I have a certain number of relay stations where my travelers are sheltered until their flights come in."

He turns to Favier: "Where are you going to lodge these two?"

"With Jean Boyat and his wife. I know them well, they are as unassuming as they are brave. They have two children old enough to understand and keep quiet. They will sleep there tonight, but for dinner, they are our guests. Do stay, too, Charles-Henri, the hostess has outdone herself for this dinner."

On the fine old wooden table is a tray with four crystal flutes.

"Your arrival certainly merits Champagne!" says our host, smiling.

"I don't know how this wretched fellow does it," Charles-Henri says. "But all the people who come to his house are entertained in a grand manner. He must have had some fine cellar in 1940 for it to be still plentiful in 1943."

He pops the cork as tradition calls for, with a loud noise, and Champagne froths in the glasses.

"This is better than the water at Montluc," Favier says, toasting Raymond. He puts his arm around my shoulders: "You don't turn up a woman like this under every cabbage!"

So I realize that Charles-Henri has filled him in on all our adventures. Jean-Pierre, accustomed to numerous changes in his surroundings, is perfectly at ease, wandering around the room and playing with the cat. Suddenly he exclaims: "Peepee!"

"Hey, you women," Favier calls out, "look after the little one. Give him some soup, and if he's tired, put him to bed. When we go to Jean's, we'll carry him."

I stand up obediently.

194

"Not you! I was speaking to my women. You're a man, you know. You fight like a man. You stay with us."

I look down at my stomach, thinking back to all my ploys with the Gestapo, that same old story of my illegal pregnancy. Is there anything masculine about that? Why is it that the greatest compliment a man can pay a woman is to tell her: you write, you work, you act like a man. When I was preparing the history *agrégation* at the Sorbonne, my teacher, Guignebert, had said to me: "You ought to sit for the male section of the *agrégation*; you have the intellectual power of a man." I had been extremely upset by that judgment, which classified me according to a stereotype.

My reply to this man, who has received us with such kindness, is in no uncertain terms: "As far as I'm concerned, I feel perfectly at ease as a woman, you know; what I did was a woman's job, and what's more, a pregnant woman's, something that would never happen to you."

There is a silence.

Charles-Henri and Raymond carefully fill their pipes as if the fate of the world depended on it. Favier is speechless; then his face wrinkles and he bursts into loud laughter: "What a woman! She isn't scared of anything. Now I understand, my boy, how she got you out of the cooler," he adds, slapping Raymond's shoulder.

"Three times," Raymond answers. "I'll tell you all about it someday."

Our little boy has quickly downed a thick vegetable cream soup. Now he is licking the bowl that was full of applesauce. He is ready to go to sleep.

It's our turn now. With Mrs. Favier and her daughter, we finish the bottle of Champagne. At dinner we are overwhelmed. A healthy soup, a genuine Bresse capon, real goat cheeses, and to accompany the applesauce, floating island, the dessert we had for the grand occasions of my childhood. But it is quite a feat these days. It takes eggs, milk, and sugar. Raymond can't get over it, and he indicates his amazement.

"Bresse is a land of plenty," Favier says. "We've got everything except wine. You have to cross the Saône to get some. Incidentally, I'm at a choice location, between the white Viré and the various red Beaujolais."

"But what about requisitions?"

"We manage; the inspectors often allow their palms to be greased. They too have families to feed. Besides, they only inspect what we let them see."

"And the Germans?"

"We hardly see any at all. According to their maps, the main road is on the other side of the Saône, and so are the big cities like Chalon, Tournus, and Mâcon. In the winter Bresse is pretty wet, so they don't come here much. Instead they concentrate their forces in the cities, or at the foot of the mountains to keep an eye on the maquis. For the time being, we are more or less left in peace."

"But what about denunciations, the Vichy police, and the Milice?"

"Here at Pont-de-Vaux we have no police in the strict sense, but rather a gendarmerie brigade. Those are mostly guys from this area, many of whom think the way we do and help us. As for the others, they don't want any 'complications'; they won't budge. Why should they be zealous when they have a nice, cozy life as it is? Any denunciations would go to the brigade office if the postal inspector and the two women letter carriers didn't intercept them. Up to now, things haven't gone any further."

He continues: "As for me, I was the mayor until 1940, a notorious Freemason and known for my anticlerical views. So in November of 1940 I was suspended from my administrative functions and replaced by the president of the veterans' organization from the war of 1914–18. I said to him: 'Well, old boy, we were in the army together, and here you are on the wrong side. So now you needn't know what I say or what I do, and you don't even want to know it. After the final victory, you won't be sorry; we'll remember it.' That's how we left it. But what worries me at present is that this idiot senses that the winds are shifting and wants to resign. Every day I have to bolster his morale and persuade him to stay on the job. You never know who might be designated to replace him, you see."

We laugh at these curious inverted relations. Favier is pleased with his performance. A thousand small wrinkles pucker the corners of his eyes; he strokes his reddish beard, which shows a few gray streaks. How old is he? Maybe my father's age; he reminds me of him a lot with his epicurean side, his pleasure in living and his generosity.

Before taking our leave, we check our identity papers once more. We are, if you please, Mr. and Mrs. Saint-André du Plessis. Raymond and Lucie are our first names. I don't know where on earth Pierre-the-forger unearthed this name. But from my experience I do know that this must be a foolproof identity. We have a good laugh over this noble name, but Charles-Henri tells us: "For all of us, you are and will remain Aubrac."

That makes Raymond's last Resistance name permanent—his pseudonym. Just as writers have a pen name and actors a stage name, fighters in the Resistance have an underground name, which has nothing to do with a false identity paper.

"Do you have any connection with the mountains of the Massif Central?" Favier asks. "What made you choose the name of one of those volcanoes? Do you know, Lucie, it suits you very well, that name."

"That name is not my name. All I ever had in the underground is a first name, Catherine, which is what I'll call my daughter. In the Resistance I had only a first name, like all the women. There were so many women that there were several Catherines, so they added our function. I was the groupes-francs Catherine. Naturally, from now on they'll call me Mrs. Aubrac, since I'm his wife. I don't complain about that. But we will have our full names. I will not be Mrs. Raymond Aubrac; I will be Lucie Aubrac."

Sensing a storm brewing, Raymond intervenes: "Maybe someday they'll call me Mr. Lucie Aubrac! Or Mr. L. Aubrac. But the name has no connection with geography, Mr. Favier."

And this is what he tells him: "Early in March, when the Vichy government decrees for compulsory labor service went into effect, many young people refused to go to Germany. Those living in cities didn't always have families to go to in the country to hide. So we quickly had to organize places where those who refused compulsory service could gather. We met in my house, at avenue Esquirol, with some leaders of the secret army of the MUR. Lucie made us pancakes."

"Yes, I ground some wheat in the coffee grinder and mixed it with a little milk diluted with water, then I browned the mixture in beef fat—it was edible."

"You bet it was! Everybody congratulated you on it. They liked coming to our house, all these guys without a family life. We still had a legal address, with a mailbox, a real home with books, a small stock of coal and provisions, beds ready for our buddies—we were a couple with a child. Those guys liked seeing that such a thing still existed—a home. Of course, at times it meant an escape into lodgings rented under an assumed name, where we took on a different identity and wore different clothes. So we became our own doubles, or rather, we had to split ourselves in two—no more husband, wife, child—to join the cohorts of lonely underground people. That wasn't always easy—right, Charles-Henri?"

"It's another kind of family," he answers, "one in which you would die for each other."

Mrs. Favier shudders at this glimpse of a life of lies, where hide-and-go-seek is no longer a child's game. Raymond senses how upset our hostess is.

"So that day we decided to send scouts into the Jura and into Savoy. Their mission was to alert the Resistance leaders. Yves Farge asked: 'Now, for contacts, what shall we call you? The name Balmont is far too well known now.' He leafed through a detective story that was lying nearby. 'Look, here's a police commissioner called Aubrac. That would suit you quite well.' And that's the name I kept in the Resistance after I got out of Antiquaille. It was never revealed, the police never knew it. There was no one available to take over the job that I had been doing, so I resumed my responsibilities. But now, because of whoever betrayed us, the Gestapo knows that a certain Aubrac was inspector-general of the secret army for the southern zone. They were able to fill in that blank on their organization chart of the Resistance."

It's time for us to leave. Charles-Henri goes too. He has plenty of places to stay. He has been moving about the area for more than a year now, and every house here opens its door for him.

Favier accompanies us to Jean Boyat's place—a small house on the edge of the neighboring village. Favier looks like a giant compared to the couple waiting for us. He is a bit condescending with them, though in an amiable way.

"Show them to their room. They are very tired, you'll have time to get acquainted tomorrow. Here is some butter and a jar of preserves, which my wife has sent for your children and their little boy."

Little Mrs. Boyat thanks him and shows us to our room, a real room, like in my parents' house. The wooden bed frame matches the looking glass and the night table. It's a high bed, with both a box spring and a woolen mattress, covered with hem-stitched sheets of linen and cotton. The bedspread, embroidered red sateen on one side and green on the other, is covered with a large red eiderdown. Jean-Pierre, now awake, snuggles under it voluptuously.

We say good night. Boubou falls asleep quickly. I made a diaper for him out of a towel. Since his return from the children's home in the mountains, he wets his bed—probably his way of demanding our care and our presence.

"Do you think, Raymond, that it's because another child is on the way, or is it his way of saying: you can see I'm too little to be separated from you?"

"Bah," Raymond says, "you mustn't always look for psychological causes."

"You're right, but it does have something to do with it. Because, you know, I've noticed that since you were in the hands of the Gestapo, you don't have asthma at night anymore."

He sneers: "So, you see, Montluc did some good . . ." I shouldn't have mentioned the prison. It's still like being skinned alive each time he talks about it.

There's a water jug and a basin on the washstand, with enough water to brush our teeth. But one has to spit into a slop bucket. That makes me nauseated. I'll brush my teeth tomorrow, in the yard.

Monday, November 8, 1943

We feel like a nuisance in the house of these good people, who stare at us as if we were Martians. I realize what it must mean to

199

an average, ordinary family to shelter two strangers who are said to have accomplished heroic deeds. All their regular habits in turmoil! If we're caught here, they will be, too. Meanwhile, they share their meager provisions, which they must make last an entire week, with strangers who came from God knows where. Will their worth be acknowledged someday? I, at least, will loudly proclaim their heroism. Doing without on a daily basis is worth as much as more brilliant deeds. They are spoiling Jean-Pierre. Mrs. Boyat melted sugar with a little butter and stuck the product on a small stick, making a lollipop for Jean-Pierre. The kid is enchanted. Raymond is supposed to stay out of sight. I'm supposed to be a relative who came with her kid to find some supplies. On account of my condition—I'm starting on the seventh month—my cousins are prospecting for me around the countryside. We even gave Mr. Boyat some money so the alibi would be valid.

At night he returns with a few eggs, ten pounds of potatoes, and a sausage. He also brings two balls of white wool, timidly saying: "I thought this might be useful for the layette." He is a rather reserved man who worries that he's not being helpful enough, and he expressed this to Favier. Favier himself has just appeared bearing a brioche hot out of the oven, made by "his women." Favier tells Mr. Boyat that what he is doing is enormous in itself and that he is risking a lot, adding: "Tomorrow night bring them to my house after dark and they'll have supper with us, the kid, too; my daughter has a surprise for him."

At night, in bed, speaking softly so as not to wake Boubou, we comment on the day's events. The rabbit stew we had at noon was a feast for them just as much as for us. They were happy to see us pleased and were a bit embarrassed by our thanks. We were careful to limit ourselves to one slice of bread; we may be eating their ration, because they don't dare use the coupons we gave them. We've got to talk to Favier about that. Apart from the meal, nothing happened. Raymond, now furnished with tobacco, smoked one pipe after another while reading an almanac. I took a little stroll with the kid, looked over the homework done by the Boyat kid, and started knitting a baby vest. Time passed slowly. Our hosts pursue their own affairs; they are discreet and ask no questions. Their orderly, spotless household and the muffled atmosphere of a foggy autumn are not conducive to conversation. After dinner, however, things liven up.

It's time for the London broadcast. Everyone gathers around the wireless set. Mr. Boyat turns the dials. Luckily, tonight the power is on. First we hear the ritornello of the jamming, finally, right on the wavelength, the three beats:[30] "This is London; today, on the umpteenth day of the struggle of the people of France for their liberation, the French speak to the French." We immediately sit up straight in our chairs, looking at one another, attentive accomplices. Jean Boyat turns the dial ten times, twenty times, trying to pick up the voices from London again. What an insane situation! We learn the news from France via the BBC. We hear of the sabotage of a dam on the Saône less than sixty miles from here; of the derailment of a trainload of gasoline near Fontaines, scarcely twenty miles away; of the execution of hostages in Bordeaux; and at Mont Valérien, near Paris, of a series of desertions in the Vichy government. After that, news from Algiers. De Gaulle is finally the sole head of a provisional government, after the attempts at bipartisan rule with Giraud, which the Americans had supported. We are jubilant hearing the account of the establishment of jurisdiction by Free France in newly liberated Corsica. Tomorrow it will be our turn! Finally, news from various fronts. The Allies are resuming their offensive in the Pacific; their navy dominates the Atlantic. The Soviet forces are resisting and now triumphantly attacking around Moscow and Stalingrad. It is certain that the winter of 1943–44 will be disastrous for the Nazis, out there in the snow. In Italy, too, the Resistance is helping Allied troops, who now have French soldiers among them.

We comment at length on the good news. It's lucky we have the BBC. People buy newspapers only to keep posted about the many ration coupons entitling them to food distributions. Every-

30. The three beats, the station signal for the French edition of the BBC broadcast, used the rhythm from the opening of Beethoven's Fifth Symphony. The rhythm also corresponded to the Morse code for the letter V, which came to stand for "victory."

thing printed has to pass German and Vichy censorship. They do not print any military information unfavorable to the Germans. When they withdraw, they say it's to gain new impetus! There is a popular song going around about the "elastic defense" in the Ukraine. Even death notices in the newspapers are falsified. Nobody dies in a French prison. No *résistants* are executed; only dangerous Jewish-Marxist terrorists have been shot down. What about the massacres of civilian populations and the extermination of hostages? These hard lessons are necessary to make people understand that the law must be obeyed and the occupying power respected. And the people saying all this are French! Everybody feels better when the BBC broadcasts, to a well-known tune, "Radio-Paris is lying, / Radio-Paris is lying, / Radio-Paris is German . . ."

After each broadcast comes a whole list of "personal messages," mysterious sentences understood only by those for whom they are meant. Parachute drops are announced; a military operation on the coast; a clandestine plane landing. These messages often seem an absurd game in an absurd world. If "Jérôme has caught sixteen trout," it may well mean that sixteen containers of weapons are going to be dropped tomorrow night on a meadow in the Limousin region.

Thursday, November 11, 1943

We have been here for four days already. Here comes Favier again, this time bringing my sister, Jeanne. She is the only being who really mattered to me until I met Raymond. We have remained very close. I don't know how she managed to track us down. At any rate, she found our hiding place. She knows we are supposed to take off for England within a few days, and she came to say good-bye. She brings me a bit of a layette. She also has brought me something to remember her by: a silver ring with a hard stone, some kind of tiger's-eye.

"Jeannot, I'll wear it until we meet again. Have you had any news from Pierrot?"

Her husband, Pierre, who has been a friend since childhood, had been able to return from the POW camp in which he was being held, thanks to an *Ausweis*, an identity paper fabricated by Jansen, the clever forger who has worked with us since the early days of Libération. Pierre was a journalist in the town of Vichy, working in a technical service of the radio. Through Georges Bidault, with whom he worked at the newspaper *L'Aube* before the war, he had been in touch with a Resistance group within the press corps.[31] Was it carelessness? Maybe. All of us were sometimes. And of course there was gossip and jealousy in that hornets' nest of Vichy. So Pierre, together with other journalists, was arrested early one morning and taken to Montluc. While we were at Dr. Joie's, Raymond told me of his amazement when, one morning in September, he met his brother-in-law; they were both carrying their latrine buckets from their cells to the prison courtyard, escorted by German soldiers. In the communal toilets, in a corner of the courtyard, they had been able to exchange a few words.

"That was how I knew," Raymond told me, "that both sisters were free, the kids were safely hidden, and my Lucie, from whom I had not had any news, was determined to get me out of there."

After Pierre's arrest, my sister came to Lyon often. Maurice helped her prepare packages, which she was able to leave at Montluc, because apparently her husband had succeeded in minimizing his case and his wife was not under suspicion.

Of course, we both used to talk incessantly of our prisoners. Through a man who had been released Jeannot learned which number Pierre's cell was, and one day we decided to signal him. Some of the cells had vents or skylights facing out toward the walls where the guards walked their beat. There was a narrow alley there with houses on the side facing the prison. One couldn't get into the houses lining the alley because German patrols watched over every inch of the area. They had recorded the names of all the inhabitants of the alley and threatened them with dire penalties, so the alley dwellers refused entry or any other contact with the outside.

---

31. Georges Bidault, journalist and editor of the Catholic newspaper *L'Aube* before 1940, was active in the Resistance. He became the head of the Catholic centrist party, the Mouvement Républicain Populaire, after the war.

Taking my sister's two little girls by the hand, like carefree young mothers, we loudly sang a nursery rhyme which the children danced to on the sidewalk: "Ne pleure pas, Jeannette, on te mariera, / Avec ton ami Pierre, celui qu'est en prison . . . [Don't cry, Jeannette, we're going to marry you, / To your friend Pierre, the one who is in jail . . .).

It was a pretty nursery rhyme, and it seemed like a magnificent idea to us, delightfully romantic and transparent to our men—for we had no doubt that they would hear it. Raymond's cell faced the courtyard, so only Pierre heard us and not for long at that, because a German patrol quickly chased us away.

Then, on the night of October 21, Raymond didn't return to Montluc. The truck that was to bring back its load of prisoners never arrived. People in the prison must have known something of the raid, and Pierre certainly realized the origins of the operation.

My sister had settled her little girls in a boarding school in October. Encouraged by my success, she remained on the warpath, trying to find some way to free her Pierre. Recently he had let her know that things were working out for him; that she should take her daughters and quietly move in with the Norgeu family in Haute-Epine. So now she is full of hope. During her short visit, she reassures us about my parents-in-law, who have found a quiet little hotel in Tassin-la-Demi-Lune, on the banks of the Saône, in a working-class neighborhood away from the center of Lyon. It's a place not frequented by the Milice.

Her visit does us a world of good. We feel as if we are still connected with a familiar world, one where we are known as we were in ordinary times: for Jeannot, her big sister; for Raymond's parents, their oldest son. People like anybody else.

Sunday, November 14, 1943

Charles-Henri is back. I wonder where he is based. Maybe he keeps moving and never stops. "It's likely," he says, "that the departure will be tonight. You're too far from the landing area here, and we can't take the risk of transporting you there at the last minute. Mémé will come and get you late this afternoon if the message is broadcast at one."

Indeed, around five o'clock a little pickup truck with "Manziat Meat Market" printed on the tarpaulin in big red letters stops at the Boyats' door. Favier, who is up on everything, also appears, with a bottle under his arm. "The stirrup cup," he says.

Mémé, the butcher, is a man my age, chubby, with thick sandy hair and a reddish complexion. Is it the open air or all the meat he eats? He hurries us along, poking for a moment in the burning fuel compartment, where small logs of wood, sheltered from the outside air, slowly burn. A full bag of wood is stowed on the running board.

"You never know whether this thing is going to work or not. Let's go while it's willing. We need time for a bite to eat before going to the airstrip."

Once again someone is taking care of us, and we three are carried off to another new destination.

"Bon voyage," the Boyats say. "Bundle up well during the night," Mrs. Boyat adds, with tears in her eyes, "Don't catch cold in this weather in your condition." Her motherly concern makes us smile.

"She's seen worse than that," Favier says, embracing us. "Okay, Lucie, go show those British that we know how to produce beautiful babies!"

At Mémé's house, Charles-Henri awaits us with his usual reassuring smile. If I were a believer, and if he were a priest, I'd choose him to be my spiritual director. There are three other men, short and broad shouldered, typical of people from Bresse. They have light complexions and their speech is a bit slow, a harsh drawl quite different from the lively, melodious language of my Mâcon people. They were just waiting for us to start dinner, which is pot-au-feu, roast meat, sausages, and cheese.

"Eat well, little lady, so you'll stay warm on the airstrip. We'll leave right after the nine o'clock radio broadcast."

The fatty broth gives me heartburn, and I can't swallow it, nor does Jean-Pierre, who's never tasted it before.

"Wait, we'll put a drop of wine in it; that'll make it go down easier."

Where are the *chabrots* of my childhood? I liked that little bit of lukewarm bouillon flavored with wine, which my grandmother allowed me to drink as a great treat. Charles-Henri, amused by my difficulty, comes to the rescue:

"It's her condition, you know. Better not force her!"

That makes Mémé laugh loudly; he asserts that I'll have a girl. "Only a girl would make so much fuss even before being born."

I'm fed up with all this, I'm tired and my stomach is upset; the smoke, the noise, the odors, everything makes me nauseated, and I don't have the courage to launch into a feminist speech— much to Raymond's relief. He was afraid I might fly into a temper, which surely would have been received much less favorably than at Favier's. At nine, the message is broadcast: "Ils partiront dans l'ivresse" (They will depart with joy). We repeat: "Ils partiront dans l'ivresse."

"Let's go."

In the sleepy village—or at least the village pretending to be asleep—the pickup's wood-gas engine snorts and rumbles like a locomotive. Half an hour later, with the little truck camouflaged between two thick bushes, we go on foot to the meadow— the airstrip, as they call it. The moon is up and it's as bright as day. The beaconing team is there, following Charles-Henri's orders; he puts people where he wants them and issues instructions: "Nobody smokes, talk in a low voice. Everybody else settle yourselves in the shadow of the hedge."

How uncomfortable I am! Sitting on the ground, with my legs stretched out in front of me—the baby doesn't like it. My back hurts. I put my arms behind me and lean back to relieve it, but that makes my calves cramp. The cold creeps up my back.

"Everybody else," meaning the team conducting the operation, the people leaving with us, and also those in charge of the Resistance mailbags, crouch on their heels. They've already opened their knapsacks and begin chewing and drinking as if this were a picnic. Raymond, sitting next to me, is nervous. His gun is in his overcoat pocket, and he keeps putting his hand inside to touch it. Boubou is asleep, stretched out on a bag, under a blanket that completely hides him. The plane will arrive at eleven-thirty at the earliest. Time passes slowly. The moon is up, and then the ground begins steaming. A light mist rises to the top of the grass, then stagnates about a yard off the ground. I can't take it any longer, I'm so tired and tense. Charles-Henri comes over to see me: "Are you all right?" I answer: "Yes" in such a faint voice that he becomes alarmed: "What's wrong?"

"I can't stand holding still any longer. I hurt all over, I wish I could get up."

"Well, get up, relax, walk up the path; stay in the shadows as much as possible—with that moon, silhouettes can be seen from way off. I'm afraid I brought you here for nothing. With this ground fog, they won't see our signals."

Raymond stands up when I do. He sticks close by me. After our second time around, we return to the group and I sit down on a suitcase. After a while, one of the men under the bushes whispers: "Better hide—this may be a German plane."

Above us, the droning noise of the plane becomes more and more distinct. There it is. We can see the plane clearly. Charles-Henri sends the agreed-upon code with his flashlight; the team has set up landing beacons. Suddenly, I am extraordinarily calm. Raymond holds my hand. The plane circles once, twice, getting closer to the ground. Then it climbs again and begins a third circle. But what are they waiting for? Why don't they land? Another wide circle, then it flies away.

"Put the lights out," Charles-Henri says. "We didn't pull it off tonight. The pilot couldn't see us. The fog smothered our lights."

The drone gets weaker and weaker, finally is no longer audible. That's it.

"Cover up the tracks," Charles-Henri orders, "and let's get out of here fast."

Somebody carries the child, who doesn't wake up. I cling to Raymond's arm. Along with all the mailbags we pile into Mémé's truck. The others ride away on bicycles. We return to Manziat down sunken lanes. There's no need for headlights, the fog doesn't reach the driver's level and Mémé knows the way by heart. We scatter rapidly. If the Germans should arrive from Mâcon or Chalon, all they'll find is a sleeping village. For the remainder of the night Mémé hides us in a sort of enclosed shed with a low ceiling. Nobody will come looking for us here. There is a good layer of straw and some blankets, and Jean-Pierre lies between us. I hear grunting on the other side of the partition. By the smell I guess it must be the pigsty. It's nice and warm in this hideout, and I fall asleep right away.

Monday, November 15, 1943

Raymond tells me he was awake all night.

After we have a bowl of hot milk and a nice slice of buttered bread, a guy from the team takes us a short distance to the house of a postman whose yard opens onto the woods. "If a German patrol should search the area," he explains, "we'll come and get you in plenty of time through the woods."

But he thinks the risk is minimal. The plane didn't land, and the German observers could see plainly by the full moon that there was no parachute drop. The man leaves our new host a hefty piece of bacon and a bit of steak for the child.

We are beginning to look like bums. We're unwashed, muddy from the wet meadow, and the straw from the shed is stuck on our clothes; we spend our day cleaning up, brushing our overcoats. We can't take any initiative, but we can still take care of appearances.

Wednesday, November 17, 1943

Another two days' wait. We're getting used to seeing Charles-Henri arrive with new orders.

"Tomorrow, you'll leave for Cuiseaux. A delivery truck from Morey's will come for you. Since Raymond speaks English, you'll have company. John was the tail gunner of a Flying Fortress that was shot down on the way back from an air raid on Turin. He parachuted down not far from here. He has absolute priority for departure. Aviators of his quality are rare and invaluable. His identity papers say he's a deaf-mute as he doesn't speak a word of French. That way there's no danger of his blundering in the event of a police search. Besides, the gendarmes around here are almost all on our side."

Thursday, November 18, 1943

So once more we are nomads, again quartered with strangers. We arrive at a farm. As far as the neighbors are concerned, the story is that we are distant relatives come for a rest. Soon enough I realize that this is mere convention—nobody is duped by it. On the first day we were welcomed discreetly, but then, day by day, the atmosphere changes. A neighbor has slaughtered a hog; he arrives with a roast and a fresh sausage he wants us to taste. And just by chance, another neighbor has made a big *clafoutis*, a tart made with plums and custard. "Since you have company," she tells our hostess, "this will be a little extra." This modest and unassuming solidarity is heart warming. Of course, my condition arouses compassion and some questions: "My poor lady, soon you're going to have two little ones; it's about time for them to come and get you"—meaning the British. They are credited with the ability to do anything. All our hopes of final escape rest on them. British radio is our only link with the free world. With its messages, news, and orders it provides the rhythm of our days. We store up whatever we hear, later sharing it and discussing it endlessly with the people who are harboring us.

Monday, November 29, 1943

Charles-Henri, ruler of our destiny, has us transferred to the Jura, together with John, the British aviator.

For the last time, sitting in the old wood-fueled Simca, which has a hard time starting, we listen to safety tips from our mentor.

"In principle, you're not taking any risk. If there is a police check, you say you gave John a ride and you don't know him; besides, from what you can tell he's a deaf-mute. As for yourselves, you're just trying to find some food. Here's the name of a hamlet where you're supposed to find at least two hundred pounds of potatoes. That's your alibi. The farmer's wife has been alerted to a possible visit. If need be, Lucie can always distract attention by fainting."

Before we leave, Bernard Morey, the local leader, regales us with a lavish meal. He is an energetic young man; his sister is an academic with a degree in literature. He is in charge of an important food business and has committed himself fully to the Resistance. With few exceptions his staff is made up of people who for one reason or another had to be camouflaged, sometimes for racial or political reasons, but mostly to escape compulsory labor service. Everybody in Cuiseaux adores him. He takes enormous risks. He openly says what he thinks, everywhere and always, and claims his excessiveness is his best protection. How long can this attitude preserve him? He is so sensitive that he realizes what all this time spent obeying orders to be cautious, letting ourselves be transferred from one place to another, and remaining passive, taking no initiative, must mean to us. He takes pains to ask our advice about actions that will be taken without us. He also tells us how important our testimony will be for the people in London. He is so good at bolstering our egos that, spurred on by that excellent meal, we feel when we leave we are setting out not just for another way station, another refuge, but on a mission of the first order.

At Bletterans, John is taken away, alone, to an isolated home where he will be easy to disguise. Our little family is entrusted to a gendarme. Mr. and Mrs. Roblin have a pretty little house with a yard in the center of town. They are people approaching retirement who, by opening their door to us, are making a break with an uneventful life. I'm reminded of the boys of my *groupe-franc*; a few of them had been members of the Communist party, others had been active in the Confédération Générale du Travail—the largest French labor union. For them, the road to disobedience had been relatively easy. The Resistance represented continuity with their past actions. But for a gendarme near the end of his career, whose life has been dedicated to respect for the establishment, what a crisis of conscience it must have been to embrace the Resistance, with its underground life and its obligatory lies.

We are deeply moved at the dinner table that night, when he says to us: "I consider it my duty as a military man to refuse to accept defeat and occupation; therefore, it is only normal that I hide you in my house. I've become a 'fence.'"

A fence! Mr. Roblin can't think of any other word to describe his position.

"After all, you're not bandits. If you're outlaws, it's only because the law has been perverted. It is no longer my law, the one that throughout my career I made people respect. You are honorable people."

He doesn't know how to justify himself, and he adds: "It may cost us dearly, my wife and myself, but I'm happy to welcome you."

As is our habit at night, once the child is asleep, Raymond and I discuss the events of the day at length, in the safe solitude of our bed. At Cuiseaux, we left behind a respected middle-class man, comfortably established in his provincial life; he is a regional leader of the secret army and moreover accepts the risk of camouflaging in his firm many young people who have refused compulsory labor service. And now we are housed with a modest civil servant who is even less prepared for the life, as he puts it, of an "outlaw." After the war, we will have to bear witness to this great diversity of commitment to the Resistance. The tirades of the Gestapo lieutenant against "All those Marxist Jews" are closely related to Paul Marion's propaganda and the Paris radio's shrill slogans, as well as the rationalizations of Darnand's Milice assassins.[32] Of course there are Jews and Communists in the Resistance, but after all, that's where they belong. But there are also people who could easily wait quietly for the war to end, and who would dare to reproach them for it later?

"All it takes is for something to click," Raymond says. "When Pétain's publisher, Lardanchet, arrived in my cell at Montluc, he had no sympathy for the Resistance. He thought he would be staying just one night. He had to stagnate for two weeks. One day they made us line up and go down to the courtyard. They marched us past the body of a man who had just been shot. An interpreter translated the prison warden's speech for us: 'This man tried to pass a message to the outside. That is strictly pro-

32. Paul Marion was minister of propaganda for the Vichy government. Joseph Darnand, head of the infamous Milice, was later sentenced to death.

hibited and punishable by death. After this assembly, you will turn over to the sergeant major of your corridor all papers and any writing instruments. Then the cells will be searched. Anyone who has kept paper or pencil will be shot immediately.' Back in our six by nine cell, I could clearly see my companion was deeply upset. He prepared his fountain pen and his notebook for the guards. During that time I split my pencil in two and extracted the lead. I added a piece of newspaper and the restored pencil to the small pile that a soldier came to collect. But where was I to hide my lead? There was no hiding place in the bare cell. Finally I slipped it under the band of the hat Mr. Lardanchet was wearing when he arrived. One day when we were both trying hard to remember a certain poem, I used the lead to write a line on the door frame. That was when I realized he was no longer the same man as when he arrived, because he thought it was an excellent trick. That's when I decided to trust him, to give him my wedding band and tell him your identity. Already, just the fact of living together had changed his opinion about the 'terrorists' described by Vichy propaganda. But what clicked for him was the sight of a man shot down for having a pencil."

Early December

The days are long in this village. From time to time we are invited to visit other families. When Pascal Copeau comes to see us, we are invited to dine with him at police headquarters. That's how we find out that all the gendarmes are on our side. It's an enormous, truly Pantagruelian meal. There is plenty of wine; everybody is optimistic. I can't spend as much time at the table anymore, I get so tired. I can't eat much at one meal, and because of the baby I have to decline the wine.

On December 4, Maurice came, bringing very bad news. In Lyon the Milice arrested part of our family and handed them over to the Germans. Maurice escaped the roundup. He is on his way to Paris, and from there to Fougères, in Brittany, where a friend of his lives. My parents-in-law are at Montluc. At night Raymond cries in my arms. He knows how much misery, filth, and sheer horror is in that prison. All I have to comfort him with is my presence and my love. We are unable to speak. Together in bed, clutching each other, we gauge our despair and our helplessness.

Sunday, December 5, 1943

In the morning our hosts and the neighbors are aware of our grief. Recognizing that they cannot express condolences, they come to tell us of the most recent events: the University of Strasbourg, evacuated and operating in Clermont-Ferrand, has been surrounded by the Milice and the Gestapo. Professors and students, boys and girls, have been arrested. Some were gunned down on the spot. We are no longer alone in this vast repression. Our family tragedy is subsumed into the tragedy of all of France.

Wednesday, December 8, 1943

In the afternoon Charles-Henri comes by to tell us that we're to change our hiding place once more. John, our Englishman, is going stark raving mad at the isolated farm where he has been for ten days. Nobody there speaks English, and he hasn't managed to learn a single word of French. Charles-Henri hopes that when the moon is full again in December, a flight can finally take us to London. While waiting for that opportunity, he is going to install us, with John, in a house, or rather a chateau, surrounded by a huge enclosed park where the men can move around and speak English without any danger.

So here we are in Villevieux. We arrive at night and leave the car in a dirt road. A small wooden gate opens into a rather poorly kept garden. Beneath the large trees, dead leaves form a thick carpet, muffling the sound of our footsteps. A dog yaps at our arrival, surely an old lapdog with that hoarse snarl.

"Shut up, Maréchal . . . " Those are the first words we hear before entering a vast warm room of indeterminate shape. An enormous hanging lamp, four feet above the table, is equipped with a single bulb. Three ladies welcome us, three sisters perfectly at ease with these strangers. Boubou is asleep, heavy in his father's arms.

"Put him down in that armchair," says the oldest sister. "Hang your coats over there. Don't put anything on this bed—the dogs sleep there, all of them, except Maréchal. He's too old to get up there. The poor beast is a bit incontinent and hardly knows what he's doing anymore."

The allusion to Pétain is clear. We look at each other, a little bewildered. Charles-Henri smiles at our amazement and offers his tobacco pouch to Raymond: "These ladies don't like Pétain, and what's more they don't mind smoke."

They both fill their pipes while our hostesses escort us to our rooms. On the second floor there is an immense corridor. At the end of it is John's room, and three doors away is ours. There's a stove. I'm overcome by the cold. In a little while they're going to light a blaze and also I'm promised a hot-water bottle for the night. The canopied bed fills a large alcove, inside of which are two small nooks: in one of these are a wash basin and a jug, in the other a pretty dressing table in the style of Napoléon III, with a mirror and a ruffled chair—the souvenirs of a nineteenth-century coquette.

At dinner, served on an embroidered tablecloth, we learn the essential facts about our hostesses. They suffered greatly during the First World War. In it they lost both their father, a career general, and their brother, a graduate of the military academy at Saint-Cyr; the oldest lost her young husband, and the other two had to give up any hope of marrying. After the war they watched their income dwindle away, and they live on the war widow's pension of the oldest sister, whose name is Louise. In the kitchen, which is Jeanne's domain, stands an enormous cast-iron range, occupying one whole side of the room. The dogs' food simmers there perpetually. On the rim of the open hearth they also warm up peelings and frozen greens for the rabbits. The large range boiler furnishes hot water for washing. Cécile, the youngest, is in charge of housekeeping and the hardest housework, the upkeep of the stoves. Every morning the tenant farmer–gardener and his wife, with their abundant progeny, come to receive their orders from the oldest sister.

One Sunday in 1942, with their usual outspokenness and their unquestioned patriotism, they confronted the village priest, who had preached from the pulpit in favor of the new state and col-

214

laboration with the Germans. The day they baptized the oldest of their dogs Maréchal, the manager of the cheese makers' cooperative, the local Resistance leader, paid them a visit. They received him most ceremoniously. He didn't quite know what to say to these ladies of the manor and started talking about the Resistance. Louise quickly interrupted him: "We were wondering when you would finally make up your mind to contact us. Very well, then. From now on you're our leader. We'll obey you. What do you expect of us?"

The cheese maker, as they call him, told Charles-Henri about this meeting. Charles-Henri had come to check out a field for parachute drops and for clandestine pickup operations. He understood immediately what a stroke of good luck this was: an isolated chateau, surrounded by a large park and a continuous wall. As soon as he saw these three "maiden ladies," as they say in these parts, he perceived their courage, their simplicity, and their determination.

Of course, the couple who work for them was informed and officially enrolled in the Resistance group. Jean, the husband, is to be a liaison agent, a courier, and a member of the reception teams. Gradually he will begin to work full-time for the movement, which partly explains the state of neglect of the park.

December 9, 1943

John and Raymond are delighted to make themselves useful, cleaning up the ponds, raking the walkways, sawing up dead wood. They talk while working. John found that Raymond was someone he could talk to who was happy to accustom himself to the English language. Cécile got out her nephew's toys for my little boy to play with. Louise's son was born in 1914, three months after his father's death in Alsace became known. Jean-Pierre is a quiet child, too quiet; for a good part of the day he plays peacefully with the dogs he adores. He doesn't talk very much. As soon as Raymond sits down anywhere, Jean-Pierre climbs on his lap. He clings to him and demands his presence every night at his bedside before going to sleep. The minute he wakes up in the morning he calls him.

And I'm starting on the eighth month and it's beginning to seem long. Still two full months to go! This is the hardest period, perhaps because I have nothing to do, maybe also because I have no idea about my future. I don't feel like doing anything to prepare for the birth. It's a little as though this baby I wanted so much, who helped me so much all summer long, has become an obstacle, even a threat to my freedom. What freedom? I am vegetating more and more. The days drift by, dreary and slow. Every morning it starts all over again, and I know this is what it will be like until the January moon. Charles-Henri told us there won't be any operation this month.

Every morning, in my room, I rekindle the wood fire that burned down during the night. On top of the stove, a jug of water I got from the faucet at the end of the corridor heats up slowly. I have to bathe Jean-Pierre, who is regressing now, wetting his bed every night to show us he needs us, or perhaps it's unconscious jealousy toward the unborn baby. I have to rinse the towels I use for his diapers. Every morning I soak some clothes—mine, John's, and Raymond's. Shirts, briefs, socks, and always those unspeakable slimy, sticky handkerchiefs . . . After that, while Raymond takes care of the child, I spend all morning dragging around this harmonious room, which warms up gradually. I hate housework because I have a hard time bending down. I have only one maternity dress; the one I wore with Jean-Pierre. Periodically I move the buttons to enlarge it enough to fit my stomach. I have a nightmare: what if it were twins? I used to dream of that. With my hands on my stomach, at night, I claim to feel two sets of movements, so much so that Raymond almost believes it. People bring me bits of layette, diapers, swaddling clothes—I can hardly get interested. Cécile washed and ironed some beautiful little linen shirts that she had embroidered for her nephew in 1914.

Every night we listen to the BBC. We can tell from their reaction whenever they recognize a voice, a name, that the Misses Bergerot have sheltered all the leaders of the Resistance and many politicians in their home. They have stories to tell about each and every one of them, and their tongues are as sharp and their sense of humor as great as their generosity.

Monday, December 20, 1943

Christmas is only a few days away. In the library, where John
and Raymond have spent hours exploring, the Misses Bergerot
have set up a crèche. Boubou makes the acquaintance of the
baby Jesus and all of a sudden realizes that his mummy, too, is
going to have a baby. He becomes more respectful of my stomach
and no longer flings himself at me so roughly; he even begins to
speak tenderly of a future little sister.

Raymond and John have decided to decorate the house. They
cut some holly, and John climbed up an apple tree to pick a
bunch of mistletoe.

Friday, December 24, 1943

I attend midnight mass with my hostesses. Everybody in this
little church stares at me. Where does *she* come from? Cécile
loudly refers to me as Cousin, blessing me with her gloved finger,
dipped in consecrated water. From our seats in the front pew,
we follow the service. Kneeling down on the straw prayer stool, I
have a hard time getting up. I am so heavy, and at this hour of the
night I'm so sleepy. My three neighbors are very attentive during
the service. Even on Christmas Eve they are pugnacious, lying
in wait for the conformist homily that will give them a chance to
make a scene. I tell them in a low voice: "For my sake, it's better
not to attract too much attention tonight." Frustrated, they take
me back through the pitch-dark night to the silent chateau.

The two men welcome us in one of the small drawing rooms,
where a beautiful fire crackles in the fireplace. A small fir tree
with a few candles merrily lights up the corner of the table.
John has cleverly folded paper to manufacture four pretty boxes.
Three of these contain a tiny piece of his captain's stripes, carefully preserved since his accident. That's a lovely gift for these
women, the daughters, sisters, and widow of officers.

For me he constructed a miniature machine gun out of wire.
The cheese merchant has sent us a roast, and Jeanne made a
bûche de Noël with real butter cream. I don't know who provided
the bottle of sparkling wine. At least the illusion of Champagne!

John, soon in high spirits, sings "God Save the King." Where are our Lyon Christmases? Where are our parents, our whole family, and all our friends? Where will we be next Christmas? For John, this evening is just an unexpected interlude in his life as a soldier, nothing more. I'm so tired, weary to the point of tears. Tomorrow, another day just like this will begin. What wish could I make as I fall asleep? Simply wish for our safety's sake that, indeed, tomorrow will be the same as today.

Here, all day long we talk of nothing but the war, all wars, and the Resistance, its victories and repression. Every night we try to listen to the BBC, in spite of the jamming. General de Gaulle is in Algiers, where the provisional government is functioning with the constituent assembly where, alongside former deputies hostile to Pétain, many of our comrades in the Resistance are seated. They are our spokesmen, and all of them, from Claudius Petit to Médéric, from d'Astier to Grenier, affirm the importance of the Resistance inside France. They stress its effectiveness in sabotaging and harassing enemy troops. All of them demand that weapons be sent quickly, enabling us to act, and they categorically refute the threat of civil war in France. "No," Claudius Petit tells the constituent assembly, "the Resistance does not want arms to carry out its little revolution, but for its liberation."

Thursday, January 6, 1944

It's Twelfth Night. Cécile made the traditional king's galette —a magnificent tart—thanks to the largesse of the neighboring farmers. Just as we are sitting down to our noonday meal, Charles-Henri arrives, his usual calm self, with his pipe between his teeth. "There probably will be a pickup operation this very night. We'll listen to the BBC at one o'clock to find out if our message is broadcast."

I go up to our room to get the clothes I washed this morning and hang them up to dry at once on the lines strung over the range. The message comes through: "Ils partiront dans l'ivresse." We wait for confirmation at seven o'clock and again at nine—and off we go. We are quite a crowd on the airstrip. The moon isn't completely full yet, but it is shining with exceptional brightness on this dry, cold night. Jean-Pierre is sleepy, as am I; standing for a long time exhausts me. To wait for the plane, we both stay in the car that brought us here. Midnight. They come for us in a hurry. The child, carried in his father's arms, doesn't wake up; I arrive on the spot with the suitcase containing the layette put together over the past months.

The beacon works well. Charles-Henri sends the signal, the plane replies with the agreed-upon letter. Then nothing. Nothing happens, the plane flies farther and farther away and doesn't come back.

There are seven or eight passengers stranded here. All the bags of Resistance mail and two months' worth of reports sit on the grass. Charles-Henri quickly organizes our return. The passengers are taken by the local leader in a pickup truck to a mill at the other end of the airstrip, Raymond and John among them. They decide that I will return with my child to the Ville-vieux chateau, where the three ladies are waiting for me. They are quite used to clandestine pickups; with their sharp hearing they already know that the plane didn't land.

Friday, January 7, 1944

The cheese maker implores me to be patient. Now we must wait for calm to return to this area. In Lons-le-Saunier, that is, about fifteen miles from here, the Germans have stationed a detail of Russian prisoners of war pressed into German military service. They are said to be ferocious, the equivalent of the Waffen ss and our Milice.

Thursday, January 13, 1944

The situation is grave. Philippe Henriot has made his debut on Radio-Paris, replacing Paul Marion, who was considered too soft. Henriot is a brilliant journalist, a formidable polemicist, and totally devoted to Nazism. Threatening and persuasive, he is capable of swaying more than one Frenchman. On the night of January 11, it is he who trumpets the news of the trial, the death sentence, and the immediate execution of Count Ciano, who had contributed to the restoration of the monarchy in Italy in September 1943. Mussolini, his father-in-law, would not sign his petition for mercy. "This is what happens to traitors," Philippe Henriot concludes.

Charles-Henri informs us that there won't be any more operations during this full moon and that the passengers who were supposed to leave on January 6 have been sent to Paris. As for Raymond and John, they come to the chateau for dinner in the evening, then return to the mill for the night. Ultimately, they end up staying here, which is more prudent than the daily comings and goings.

Now I have become the subject of concern. I'm starting the ninth month, and I yield more and more to the vegetative fatalism of pregnant women. I no longer feel responsible for myself. I allow myself to be taken care of, which has been the case for three months. My passivity is equaled only by my trust. Charles-Henri is the master of my destiny. He is fully conscious of this. If he could find a solution tomorrow, he would be relieved. But he does not make decisions alone; he depends on the services of London.

For the February moon, departures are planned between the fifth and the fourteenth. He asks me: "Will you be able to hold out until then?" My little boy was born a bit prematurely; for a second baby, the chances are increased. Measures have to be taken. First, we must be closer to Lons-le-Saunier; then we must contact a doctor and reserve a place in the maternity clinic.

"Villevieux needs to return to calm," Charles-Henri says. "Everybody around here knows everything. Everybody is committed, and they all talk too much. Since they haven't yet suffered any harsh blows, nobody thinks of taking precautions. For a while we're going to cut our links with the chateau and the village completely."

I know I'll miss the way I lived here, the kindness and the conversations with my hostesses. Jean-Pierre, who was coddled for more than a month by three grandmothers and fell asleep between the paws of the dogs, thinks this departure is perfectly natural. Only one thing matters to him: not to lose sight of his parents, above all his father. I, however, was to be separated from Raymond one more time.

Thursday, January 20, 1944

I am housed at Chilly-le-Vignoble, very close to Lons-le-Saunier, with two schoolteachers. He, though still in a legal situation, is the head of a maquis unit. They have a little girl about twelve years old, who immediately adopts my little boy. Raymond and John stay with another family on the outskirts of the village, but we will see each other every day.

Mrs. Cazeau, my hostess, accompanies me to the hospital in Lons-le-Saunier. A physician, Dr. Michel, who has been taking care of members of the Resistance for a long time, examines me. My baby has dropped, he reports. "You have less than a month to wait."

I tell him I'm sure of the date of conception: May 14. "Well, then," he says, "the birth will take place between February 10 and 15." He knows I'm waiting for a flight to London; he also knows of my past activities and Raymond's role. Since we started on our peregrinations, back and forth between hiding place and aborted departure, a sort of legend has accompanied us. People invariably ask Raymond to tell of his arrest in Caluire, and then I'm obliged to follow suit with the attack on the German pickup truck. During one of my rare moments of reflection, I say to the doctor that this must be how heroic epics are born. I am sure to arrive in England as the woman-with-the-submachine-gun-who-saved-her-husband. Later, when the war is over, I'll have a hard time escaping that cliché. And yet the escape that saved my love is only one deed among the mass of heroic actions accomplished over the years of resistance.

"Yes," the doctor replies, "but such deeds keep up our morale. In any event, you'll have a bed ready here for your confinement. If you do leave in February, come see me the day before. You will be almost due then, and I'll give you some advice for the trip."

The trip! On February 7, Charles-Henri is back again.

"It's set for tomorrow," he says. "I'm ready, and so is the team. I got the okay from London in yesterday's three broadcasts. Today they repeated it. My station signal is 'From Carnival to Shrove Tuesday,' and the message giving the okay is 'My father cherishes a hope.' It's set for tomorrow. Listen carefully to the three broadcasts today. After my station signal, when you hear "Nous partirons dans l'ivresse," get ready. There will be a lot of you this time, at least eight. For the first time, the British are sending a twin-engine plane, a Hudson. The airstrip isn't far from here; it's large, well cleared, and the ground is frozen solid. So there's no problem. It's so close to Lons-le-Saunier that the Germans won't have time to realize how daring we are. See you tomorrow night, Lucie."

Tuesday, February 8, 1944

By twelve-thirty we've taken up position at the radio set. We can't afford to miss the one o'clock broadcast. Despite the jamming, we hear the string of "personal messages." All of a sudden: "From Carnival to Shrove Tuesday; nous partirons dans l'ivresse!" The message has come through. Raymond and I look at each other. We are sure that tonight all will go well and that we'll be leaving. With joy? That's another matter. Three (soon to be four) people will be saved, but what about all those who remain in France, parents, friends in the underground. Our pillaged, tortured France fighting on without us. We decide to go to Lons-le-Saunier to see Dr. Michel. He examines me quickly. "It will be soon, very soon. I'm going to prepare a laudanum solution for you. It's an opiate. On the airstrip, before the departure, you must administer it to yourself by means of a douche. That way we may prevent labor from starting during the trip; its effect lasts about forty-eight hours. Don't linger in Lons-le-Saunier now. They have stationed the worst ss here, with a group of Russians from the Vlassov army. Everybody is scared; the day before yesterday they invaded the boarders' quarters at the lycée. It was awful. I fear they may come to the hospital next. Get back to Chilly quickly—bon voyage!"

At seven the message comes through again. In the village, Mr. Cazeau has alerted the men of his group. Commanded by the cheese merchant from Bletterans, they will be in charge of protecting the airstrip. Charles-Henri has his team in readiness. Their job is to gather the passengers together near the airstrip. My suitcase is ready. Raymond took his pistol apart and greased it. Being pessimistic, he fears another bungled departure and is worrying about me.

After the failure on January 6, he wanted to resume contact with the active Resistance. I couldn't prevent him from taking the train to Paris. On the place des Vosges he found a place to stay with a childhood friend of mine. After that he stayed with an ear and nose specialist in the fifteenth arrondissement. He tried, in vain, to learn his parents' whereabouts. When he met our Resistance comrades, he proposed to them that he resume his activity. Luckily, wisely, Copeau persuaded him to come back to the Jura. "You can't leave Lucie now. It's her turn to need you. You are expected in Algiers. We count on men like you who know the Resistance inside France to lend d'Astier a hand. You have been designated as a member of the constituent assembly, don't forget—so you have no right to shirk your obligations."

Raymond gave in, but since his return he can't keep still. He passionately follows the advances of Allied troops in Italy and curses the fact that he can't fight. As for me, I'm protected from such impatience by my pregnancy. Ever since Raymond's escape on October 21, 1943, I have been certain that my daughter would be born in London. Today, I say good-bye forever to those around me.

A Citroën comes to pick us up after the nine-fifteen broadcast. Charles-Henri checks our equipment. Our little boy is covered with woolens; he is wrapped in a rabbit-skin overcoat, made by the farmers' wives neighboring the chateau in Villevieux. This enormous fur coat, a bit stiff and slightly smelly, was prepared for our aborted departure on January 6. Charles-Henri advises us to turn it inside out. There is no heat in the plane, he points out. He has repeated the same recommendations for all the passengers: several layers of clothing and, underneath one's overcoat, a thick padding of newspaper—the best insulating material for this kind of expedition.

Looking like balloons, we climb into the venerable old Citroën provided by a farmer who had hidden it in his barn, where it was camouflaged under the hay. He inflated the tires with a hand pump and is sacrificing a little of his gasoline reserve. It's about fifteen miles to the airstrip. After nine or ten miles, some kind of smoke comes out from under the hood, the engine hiccups and falls silent. A catastrophe! The farmer forgot to pour water into the cooling system. We finish the trip on foot, over small dirt paths. John carries my suitcase with the layette. Raymond carries Boubou, who is wide awake and happy on his father's shoulders. I drag along, out of breath, carrying my bag containing the douche and the vial with the laudanum solution.

This is no time to break down, but I'm terrified by this moonlight procession, with its protective escort. If there is an alarm, I cannot run, and this unforeseen march may induce labor. So I decide to administer the laudanum enema without waiting any longer. The leader of the group is stunned when I ask him to leave me alone for five minutes in the shelter of a bush. I don't give him any details. He offers to carry me. I reassure him and promise that everything will be all right. When I return to my place in the group, everyone looks at me, worried. All that's missing now would be to see me with a newborn baby in my arms! We have to hurry; the plane is scheduled for any time after eleven.

There are lots of people at the airstrip, where I arrive in a sweat. Among the passengers is a doctor called Trompette, who is in charge of the underground health services. He dispels the climate of apprehension by explaining that childbirth is the most natural act in the world. Moreover, he says with a laugh, he is equipped with a pair of scissors and a spool of thread for the umbilical cord. He assures us that everything is going to be fine. The ground crew is setting up the beacons. The weather is milder now, but it is still clear. At eleven the plane arrives. It looks enormous and makes a terrifying noise. It touches down, passes us at top speed, then slows down at the end of the runway. Several passengers get off and are whisked away at once. With its two engines still throbbing, the plane heads back to where it will take off. But little by little it begins to labor, then stops. It is bogged down where the sudden thaw has softened the ground.

The ground crew, the passengers, everybody must join in

pushing the plane to its starting point. Then the passengers quickly climb on board. All that remains is to unload the weapons and the ammunition cases, replacing them with mailbags. But before this operation, the pilot decides to try moving the plane. The engines turn, but the plane doesn't budge and gets bogged down even more. Everybody else has to get off, but I'm told to stay on board with the child. I can hear the navigator coordinating the men's efforts: "Go, hop, hop." Nothing happens.

Despite his responsibilities, Charles-Henri comes to tell me what's happening. His assistant has left for the neighboring villages to recruit more men and some oxen and horses. Through the portholes I see a mass of people bustling around in silence. The men stand under the wings, horses and oxen are harnessed to the plane's nose. At the "hop" signal, the animals pull, the men lift the wings of the plane with their shoulders. What a nighttime procession! The Germans are less than fifteen miles away.

All the gendarmes from Bletterans are on the roads around the airstrip. They will turn back any curiosity seekers and will guard the maneuver in case anything untoward happens.

I see Charles-Henri talking with the pilot. From the door of the plane Raymond tells me that the crew want to destroy the machine and quickly head for Spain. Charles-Henri keeps talking and finally comes toward me with the pilot. The latter shakes my hand and Charles-Henri translates: "He congratulates you for what you have done. For your sake, he will make one more try—the last. He has already passed the safety margin in time allotted for his return flight. John and Raymond are going with you. Your husband urges that the mail should also be taken on board. So we'll unload the crates, the three of you get settled with the mailbags, and then it's up to God!"

The plane is brought back to the starting point. Animals and men get out of the way. After the crates are unloaded and the mailbags hoisted aboard, John, Raymond, the pilot, and the navigator climb in. Just before the door closes, Raymond finally abandons his gun and gives it to one of the men on the ground. In front of the wheels, using picks and shovels, the ground crews have cut a deep rut where the villagers have heaped branches and bundles of sticks. Charles-Henri is at his post to direct the maneuver. The engines turn again, the plane shakes, starts rolling, makes an enormous bounce over a bump at the end of the runway, and takes off. One last look. Charles-Henri is standing with both arms raised high and thumbs up, imitated by the whole team. I feel launched toward the sky, en route to freedom.

It is two o'clock in the morning. John, deep in conversation with the navigator, is already home. Covered with mud, freezing cold, deafened by the noise of the engines, worried by the creaking of the metal, we three seated on the floor of the cabin are emigrants full of hope, anxious about the land that is to welcome us. Jean-Pierre is stretched out on the floor asleep, with his head on his father's lap. I am overcome with weariness. The laudanum has made me a little woozy and I can't control the horrible waves of nausea. The plane flies first high, then low. Its zigzagging makes me dizzy. But it is necessary if we are to escape enemy detection from one direction and antiaircraft fire from another. It's a nightmarish trip.

Through the nearest porthole I can see the Loire, the mouth of the Seine, and then the Channel. The pilot is worried because the radio antenna broke during the maneuvers on the muddy ground. There is no way to identify ourselves to the British air defenses. He will be even more alarmed when he finds out that he could get through without being detected!

It is almost seven o'clock in the morning when we land. Our arrival is met with great enthusiasm. They had given up on us because we were three hours late. No word by radio. I climb down the ladder from the plane with difficulty. Jean-Pierre is barely awake. Raymond is gray with fatigue. John is feeling chipper—a captain in the British army again, overnight. At the air base our pilot is greeted with an ovation and the congratulations of his commander. We are led into a large reception hall, a sort of mess, where they pass around hot coffee and marvelous rolls. The base commander greets me, asking if yesterday I still believed the departure attempt would succeed.

"Of course: there is a French proverb, Never two without three, and the third is always good."

He speaks French quite well, translating for me our pilot's most recent anxiety: during the flight he had retracted the landing gear, as usual, but when the time came to release the gear he realized that the wet mud covering the wheels had probably frozen during the flight, so we would have to prepare for a belly landing. Fortunately, there wasn't a problem.

Having exhausted all my potential for worrying, I nonchalantly reply: "Bah, we've seen worse," to everyone's astonishment.

The pilot has a request. He would like to have the wooden clogs our little man is wearing. "They'll be our mascot," he says. I gladly give them to him, which is why Jean-Pierre arrives in London wearing only his socks.

On the bus into town, Jean-Pierre, now fully awake and with a good breakfast inside him, is curious about everything and babbles constantly. "Mama, look, in this country the fish swim in the sky." Above us the air defense balloons, shaped like great long whales, perform guard duty over the city, swaying at the end of ropes holding them captive.

Raymond is taken in charge at the first stop. They let him off at "Patriotic School," the prison-hotel where any foreigner coming from the Continent must stay for interrogation by the Intelligence Service. I am so obviously ready to give birth that I am spared these procedures. They take me to Hill Street, which is the seat, in London, of the Interior Department of the government of Free France. D'Astier, our Bernard, the head of Libération, had been there and many others: his deputy, Georges Boris, the editor of the newspaper La Lumière before the war; François Coulet, who had an impressive war record; Crémieux-Brilhac, who had recently carried out an unbelievable escape from a German POW camp for officers, via the USSR.

Everyone gathers around me. Jean-Pierre takes over the place, fiddling with the typewriters and melting the hearts of the secretaries, who give him cookies and candy from their desks. I feel miserable in my old muddy overcoat with my long, drab hair and my face swollen from a sleepless night. I no longer know where I am, in what sort of a world, on what planet. All around me people in civilian clothes or in uniform are smiling; they are gentle and courteous and talk about the secrets of our clandestine lives without being cautious. I am free, among free men and women who want to know everything. I feel like I have just come from a place where someone is seriously ill. They are all asking me for news of one they hold dear: France. It is overwhelming. Here I am, preceded by that legend of escape and of raids. They expect me to talk. I can't take any more. The uncomfortable chair. All these faces. That pale tobacco smoke that makes me feel sick. I think I'm going to faint. One of the secretaries notices, and an official car carries me off with my son and my suitcase. The driver is a uniformed woman. I look at her with respect.

"My name is Lucie, like yours," she tells me. "I volunteered for the Free French forces, and I hope to end the war in France."

She takes me to a luxury hotel, the Savoy, where a good room awaits me and a bathroom with nice warm water. What a delight! To wash with real soap that smells good and lathers. Jean-Pierre and I splash around for a good long while. I teach him to make bubbles by blowing into his soapy half-clenched fist. We're happy. In the fireplace there is a good coal fire that burns without a flame—the nuggets of coal are like glowing eggs, and just as red after four or five hours. We sleep through lunch time. I dare not leave the room. A maid brings me a tray with some tea, milk, and doughnuts.

There is also a letter: d'Astier informs me that a nurse will take care of Jean-Pierre tonight, because he is coming to take me to dinner with Frenay and Kessel.[33] I don't feel up to it, having nothing decent to wear, but I can't refuse. He will come at eight, unless the traffic is stopped by an air raid. Bombardments are frequent, especially when the moon is full. So the moon dictates the rhythm of my life. In Lyon it cheered me on when I was alone at night, on the avenue Esquirol. It was the promise of departure during our vagrant winter months. Here in London, the moon means German bomb attacks will be more precise, more destructive. Because of that risk, we go to a basement restaurant that is frequented particularly by French-speaking people. The cloakroom is at the bottom of the stairs. I take off my old overcoat, worn during the Jura winter; snippets of newspaper

33. Joseph Kessel (1898–1971) was a Russian-born Jewish writer and a member of the French Academy.

are still stuck in the lining from when I tried to get rid of my padding in the RAF hall. They scatter on the floor like confetti, to everybody's great surprise. On the little counter in front of the cloakroom attendant, an ash tray is overflowing, not with cigarette butts but with barely smoked cigarettes. I instinctively start to retrieve that wealth, but stop just in time. I still have to unlearn a lot of habits. Already I've begun to realize the reverse effort our comrades had to muster when they were parachuted into France.

I feel ugly, heavy, and weary; I don't know how to respond to the affectionate words spoken by Frenay, Kessel, and d'Astier. Each of us is served a plate holding a pork chop accompanied by a handsome portion of noodles. What a feast! I eat heartily. I soon notice that the three men just eat the eye of the chop and scarcely touch the noodles. My plate is empty and mopped clean. With some longing and regret I watch the plates, still full of pasta in that tasty gravy, all that nice crispy fat and meat still on the bone, being removed.

The singer Anna Marly is the attraction at the restaurant. All three men know her well and introduce us. She has just composed the music for the "Partisans' Song," written by d'Astier and Kessel. The BBC broadcast it in January and the entire Resistance immediately adopted it. She is going to sing it for us. Through the hubbub of conversations at the other tables I listen with all my soul. Here I am, in tears, thinking of those I left behind in France. I am pathetic in my worn dress, misshapen, weary, with my omnipresent belly. Some diners at the nearest tables, Canadian officers, fall silent and look at me, somewhat embarrassed. Then Anna Marly, scarcely having strummed the last chord of the last line on her guitar, whirls out between the tables in her long black dress, gaily belting out "Alouette, gentille alouette . . ."

I am destroyed. Kessel doesn't take his eyes off me; he grabs my shoulders: "Come on, little one—that's life! Don't cry anymore. I'm going to show you something." He picks up his glass, empties it, then bites off the rim, chews, and swallows. I have just recovered from my amazement when I see Raymond arriving. He is escorted by a British officer, half-guide, half-guard. He has managed to get permission to come see me for a few minutes in spite of the rigorous regulations of "Patriotic School."

At the hotel Jean-Pierre is fast asleep. Once more I'm alone in a room for transients. Once more Raymond is being kept from me by force. But this time his prison is gilded and the interrogation a mere formality.

Twenty-four hours ago I was in the Jura mountains. Our shadows furtively departed on a plane sent from England. The same shadows waited while the residents of a nearby village freed the bogged-down plane on that rain-soaked meadow. There was no need for words. The British pilot, the farmer with his oxen, the saboteur who had just arrived, the leader of the health services who was about to leave, our persecuted family, Charles-Henri with his team, all were united by the same fight, with the same awareness of risks, of failures, and of success.

Yesterday I was a member of the underground, in constant danger, deeply anxious about this baby who is ready to be born; today my fight is over. We're in London, with Raymond, safe, heroes of a story filled to the very end with unforeseen episodes. The grueling departure of that big Hudson machine, torn out of the Jura mud by the solidarity of an entire village, was the end of our adventure.

Not quite for me. With my comrades of the Resistance, we rescued Raymond. Today, on February, 11, 1944, we are in England because certain French people and a British crew took unheard-of risks. One task still remains, which I alone can accomplish: to bring into the world the baby of love and of hope.

Wasn't that what the message from the Royal Air Force to Charles-Henri had promised: "The father cherishes a hope"?

EPILOGUE

Forty Years Later . . .

Early in 1983, France obtained the extradition and subsequent transfer of Klaus Barbie to Lyon, where he was to be sentenced. He had been the head of the Gestapo in that city during the occupation.

Emotions in France ran high. Certain collaborators and some of Barbie's informers must have feared that the "Butcher of Lyon" would spill the beans, revealing the names of the people who had helped him.

They had no need to worry. The fundamental basis of his deplorable notoriety was the arrest, on June 21, 1943, and the eventual torture and death of Jean Moulin. French law, however, does not permit sentencing for the repression of the Resistance. There is a prescription against everything concerning war crimes. The trial therefore would cover crimes against humanity, which are imprescriptible, namely, the savage annihilation of hostages and innocent children.

This made Barbie's defense quite simple. He had only to distract public opinion by a strategy that deliberately ignored the assassinations, since he could not deny them. His defense did just that. Barbie still had the same enemies: all those men and women who took part in the Resistance. He found new allies, and together they busied themselves spreading around dirt wherever he believed it was possible to tarnish the *résistants*. If his defense could succeed in sowing doubt in public opinion, by suggesting that Jean Moulin, under arrest and confronted with the plan to deliver him to the Gestapo, had no recourse other than suicide, then Barbie would be victorious once again. He would have obscured the fact that Jean Moulin fought until death to preserve the secrets of the clandestine struggle, and that the *résistants*, whatever their political affiliation, put up a solid front before the enemy. If he prevailed in his tactics, he, the Nazi torturer, would have succeeded in putting the Resistance on trial.

Having known the men of those early days of struggle, those with whom we were reunited, many of whom today can no longer answer the roll call, I don't want Barbie and his friends to insult them, or us, or to trivialize with their slander the glorious and tragic history of the Resistance.[34]

34. In 1987 in Lyon, Klaus Barbie was sentenced to life imprisonment. Despite all the efforts of reactionaries and so-called revisionists to deny the existence of Nazi death camps, and a very clever attorney, justice prevailed in this long and spectacular trial. Earlier that year the Aubracs had won a libel suit against Barbie's lawyer, Jacques Vergès, who slandered them in the most vicious way. Other witnesses, too, testified about torture inflicted by Barbie. The death of René Hardy, whose "flight" from Caluire suggested his cooperation with the Gestapo, prevented complete elucidation of his role.

AFTERWORD

From June 6 to August 15, 1944, the Allied forces together with the "New French Army" fought the Germans in the Liberation of France. General Eisenhower estimated the contribution of the French Resistance in this struggle as the equivalent of fifteen divisions.

We had enlisted in the Resistance as a voluntary move, aimed at recovering our freedom and confirming the dignity of the human being. Mission fulfilled. Our pledge was completed. After our country had been reconstructed, we each returned to our own lives. However, those of us who had served kept a spirit of solidarity, even a sense of still being united in a mission, which sometimes surprised our society, so divided by politics, ideology, religion, or social class.

For us, the *résistants*, memory is our resource; whenever racism or fascism tries to reappear, our watchfulness draws us together. We then become partners once again in a struggle that has been our source of pride, and for this we also struggle to keep the young from forgetting.

Since the events recorded in this book, almost fifty years have passed. Here are the stories of some of those I mentioned:

Bernard, who was Emmanuel d'Astier de la Vigerie, had been the founder of our Resistance group Libération-Sud. He became a member of General de Gaulle's cabinet during the Liberation.

After the war he was a member of Parliament, then manager of a daily newspaper and once again a journalist, as he had been before the war. He is now deceased.

Max was Jean Moulin, de Gaulle's representative in France and founder and chairman of the National Resistance Council (CNR). He was arrested at Caluire by Klaus Barbie and tortured; he died without uttering a word. He is now the emblematic figure of the French Resistance, and his funerary urn has been installed in Le Panthéon in Paris.

Pascal Copeau, who took over direction of Libération-Sud when Bernard was recalled to London, became a member of the CNR. After the war he was a member of Parliament, and also returned to his prewar occupation as a newspaper and broadcast journalist. He is now deceased.

Charles-Henri is Colonel Paul Rivière. He remained in the army after the war and served as French military attaché in Prague and Tokyo. He is now retired.

Maurice David, my husband's cousin, returned to his prewar business; he is now deceased.

Serge Ravanel, leader of the groupes-francs, was named a colonel in the French Army. Later he returned to civilian life as an engineer and manager, and is still active as a consultant.

Pierre-des-faux-papiers, our counterfeiter, is Pierre Farelle. During the Resistance he was arrested, tortured, and deported to a concentration camp. He returned and resumed his prewar business.

The members of my groupe-franc: several were killed in fighting with the Milice and Gestapo during the last year of German occupation. After the war, three volunteered for service with the mine-clearance organization. Most of the survivors returned to their prewar occupations and are now retired.

Boubou, my little son, is now Jean-Pierre Aubrac, an engineer following his profession in Dakar. He has two children, Gilles and Marianne.

Catherine, my daughter who was born in London on February 12, 1944, is the director of a Grenoble social facility group. She is married to a university professor and they have four children.

Elisabeth, our second daughter, was born in Paris in 1946. She teaches in a secondary school; her husband is also a university professor. They have three children and live in Paris.

Raymond Aubrac, my husband, was a member of the Consultative Assembly in Algiers, and returned to France with the landing forces in Provence in August 1944. He was appointed Commissaire Régional de la République by de Gaulle. In 1945 he resumed his work as an engineer, first at the Ministry of Reconstruction (where he was responsible for mine clearance throughout France), and then with a private firm. Later he was an adviser to the newly independent government of Morocco, and finally served with the United Nations' FAO bureau in Rome and at the General Secretariat in New York. He was associated with Henry Kissinger and Kurt Waldheim during the negotiations ending the Vietnam War. Raymond is still active in technical assistance programs for developing countries.

Lucie Aubrac: as for myself, at the time of the Liberation I was given a mission to help in the establishment of the new Public Administration in Normandy. I became a member of the Consultative Assembly in Paris, then a member of the Second World War Historical Committee. Subsequently I resumed my teaching career and taught at schools in Paris, Rabat, and Rome. I retired in 1966 and am still very active in movements against racism and in remembrance of the Resistance. Raymond and I live sometimes in Paris and sometimes in the south of France.

My parents, who had been wine dressers in Burgundy, are now dead.

Raymond's parents were arrested by Paul Touvier's Milice and handed over to Klaus Barbie's Gestapo. They were killed at Auschwitz.

Lucie Aubrac, France, July 30, 1992